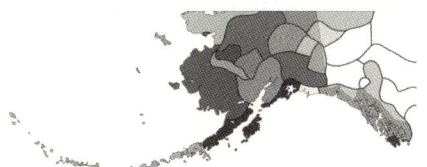

Alaska Native
        Studies Council

TRANSFORMING THE UNIVERSITY:

ALASKA NATIVE STUDIES

IN THE 21ST CENTURY

Proceedings from the Alaska Native Studies Conference

APRIL 4–6, 2013

ANCHORAGE, ALASKA

UNIVERSITY *of*
ALASKA ANCHORAGE

TRANSFORMING THE UNIVERSITY:

ALASKA NATIVE STUDIES

IN THE 21ST CENTURY

Proceedings from the Alaska Native Studies Conference 2013

EDITORS:

Beth *Ginondidoy* Leonard, Jeane *Táaw xíwaa* Breinig,
Lenora *Ac'aralek* Carpluk, Sharon *Chilux* Lind,
and Maria *Shaa Tláa* Williams

TWO HARBORS PRESS
MINNEAPOLIS, MN

Two Harbors Press
322 First Avenue N, 5th floor
Minneapolis, MN 55401
612.455.2293
www.TwoHarborsPress.com

ISBN-13: 978-1-62652-813-0
LCCN: 2014936698

Distributed by Itasca Books

Book Design by Sophie Chi

Printed in the United States of America

Alaska Native Studies Conference Proceedings 2013
Transforming the University: Alaska Native Studies in the 21ˢᵗ
Century
Editors:
Beth *Ginondidoy* Leonard, Senior Editor, Associate Professor of
Indigenous Studies, UAF
Jeane *Táaw xíwaa* Breinig, Associate Dean for Humanities and
Professor of English, UAA
Lenora *Ac'aralek* Carpluk, Ikautaq Project Coordinator, UAA Center
for Human Development
Sharon *Chilux* Lind, Assistant Professor, College of Business and
Public Policy, UAA
Maria *Shaa Tláa* Williams, Director and Associate Professor of
Alaska Native Studies, UAA

Editorial Review Board:
Ray Barnhardt, Professor Emeritus of Cross-Cultural Studies, UAF
Alisha Susana *Englartaq* Drabek, Executive Director, Alutiiq
Museum
Phyllis Fast, Professor of Anthropology and Liberal Studies, UAA
Liza Mack, Indigenous Studies PhD Student, UAF
Gordon Pullar, Associate Professor of Rural Development, UAF
Roy Roehl, Assistant Professor of Secondary Education, UAF
Thomas Swensen, Assistant Professor of Native Arts and Culture,
Arizona State University
Miranda Wright, Director and Associate Professor of Alaska Native
Studies and Rural Development, UAF

CONTENTS

Part III Indigenous Worldview, Language, and the Arts

Part IV The Alaska Native Claims Settlement Act (ANCSA)

Statement from University of Alaska Leaders

The University of Alaska takes great pride in having supported another important milestone in our efforts to uphold the institutional responsibility we owe to the Native citizens of Alaska. The Alaska Native Studies Conference in April, the first of its kind, was a resounding success. Plans are already under way for 2014/2015, and each of our major administrative units, in turn, will share the host duties. Alaska Native history, art, health, education, development, language preservation, and Native knowledge systems and ways of knowing are all subjects of research, deep interest, and cultural concern across Alaska's university. This conference showcased a world-class venue for these and other important Alaska Native matters. The University of Alaska is endowed with a premier cadre of brilliant Indigenous scholars. Now they have organized themselves into a forceful academic voice for promoting the university's many and varied Native Alaskan interests, and I expect to see all three major administrative units in the University of Alaska system

Photo Credit: Rob Stapleton

Marie *Arnaq* Meade, giving the Blessing at the Alaska Native Studies Conference 2013 during the Opening Session.

derive significant overall mission benefits as a result. I fully support their initiative.

President Patrick Gamble University of Alaska

UAA was privileged to host the first ever Alaska Native Studies Conference. Drawing more than 300 people, with speakers and presenters from around the world, this historic conference highlighted the importance of better integrating Alaska Native and Indigenous knowledge in all that we do as a university and community. The conference exceeded all expectations,

Photo Credit: Rob Stapleton

Chancellor Tom Case, University of Alaska Anchorage at the opening session of the Alaska Native Studies Conference 2013.

generating the passion and energy for transformation. I am proud that this seminal conference took place at UAA and encourage and support the continued work needed to transform the ways we teach and learn in the 21st century.

Chancellor Tom Case
University of Alaska Anchorage

It was a great honor to host the first-ever Alaska Native Studies Conference in April 2013 at the University of Alaska Anchorage. As we look forward to new initiatives in the areas of teaching, research, and public service and examine our role supporting the expansion of Indigenous studies, we are very proud of the success of the April 2013 event and look forward to upcoming conferences. I personally am very pleased that we have produced the first *Alaska Native Studies Journal*, which includes proceedings from the conference.

The conference, "Transforming the University: Alaska Native Studies in the 21st Century" and the pre-conference symposium, The Things We Make, clearly demonstrated the power and new paradigms being developed in Indigenous and Alaska Native scholarship. As Alaska Native faculty are growing in numbers here throughout the University of Alaska system, we as administrators must recognize the new epistemologies, new pedagogies, and new approaches that are being presented and assist in the incorporation of these new ideas into our university system. Sponsoring conferences and providing support for the publication of new work is a first step.

As Provost of the University of Alaska Anchorage I was very humbled by the number and diversity of people attending. The conference and pre-conference symposium created excitement beyond my wildest expectations. The conference attendees and I were inspired by the keynote address of Distinguished Professor Graham *Hingangaroa* Smith of New Zealand, who specifically mentioned and highlighted his professional relationship with Alaska Native scholar Oscar *Angayuqaq* Kawagley and his work on Indigenous knowledge systems. I was also impressed with the pre-conference symposium, which focused on Alaska Native art. Alvin Amason, who is establishing an Alaska Native art program here at UAA after his distinguished career at the University of Alaska Fairbanks, was one of the main organizers of this daylong gathering that hosted almost two dozen Alaska Native artists. This one-day gathering clearly illustrated the power of Alaska Native art and included well-known established artists as well as new young and up-and-coming artists who are creating new work in the areas of film, video, performance art, music, and the traditional arts. The main conference was able to host a new reading by writer Ishmael *Angaluuk* Hope, who also participated in the pre-conference.

Photo Credit: Rob Stapleton

Provost Elisha "Bear" Baker, University of Alaska Anchorage, at the opening session of the Alaska Native Studies Conference.

Words cannot describe the energy that the conference attendees brought with them. Individuals traveled from all parts of Alaska, including representatives from Ilisaġvik College, which remains Alaska's only tribal college, as well as individuals from Canada, Greenland, and New Zealand. The success of the conference and this journal publication are clear indicators that new opportunities to elevate the importance of Alaska Native and, more broadly, indigenous peoples contributions are valued by the university.

Elisha "Bear" Baker IV, Provost
University of Alaska Anchorage

The launch of the new *Alaska Native Studies Journal* is a significant step forward for the University of Alaska in fulfilling its mission to advance and disseminate knowledge related to Alaska's Indigenous peoples. This journal will provide scholars a venue to share vitally important work that will help shape Alaska and its future.

Dana Thomas
Vice President for Academic Affairs
University of Alaska Statewide

The University of Alaska Southeast is pleased to host the 2014 Alaska Native Studies Conference in Juneau in March 2014, building on the extraordinary success of the first conference in 2013. We look forward to working with the Tlingit, Haida, and Tsimshian peoples of southeast Alaska and participants from across Alaska in a spirit of *Woocheen* ("working together," in the Lingít language). Southeast Alaska will be an enriching setting for continuing efforts to infuse Indigenous knowledge, languages, and values in the university for the benefit of our students.

Provost Richard A. Caulfield
University of Alaska Southeast

Photo Credit: Rob Stapleton

Registration for the conference at the Wendy Williamson Auditorium
on the UAA Campus.

Acknowledgments

Thank you to the conference sponsors, which include Provost Baker, University of Alaska Anchorage, the Arctic Slope Regional Corporation, NANA Development, the Alaska Dispatch, CRW Engineering Group, University of Alaska Southeast, and Agnew-Beck Consulting.

The editors of the *Alaska Native Studies Journal* wish to thank the members of the inaugural *ANSJ* editorial review board for their thorough, professional, and timely reviews of the manuscripts, and assistance in shaping the structure and content of the journal:

Ray Barnhardt, Professor of Cross-Cultural Studies, UAF
Alisha Susana *Englartaq* Drabek, Executive Director,
Alutiiq Museum
Phyllis Fast, Professor of Anthropology and Liberal Studies, UAA
Liza Mack, Indigenous Studies PhD Student, UAF
Gordon Pullar, Associate Professor of Rural Development, UAF
Roy Roehl, Assistant Professor of Secondary Education, UAF
Thomas Swensen, Assistant Professor of Native Arts and Culture,
Arizona State University
Miranda Wright, Director and Associate Professor of Alaska
Native Studies and Rural Development, UAF

PART I
DECOLONIZING THE UNIVERSITY

"The basis for Indigenous theorizing, Indigenous knowledge elements, have been done. There needs to be further work and needs to be the defense, if you like, of the Native studies elements. To make them more effective, more meaningful, and more connected to

Photo Credit: Rob Stapleton

Keynote speaker
Graham *Hingangaroa* Smith

our community aspiration. And to reflect the Indigenous knowledge framework that's been laid out."

Excerpt from Keynote address by Distinguished Professor Graham *Hingangaroa* Smith at the 2013 Alaska Native Studies Conference.

Why do we need an Alaska Native Studies Council?

Statements from the 2013 Alaska Native Studies Council members: Beth *Ginondidoy* Leonard (Deg Hit'an Athabascan), Maria *Shaa Tláa* Williams (Tlingit), Jeane *T'áaw xíwaa* Breinig (Haida), *Ac'aralek* Lolly Carpluk (Yup'ik), and Sharon *Chilux* Lind (Aleut).

Introduction

The Alaska Native Studies Council started as an informal gathering of affiliated Alaska Native faculty across the different University of Alaska campuses beginning in the fall of 2011. The University of Alaska has just a handful of Alaska Native faculty, and the goal of organizing monthly teleconferences was to share respective activities, courses, plans, and curriculum development. The monthly teleconferences initiated an exchange of ideas, including the formation of the Alaska Native Studies Council in late 2011. In April 2012 during an in-person meeting at the Bilingual Conference at the Sheraton Hotel in Anchorage, Alaska, the council formulated plans to have a conference. During one of the earlier meetings, Lance *X'hunei* Twitchell (Tlingit) of the University of Alaska Southeast campus said that he wanted to see an Alaska Native Studies Conference, thus planting the seed for a statewide gathering. The April 2012 meeting solidified the goal of creating and planning the first-ever Alaska Native Studies Conference; at that meeting the group established the chair and cochairs of this exciting endeavor. At the April meeting the participants included Lance *X'hunei* Twitchell, Beth Leonard, Lolly Carpluk, Maria Williams, Jeane Breinig, Paul Ongtooguk, Sharon Lind, Dalee Sambo Dorough,

April Counceller, and Gordon Pullar.

The University of Alaska Anchorage was willing to take on the responsibility of hosting the conference, and discussion of having an April 2013 conference in Anchorage was set in motion. Jeane Breinig (Haida) and Associate Dean at the University of Alaska Anchorage drafted a budget and a funding request to University of Alaska Anchorage Provost Elisha "Bear" Baker, which he approved. Subsequent planning meetings started in May 2012 and led to the successful April 4–6, 2013, conference, which hosted panels and workshops, with more than 300 individuals in attendance. It was a magical three days, including the pre-conference (The Things We Make) and the inspiring keynote address by Distinguished Professor Graham *Hingangaroa* Smith from New Zealand.

The following are brief statements from various individuals involved in the planning of the conference and comprise the reason why the Alaska Native Studies Council was formed.

Photo Credit: Rob Stapleton

Chair and cochairs of the Alaska Native Studies Council. L–R: Jeane *T'áaw xíwaa* Breinig (UAA), Beth *Ginondidoy* Leonard (UAF), Maria *Shaa Tláa* Williams (UAA), Lance *X'hunei* Twitchell (UAS), and Sharon *Chilux* Lind (UAA).

Statement from Beth *Ginondidoy* Leonard

I am Deg Hit'an Athabascan and originally from Shageluk, a community on the Innoko River in interior Alaska. My father is James Dementi, who was raised in the traditional Athabascan subsistence lifestyle. My mother is the late Reverend Jean Dementi, originally from California. I am currently an Associate Professor of Indigenous Studies with the Center for Cross-Cultural Studies at the University of Alaska Fairbanks. As faculty, I work closely with the Indigenous Studies PhD students and am a member of the Indigenous Studies PhD Steering Committee.

During my time at UAF—ranging from my student years beginning in 1988 to my tenure-track appointment in 2007 with the School of Education—I have benefitted from the many constructive changes initiated by faculty and staff who have been working for decades to ensure Alaska Native student success. As tenured faculty, I seek to "pay forward," or share this support and guidance with our Alaska Native graduate students; many Alaska Native students enter our programs with numerous prior personal and professional successes and significant "funds of knowledge" that contribute expertise and validity to our diverse fields of study.

Fostering relationships, reciprocity, responsibility, and respect: Validating the formation of an Alaska Native Studies Council

Indigenous communities throughout the world have long been engaged in research that has generated complex systems of knowledge. However, these systems have only recently been recognized as valid scholarly knowledge within the academy, thanks to the work of Indigenous and non-Indigenous scholars who continue to advocate for, and legitimize, Indigenous theory and methodologies.

The University of Alaska Fairbanks (UAF) recently sanctioned a series of strategic pathways, goals, and core themes, several of which directly reference Indigenous and Alaska Native peoples. UAF's "Research and Scholarship Strategic Pathway" includes the following goals: "Increase research programs that address the Arctic and its Indigenous people" and "document and disseminate Indigenous knowledge" (http://www.uaf.edu/ strategic/2010/goals/index.xml#i). In addition, one of the newly adopted core themes from the mission statement focuses on connecting "Alaska Native, Rural, and Urban Communities by Sharing Knowledge and Ways of Knowing" (http://www.uaf. edu/uaf/about/mission/).

In order to achieve these goals, UAF and the UA system need consistent, *collaborative* guidance and oversight from Alaska Native faculty, staff, and students, many of whom provide critical links to Alaska Native communities— communities from which "Indigenous knowledge[s]" is generated. Also, communities must have ownership of the processes and protocols through which Indigenous knowledge is both "documented and disseminated." The formation of a University of Alaska Statewide Alaska Native Studies Council will fundamentally shape and transform relationships within and outside of academia, enhancing recruitment of Alaska Native scholars, increasing opportunities for collaboration and power-sharing with Alaska Native and Indigenous communities, and advancing the validity of Indigenous theory and methods within the academy.

Statement from Maria *Shaa Tláa* Williams

I became the Director of the Alaska Native Studies program at the University of Alaska Anchorage in the fall of 2011. I was born and raised in *Tikahtnu* (Anchorage) and was excited to return home after teaching for more than ten years at the University of New Mexico. My greatest concerns and missions include: 1) how to strengthen Indigenous communities and protect Alaska's lands and 2) how to effectively change educational strategies for Alaska Native students.

These goals are shared by many, if not all Alaska Native people, and as an educator, I know that education is a key to attaining sustainable communities in rural and urban Alaska and creating a new foundation for the future of Alaska Native people.

The education for the Indigenous population of Alaska can no longer continue to be overlooked, and demographics are a powerful argument. According to the 2010 study by Indigenous educators Susan Faircloth and John W. Tippeconnic III, Alaska has the highest percentage of Indigenous K–12 students (1). The percentage of Alaska Native students in K–12 is 26.3 percent, so one in every four students in Alaska is Alaska Native. The next-highest Indigenous student populations include Oklahoma at 18 percent, Montana at 11.3 percent, and New Mexico at 11.1 percent.

Although Alaska has the highest percentage of Indigenous students per capita in the United States, the graduation rates remain low. Alaska's overall graduation rate is 67.6 percent, but for Alaska Natives it is 46.8 percent. Less than half of our young people are graduating from high school. This is a crisis. One of the issues is that Alaska has to recruit more than 50 percent of K–12 educators from outside of the state. Alaska is not growing its own educators. We need to have a revolution in the educational system. We need to change our K–12 educational system, grow our own educators, and create our own Alaska-centric and Native-centric curriculum in order to achieve this goal. The very young demographics of Alaska Native people show that we are at a tipping point. If we do not immediately start with a revolution in education, we are looking at disastrous circumstances, both economically and socially. If we do not initiate major change in K–12 education, we cannot address the future.

My dream is to have *all* of our young Alaska Native students graduate from high school. We need our own teachers, bankers, veterinarians, businesspeople, entrepreneurs, doctors, dentists, nurses, contractors, electricians, aviators, etc. in order to have sustainable communities. Again, if we look at the demographics, they indicate we are at a very powerful moment in history. (2)

- Median age of Alaska Native people is 24 years of age
- More than 44 percent of Alaska Native people are *under* the age of 19 years
- One-third of the Alaska Native population is in the K–12 age group

The Alaska Native Studies Council and the recent Alaska Native Studies Conference brought many individuals together that are working in their communities and developing educational strategies that will effect positive change. We have the opportunity to share ideas and strategies and learn who was doing what in the various regions of Alaska. It was inspiring to hear of the efforts across Alaska from Barrow to Atka and from Nome to Ketchikan. We can move forward and work together, and the Alaska Native Studies Council can be a major agent of change. We can address policies and enact changes at the statewide and federal level. Our annual conferences can help us network among each other and support our various initiatives. This is why I believe we need the Alaska Native Studies Council, and annual conferences and gatherings.

Endnotes

i. Faircloth, S. C. and Tippeconnic, J. W. III. (2010). *The Dropout/graduation Crisis Among American Indian and Alaska Native Students: Failure to Respond Places the Future of Native Peoples at Risk.* The Civil Rights Project/*Proyecto Derechos Civiles* at UCLA and the Pennsylvania State University, Center for the Study of Leadership in American Indian Education, January 2010.

ii. Alaska Native Policy Center (2004). Our Choices, Our Future: Analysis of the Status of Alaska Natives Report 2004. Prepared for the Alaska Federation of Natives.

Statement from Jeane *T'áaw xíwaa* Breinig

Knowing our History, Charting our Future

In 1995 I arrived as one of the first two Alaska Native tenure-track faculty members hired at the University of Alaska Anchorage (UAA). I had just completed my PhD in English at the University of Washington and was beginning my academic career with only one semester of teaching experience. The other faculty member was Edgar Blatchford, hired in Journalism and Public Communication (JPC). He was new to academia as well, and brought a long history of newspaper publishing and significant Alaskan public service. Neither of us knew much about how universities function. Given that university departments seem to operate as "silos," we found little time to interact, commiserate, and strategize over our mutual challenges navigating a new and daunting system. I struggled to learn how to teach, and Edgar struggled to find his place in JPC.

Fortunately Elaine Abraham, an accomplished Tlingit matriarch who was well respected within Alaska Native communities, had recently assumed the new position as director of the fledgling Alaska Native Studies (AKNS) program; she was the warm, welcoming presence I needed as I tried to figure how to stay connected with Native peoples while learning what my career as an English faculty member would entail. I am grateful for Elaine's kind and loving spirit and her gentle ability to reach out to me in this strange new place—a place I was uncertain I belonged. Native Student Services (NSS) and AKNS provided two places where I felt at home because I could visit and laugh with Native students and staff.

The Alaska Native Studies program, created just before Edgar and I arrived, arose from strong student pressure. The University of Alaska Anchorage sits in Alaska's largest urban center and enrolls significant numbers of Native students but has never offered many courses directly related to their histories, cultures, or languages. Students held rallies and advocated for Indigenous-studies courses, including Native languages, Native cultures, and topics related to their unique political situations. Elaine Abraham, then serving as director of NSS, was tapped to lead the new program. As a strong Tlingit woman, fluent in her language and grounded in her cultural traditions, she nurtured the program from the ground up, working with faculty in the Political Science department to develop a minor with both policy and language strands.

Unfortunately, most UAA faculty and administrators did not appreciate or understand how Elaine's traditional Tlingit values and upbringing might contribute to academia. Although she holds an M.Ed., her lack of a PhD and knowledge about university processes and procedures made it difficult for her to accomplish all her programmatic goals before she retired and returned home to Yakutat.

Since then, several different directors have led AKNS. Each person brought particular strengths and weaknesses to the position. From my perspective, the lack of role models and no sustained mentoring led to their undoing. Most left disillusioned and disheartened, wondering if changing the system was possible. Given the small pool of Alaska Natives with both advanced academic degrees and program-building experience, it is no wonder UAA's Alaska Native Studies program has never reached its full potential.

Fast-forward to 2009. Both Edgar and I were tenured Associate Professors and we were no longer the only Alaska Native tenure-track faculty at UAA. Phyllis Fast in Anthropology and Liberal Studies, and Dalee Sambo Dorough in Political Science have joined our ranks. The Alaska Native Studies program also includes two part-time term positions staffed by Alaska Native faculty.

This same year, Nancy Furlow (Tlingit), doctoral candidate and the interim AKNS director for five years, and I initiated an Alaska Native Studies retreat to create a plan to move the program forward. Nancy suggested we include Alaska Native faculty and other allies from all three University of Alaska campuses—University of Alaska Fairbanks (UAF), and University of Alaska Southeast (UAS) Juneau—to strengthen our statewide impact. We initially held a face-to-face meeting, followed by several videoconferences. Within the state system, UAF has the most Alaska Native faculty and the most academic programs supporting Alaska Native students. UAS has the fewest. We recognized the need to collaborate and begin discussions about whether or not it might be possible to develop one Alaska Native Studies degree across the campus system using distance delivery. We began talking about how to build upon regional strengths, rather than competing against each other. We began talking about whether Native languages can realistically be offered via videoconferencing.

The conversation continued amidst a national search for a permanent AKNS director. In 2011 Maria Williams

(Tlingit) was hired; she has a PhD in Ethnomusicology and is a former associate professor of Music and American Indian Studies at the University of New Mexico. In her first year, she reinvigorated discussions and teleconferenced meetings with statewide Alaska Native faculty. Through the 2012–13 planning year, we gained strength from each other and formally established the Alaska Native Studies Council. We recognized the critical need to band together to address Alaska's abysmal failure to educate our children adequately across the system from K-12 through higher education.

The first Alaska Native Studies conference, held April 4–6, 2013, unleashed a powerful force. With more than 300 attendees from across the state, the presentations highlighted Alaska Native academic and community voices—people uniquely positioned to tackle significant problems embedded in Alaska's education system. The conference made evident the significant role the Alaska Native Studies Council might play in transforming our state's education system. The newly formed Alaska Native Studies Council is strategically positioned to provide guidance on available and needed Alaska Native research topics, on Indigenous pedagogical strategies, and on what programs or resources might best serve Native students. Perhaps most important, the Alaska Native Studies Council is uniquely positioned to develop and mentor the next generation of Alaska Native PhDs.

Statement from *Ac'aralek* Lolly Carpluk

Why we, as Indigenous faculty, staff, students,
& communities, need an
Alaska Native Studies Council & Conference

Kuiggpagmiungunga As'arcaryarmek/I am from the Yukon River area, from As'aryarmek, the Yup'ik name for Mountain Village. I was born and raised there. My parents are Cunicuar Johnny and Yungersaq Mary Ann Sheppard. I come from a family of eight younger siblings, over 25 nieces and nephews, over 15 great-nieces and -nephews (or my grandchildren through the Yup'ik kinship terminology), and a large extended family up and down the Yukon River and the Bering Sea coastline. With as large a family as I have, my life's work has been invested in education at all levels, but mostly at the university/educator/community partnership level. Most important, I have been fortunate to have learned from Elders and collaborated with the trailblazers in Indigenous epistemologies in education statewide, nationally, and internationally.

I begin with the present; although we as Indigenous faculty, staff, students, consultants, visiting professors, Elders-in-residence, etc. may be employed or consulted by the University of Alaska system, we do not separate ourselves from who we are as Indigenous Peoples in our workplaces. We are Indigenous People first, and it has an influence on how we direct our focus/energies in the workplace.

*This is why we need an Alaska Native Studies Council, to receive that affirmation and confidence that we indeed can be **who we are as Indigenous People** in any environment and still have our work valued.*

I also begin with the past. The Yup'ik values were taught to me by my grandparents, parents, aunts, uncles, cousins, and friends as they also were taught the same guiding principles. These values ensure the survival of the next generation of our people and the land we live on. The Yup'ik values are instilled in us at a very young age and shape our worldview.

Imagine if we, as Indigenous Peoples, had to be led by a newcomer to the village or region every year, or every five or ten years, with the newcomer having to learn from the beginning how to survive in our specific geographic region—we, as a peoples, would have perished a long time ago.

This is why we need the Alaska Native Studies Council, we come from all parts of Indigenous Alaska, and we carry with us **those values that continue to guide us in our life that sustains us as a people** (and oversees the stewardship of the Earth). We can call on each other and "get it!" We don't have to do a lot of explaining because the other person "gets it" and can give us advice or just listen. We have our Indigenous values instilled in us as guiding principles.

I also want to share the places I've worked with Indigenous high school students, undergraduate and graduate students, faculty, staff, and Elders. My experience has been mostly at the University of Alaska Fairbanks campus and University of Alaska Statewide with various grant partnerships, where I would have loved to have a statewide Indigenous faculty or staff to call on for guidance. It was a struggle to initiate networks due to minimal numbers of Indigenous faculty and staff and to the nature of grant programs and their eventual closures. Additionally, I have developed and taught undergraduate and graduate courses where I would have loved to have had an Indigenous faculty or staff to call on to ask for advice on developing Indigenous-based undergraduate and graduate courses.

This is why we need an Alaska Native Studies Council, **to be able to have another Indigenous colleague to call on for assistance, for understanding, for hearing** *the affirmation of "I/ We get it, We understand! Or this is a suggestion of how you might go about your situation."*

In the various work environments, there are Western-based professional-development workshops, institutes, and training formats that tie in with improving the work that we do; some are required and paid for by our employers and others are suggested, and we are expected to pay for the expenses. They do make a difference. On the other hand, when we as Indigenous People are hired as faculty, staff, etc. to develop an Indigenous component at the university or school-district level, we are expected to already "know it all" without any professional development that is Indigenous-based.

This is why we need an Alaska Native Studies Council conference, **it is one venue for Indigenous based "professional development," we need to nurture and strengthen our Indigenous perspective** *so that we can continue to guide our students and colleagues in the complex academic environments we are part of.*

Last, to have spent over 20 years working with our Indigenous students, faculty, and staff or working in K–12 public schools and higher education as they navigate the mostly Western-based academic environment, we still need to find ways to strengthen our voices from an Indigenous perspective to enhance their educational experience.

This is why we need an Alaska Native Studies Council, **for Indigenous Peoples to have a voice in our educational endeavors and to be valued for our contributions in sharing an Indigenous perspective** *that enhances and equalizes the educational and work environment.*

Statement from Sharon *Chilux* Lind

The year 2011 was the 40th anniversary of the passage and implementation of the Alaska Native Claims Settlement Act (ANCSA). In 1971, through this act, the United States Congress addressed the land claims of the aboriginal peoples of Alaska. It was impossible to foresee the future over 40 years ago when Congress passed ANCSA. Who knew back then that ANCSA would create the 12 unique, successful, and diversified entities that would help shape the state of Alaska and provide a future and a means to preserve the many cultures of Alaska Native peoples for generations to come?

Collaboration on curriculum development and research focused on ANCSA will be a critical component and just a piece of what this Alaska Native Studies Council could work on. The partnership of Alaska Native educators through this council will enhance efforts in the classroom and result in better-equipped students in the future.

Part II
Decolonizing Education

Cross-Institutional Collaborations in Indigenous Education

Ray Barnhardt

Abstract

Native peoples in Alaska have usually been the subjects of research rather than the ones responsible for conducting it. However, the role of Alaska Natives in research is changing due to a concerted effort on the part of the University of Alaska and Native people themselves to develop new programs aimed at recruiting and preparing Native scholars in all academic fields who can take on leadership roles and bring an Indigenous perspective to the policy arenas at the local, state, national, and international levels. This article will describe the activities under way, their rationale, and the implications for research.

Key words: Indigenous Education, Alaska Natives, Indigenous Knowledge Systems, Higher Education, Native Ways of Knowing

The author is a professor of cross-cultural studies at the University of Alaska Fairbanks, where he has been involved in teaching and research related to Native-education issues since 1970. He has served as the director of the Cross-Cultural Education Development Program and the Center for Cross-Cultural Studies and has positioned his work at the nexus between Indigenous and Western knowledge systems. Much of the work presented in this article was developed in collaboration with Angayuqaq Oscar Kawagley and is included in his honor.

Introduction

Indigenous peoples throughout the world have sustained their unique worldviews and associated knowledge systems for millennia, even while undergoing major social upheavals as a result of transformative forces beyond their control. Many of the core values, beliefs, and practices associated with those worldviews have survived and are beginning to be recognized as having an adaptive integrity that is as relevant for today's generations as it was for past generations. The depth of Indigenous knowledge rooted in the long inhabitation of a particular place offers insights that can benefit everyone, from educator to scientist, as we search for a more satisfying and sustainable way to live on this planet.

Actions taken by Indigenous peoples themselves over the past 20 years have begun to explicate Indigenous knowledge systems and ways of knowing in ways that demonstrate their inherent validity and adaptability as complex knowledge systems with a logic and coherence of their own. As this shift evolves, it is not only Indigenous people who are the beneficiaries, because the issues that are being addressed are of equal significance in non-Indigenous contexts (Barnhardt and Kawagley 2005). Many of the problems that are manifested under conditions of marginalization have gravitated from the periphery to the center of industrial societies, so the new insights that are emerging from Indigenous societies are of equal benefit to the broader community.

The tendency in past education and research initiatives aimed at engaging Indigenous people, most of which were designed from a non-Indigenous perspective, has been to focus on how to get Indigenous people to understand the Western/ scientific view of the world. Until recently there was very little attention given to how Western scientists and educators might better understand Indigenous worldviews, and even less on what it means for participants when such divergent systems coexist in the same person, organization, or community. It is imperative, therefore, that we come at these issues on a two-way street, rather than view the problem as a one-way challenge to get Indigenous people to buy into the Western system. Indigenous people may need to understand Western society, but not at the expense of what they already know and the way they have come to know it. Non-Indigenous people, too, need to recognize the coexistence of multiple worldviews and knowledge systems, and find ways to understand and relate to the world in its multiple dimensions of diversity and complexity.

Background

The aspirations of Indigenous peoples extend beyond serving in a passive or advisory role in response to someone else's policy or research agenda; they include shaping the terms of that agenda and serving as active participants in its implementation. One of the most persistent constraints in fulfilling those aspirations is for Indigenous peoples to be recognized as having the qualifications and expertise to be valued partners in the research and policy-making process. One of the most promising strategies to overcome those constraints has focused on the preparation of Indigenous scholars who have a high level of research and policy expertise and an in-depth understanding of the dynamics at the interface between Indigenous knowledge systems and Western institutions.

In 2004 the Arctic Council issued the *Arctic Human Development Report* (AHDR), which highlighted the following as significant factors influencing the lives of Indigenous peoples of the Arctic: controlling one's own destiny, maintaining cultural identity, and living close to nature (Arctic Council 2004). Key to alleviating the negative effects and strengthening the positive contributions of these factors in peoples' lives and well-being is the need for education and research efforts initiated in the Arctic by Indigenous peoples themselves and by local institutions. As indicated in the AHDR:

Economic models and policies in modern Arctic societies are traditionally designed and legitimated in administrative and political institutional contexts outside the Arctic. A key concern of future research should be to have a critical look at these contexts aiming at gaining new grounds for decision-making . . ..

> Indigenous peoples of the Arctic have managed to carve out political regions in which they make up the majority, or at least a significant part of the population. Based upon this reality, Indigenous peoples and communities are now actively involved in setting research agendas. It is thus obvious that research agendas set by Indigenous peoples themselves or reflecting Indigenous cultures will be a key factor in setting research priorities for the next decade (Arctic Council 2004).

While these issues are of critical concern for Indigenous peoples and communities in the circumpolar region, their significance is by no means limited to the Arctic—these are issues of broad international importance, as reflected in the

United Nations report on the *Status and Trends Regarding the Knowledge, Innovations and Practices of Indigenous and Local Communities* (Helander-Renvall 2005).

Recognizing the need to address these issues in a systematic way, the US National Science Foundation, Office of Polar Programs convened a "Bridging the Poles" workshop in Washington, DC, in June 2004, bringing together scientists, educators, and media specialists to outline an education and research agenda for the International Polar Year (IPY). Among their recommendations was the following: "Communication with Arctic indigenous peoples must include developing a new generation of researchers from the Arctic who actively investigate and communicate northern issues to global populations and decision makers . . .." (Pfirman et al. 2004).

The workshop participants then outlined the following objectives regarding the engagement of diverse communities:

- Arctic residents, including Indigenous populations, are meaningfully engaged in developing and implementing polar research, education, and outreach, including community concerns and traditional knowledge, with an increase in the number of Arctic residents—especially indigenous Alaskans—with PhDs.

- Focus on building capacity *within* indigenous communities for conducting research (including local collection of data) and education/outreach in both traditional and nontraditional venues. Community-based educational components should be developed for existing and planned long-term observation networks . . . tailored by community members to address community-relevant issues, and to involve both native elders and scientists. Arctic research projects by Native people, for Native people, will involve finding funding sources and connecting them with Native communities.

• Recognizing that the Native peoples have knowledge and tradition to share with other populations is an important first step towards their involvement. Their presence in the field of education, both traditional and non-traditional, will assist in encouraging more Natives, and in providing a bridge to other cultures . . . (Pfirman et al. 2004).

Since Western scientific perspectives influence decisions that impact every aspect of Indigenous peoples' lives, from education to fish-and-wildlife management, Indigenous people themselves have taken a strong active role in reasserting their own traditions of science in various research and policy-making arenas. As a result, there is a growing awareness of the depth and breadth of knowledge that is extant in many Indigenous societies and its potential value in addressing issues of contemporary concern, including the adaptive processes associated with a rapidly changing environment.

The incongruities between Western institutional structures and practices and Indigenous cultural forms are not easy to reconcile. The complexities that come into play when two fundamentally different worldviews converge present a formidable challenge. The specialization, standardization, compartmentalization, and systematization that are inherent features of most Western bureaucratic forms of organization are often in direct conflict with social structures and practices in Indigenous societies, which tend toward collective decision-making, extended kinship structures, ascribed authority vested in elders, flexible notions of time, and traditions of informality in everyday affairs (Barnhardt 2002). It is little wonder, then, that Western bureaucratic forms have been found wanting in addressing the needs of traditional societies.

Indigenous societies, as a matter of survival, have long sought to understand the irregularities in the world around them, recognizing that nature is underlain with many unseen patterns of order. For example, out of necessity, Alaska Native people have long been able to predict weather based upon observations of subtle signs that presage what subsequent conditions are likely to be. With the vagaries introduced into the environment by accelerated climate change in recent years, there is a growing interest in examining the potential for complementarities that exist between what were previously considered two disparate and irreconcilable systems of thought (Krupnik and Jolly 2001; Barnhardt and Kawagley 1999).

Intersecting Worldviews: The Alaska Experience

The 16 distinct Indigenous cultural and linguistic systems that continue to survive in communities throughout Alaska have a rich cultural history that still governs much of everyday life in those communities. For over six generations, however, Alaska Native people have been experiencing recurring negative feedback in their relationships with the external systems that have been brought to bear on them, the consequences of which have been extensive marginalization of their knowledge systems and continuing dissolution of their cultural integrity. Though diminished and often in the background, much of the

Native knowledge systems, ways of knowing, and worldviews remain intact and in practice, and there is a growing appreciation of the contributions that Indigenous knowledge can make to our contemporary understanding in areas such as medicine, resource management, meteorology, biology, and in basic human behavior and educational practices (Kawagley et al. 1998; James 2001).

In an effort to address these issues in a more comprehensive way and apply new insights to address long-standing and seemingly intractable problems, in 1995 the University of Alaska Fairbanks, under contract with the Alaska Federation of Natives and with funding support from the National Science Foundation Rural Systemic Initiative Program, entered into a ten-year applied-research endeavor in collaboration with Native communities. The activities associated with the Alaska Rural Systemic Initiative (AKRSI) were aimed at fostering connectivity and complementarities between the Indigenous knowledge systems rooted in the Native cultures that inhabit Alaska and the formal education systems that have been imported to serve the educational needs of Native communities. The underlying purpose of these efforts was to implement a set of research-based initiatives to systematically document the Indigenous knowledge systems of Alaska Native people and to develop educational practices that appropriately incorporate Indigenous knowledge and ways of knowing into the formal education system. The initiatives in Table 1 below constituted the major thrusts of the AKRSI applied-research and educational-reform strategy.

Table 1: AKRSI Educational Initiatives

*Indigenous Science Knowledge Base *Multimedia Cultural Atlas Development *Native Ways of Knowing *Elders and Cultural Camps/Academy of Elders *Village Science Applications/Science Camps and Fairs *Alaska Native Knowledge Network/Cultural Resources and Web Site *Mathematics/Science Performance Standards and Assessments *Alaska Standards for Culturally Responsive Schools *Native Educator Associations/Leadership Development

Table 1: AKRSI Educational Initiatives

Over a period of ten years, these initiatives served to strengthen the quality of educational experiences and consistently improve the academic performance of students in participating schools throughout rural Alaska (AKRSI Annual Report 2005). In the course of implementing the AKRSI initiatives, we came to recognize the depth of insights that exist within Indigenous knowledge systems, as well as at the intersection of converging knowledge systems and worldviews. Figure 1 below captures some of the critical elements that come into play when Indigenous knowledge systems and Western science traditions are put side by side and nudged together in an effort to develop more culturally sensitive interaction.

Figure 1: Indigenous Knowledge and Western Science Traditions

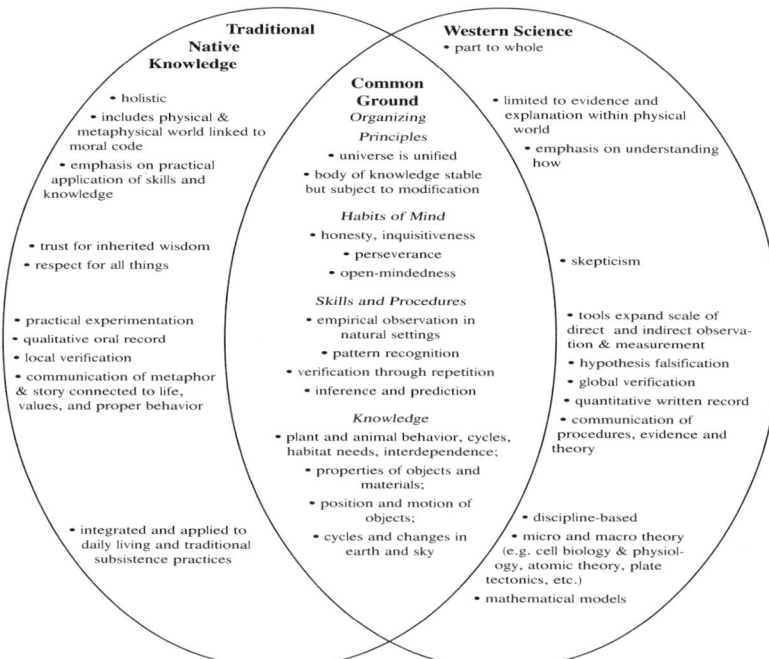

Figure 1: Indigenous Knowledge and Western Science Traditions

The implications for the research and education processes imbedded in the three domains of knowledge represented in the overlapping ovals are numerous and of considerable significance. From a Hegelian perspective, they could be characterized in terms of thesis, antithesis, and synthesis—the latter being the "common ground" depicted in the diagram. The list of qualities associated with each of the three knowledge domains lend themselves to a comprehensive research-policy agenda in their own right. In the *Handbook for Culturally Responsive Science Curriculum* prepared by AKRSI for Alaska schools, Sidney Stephens explains the significance of the various components of this diagram as follows: "It has to do with accessing cultural information, correlating that information with science skills and concepts, adjusting teaching strategies to make a place for such knowledge, and coming to value a new perspective" (Stephens 2000).

With these considerations in mind, the Alaska Rural Systemic Initiative served as a catalyst to promulgate reforms focusing on increasing the level of connectivity and complementarities between the formal education systems and the Indigenous knowledge systems of the communities in which they are situated. In so doing, AKRSI attempted to bring the two systems together in a manner that promotes a synergistic relationship such that the two previously disparate systems join to form a more comprehensive and holistic system that can better serve all students, not just Alaska Natives, while at the same time preserving the essential integrity of each component of the larger overlapping system. The implications of such an approach as it relates to Indigenous knowledge systems extend far beyond Native communities in Alaska, as indicated by Battiste in her comprehensive literature review *Indigenous Knowledge and Pedagogy in First Nations Education* (Canada):

> Indigenous scholars discovered that indigenous knowledge is far more than the binary opposite of western knowledge. As a concept, indigenous knowledge benchmarks the limitations of Eurocentric theory—its methodology, evidence, and conclusions— re-conceptualizes the resilience and self-reliance of indigenous peoples, and underscores the importance

of their own philosophies, heritages, and educational processes. Indigenous knowledge fills the ethical and knowledge gaps in Eurocentric education, research, and scholarship. By animating the voices and experiences of the cognitive 'other' and integrating them into the educational process, it creates a new, balanced centre and a fresh vantage point from which to analyze Eurocentric education and its pedagogies (Battiste 2002). When engaging in the kind of comparative analysis of different knowledge systems outlined above, any generalizations should be recognized as indicative and not definitive, since Indigenous knowledge systems are diverse themselves and are constantly adapting and changing in response to new circumstances. The qualities identified for both Indigenous and Western systems represent tendencies rather than fixed traits and thus must be used cautiously to avoid overgeneralization (Gutierrez and Rogoff 2003). At the same time, it is the diversity and dynamics of Indigenous societies and their emergence as a field of study in their own right that we continue to capitalize upon.

The expansion of the knowledge base associated with the interaction between Western science and Indigenous knowledge systems has contributed to an emerging body of scholarly work regarding the role that local observations and Indigenous knowledge can play in deepening our understanding of human and ecological processes, particularly in reference to the experiences of Indigenous peoples. Most critical in that regard, for purposes of bringing Indigenous knowledge out of the shadows in Alaska, has been the seminal scholarly work of Angayuqaq Oscar Kawagley, whose research has revolutionized our understanding of the role of Indigenous worldviews and ways of knowing and their relevance to contemporary matters (Kawagley 1995). As the first Yupiaq to receive a PhD, his insights opened the door for Indigenous perspectives to take on new life as a lens through which to better understand the world around us. The Alaska Native organizations and personnel associated with the Alaska Rural Systemic Initiative, including Angayuqaq, played a pivotal role in developing the conceptual and political underpinnings on which a new PhD program in Indigenous Studies has been developed at the University of Alaska Fairbanks.

The Alaska Federation of Natives urged the development of advanced graduate studies addressing Indigenous concerns with a formal resolution adopted in 2004. Over the next two years we assembled a list of over 100 Alaska Native people with master's degrees who expressed an interest in pursuing a PhD. Drawing upon the inspiration and success of the Maori people in New Zealand in preparing over 500 Maori PhDs over a five-year period, we acquired planning funds from the Andrew W. Mellon Foundation, and in the fall of 2007 we brought together 55 Alaska Natives with PhD aspirations for an Indigenous PhD Planning Workshop. Out of this workshop we were able to identify the areas of interest around which a new PhD program could be built, as well as the support structure and delivery system that would be needed to implement the program. The five areas of emphasis around which the program has been implemented are Indigenous education, languages, research, leadership, and knowledge systems.

Research And Policy Strategy

The new PhD program in Indigenous Studies integrates the tools and approaches of the natural and social sciences in a cross-cultural and interdisciplinary framework for analysis to better understand the emerging dynamic between Indigenous knowledge systems, Western science, and higher education. Our focus has been on the interface between Indigenous knowledge and Western science on an international scale with opportunities for cross-cultural collaboration among Indigenous peoples from around the world. With numerous research initiatives currently in various stages of development and implementation, there is an unprecedented window of opportunity to open new channels of communication between scientists, policy makers, and Indigenous communities, particularly as they relate to those research activities that are of the most consequence to Indigenous peoples (e.g., effects of climate change, environmental degradation, contaminants and subsistence resources, health and nutrition, bio/cultural diversity, Arctic observation networks, natural resource management, economic development, resilience and adaptation, community viability, cultural sustainability, language, and education).

To the extent that there are competing bodies of knowledge (Indigenous and Western) that have bearing on a comprehensive understanding of particular research initiatives associated with Indigenous-related themes, we propose to offer opportunities for Indigenous PhD candidates to be embedded with ongoing research initiatives to contribute to and learn from the research process. In addition to conducting research on the inner dynamics of Indigenous knowledge systems, the PhD students are also examining the interplay between Indigenous and Western knowledge systems, particularly as it relates to scientific processes of knowledge construction and utilization.

Related Resources And Initiatives

In January 2005 the University of Alaska Fairbanks and the Alaska Native Science Commission organized an international Indigenous Knowledge Systems Research Colloquium, which was held at the University of British Columbia, bringing together a representative group of Indigenous scholars from the US, Canada, and New Zealand "to identify salient issues and map out a research strategy and agenda to extend our current understanding of the processes that occur within and at the intersection of diverse world views and knowledge systems." A second gathering of Indigenous scholars took place in March, 2005 and focused on the theme of "Native Pedagogy, Power, and Place: Strengthening Mathematics and Science Education through Indigenous Knowledge and Ways of Knowing." In Table 2 below is a list of research topics identified by the participants in these two events as warranting further elucidation as they relate to our understanding of the role of Indigenous knowledge systems in contemporary research and education contexts.

Table 2: Research Topics Identified by Indigenous Scholars from the U.S., Canada and New Zealand

Native Ways of Knowing	Indigenous Language Learning
Culture, Identity and Cognition	Ethno-mathematics
Place-based Learning/Sense of Place	Oral Tradition/Story Telling & Metaphor
Indigenous Epistemologies	Disciplinary Structures in Education
Indigenizing Research Methods	Cultural Systems and Complexity Theory
Cross-generational Learning	Ceremonies/Rites of Passage
Culturally Responsive Pedagogy	Technologically Mediated Learning
Native Science/Sense Making	Cultural & Intellectual Property Rights

Table 2: Research Topics Identified by Indigenous Scholars from the US, Canada, and New Zealand

Drawing on the seminal work of the distinguished scholars who participated in these meetings, the research agenda outlined above is intended to advance our understanding of the existing knowledge base associated with Indigenous knowledge systems and will contribute to an emerging international body of scholarly work regarding the critical role that local knowledge can play in our understanding of global issues (Barnhardt and Kawagley 2005).

Alaska Natives have been at the forefront in bringing Indigenous perspectives into a variety of policy arenas through a wide range of research and development initiatives. In the past few years alone, the US National Science Foundation has funded Alaska projects incorporating Indigenous knowledge in the study of climate change, the development of Indigenous-based math curriculum, a geo-spatial mapping program, the effects of contaminants on subsistence foods, observations of the aurora, and alternative technology for waste disposal. In addition, Native people have formed new institutions of their own (the Consortium for Alaska Native Higher Education, the Alaska

Native Science Commission, and the First Alaskans Institute) to address some of these same issues through an Indigenous lens. A major limitation in all these endeavors, however, has been the lack of Indigenous people with advanced degrees and research experience to bring balance to the Indigenous knowledge/ Western science research endeavor.

One of the long-term purposes of the current initiative is to develop a sustainable research infrastructure that makes effective use of the rich cultural and natural environments of Indigenous peoples to implement an array of intensive and comparative research initiatives, with partnerships and collaborations in Indigenous communities across the US and around the Indigenous world. These initiatives are intended to bring together the resources of Indigenous-serving institutions and the communities they serve to forge new configurations and collaborations that break through the limitations associated with conventional paradigms of scientific research. Alaska, along with each of the other participating Indigenous regions, provides a natural laboratory in which Indigenous graduate students and scholars can get firsthand experience integrating the study of Indigenous knowledge systems and Western science.

The timing of this initiative is particularly significant, as it provides a pulse of activity that capitalizes on new Indigenous-oriented academic offerings that are emerging from institutions around the world (Alaska Native Knowledge Network 2007).

While the University of Alaska Fairbanks has had a dismal track record of graduating only four Alaska Natives with a PhD over its entire 90-year history, there is now a strong push, due in large part to the initiative of Alaska Native students and leaders, to bring resources to bear on the issue. This includes drawing upon programs and institutions from around the world to provide students with an opportunity to access expertise from a variety of Indigenous settings, as well as to identify Indigenous scholars to serve as a member of their graduate advisory committee to help guide their research in ways that foster cross-disciplinary collaboration and comparative analysis.

At the same time, students from partner institutions engaged in related research are eligible to participate in UAF-sponsored courses and research initiatives with a comparable goal of promoting scholarly cross-fertilization and synergy. Video and audio conferencing and Internet-based technologies are utilized to support an array of course offerings and joint seminars on topics of interest to a cross-institutional audience. Such shared course offerings linking faculty and students across multiple institutions have already been piloted, and the infrastructure is in place to expand to the program areas outlined above. Partner institutions bring unique perspectives to the research initiatives that serve to inform and expand the capacity of the overall effort. Close attention has also been given to addressing issues associated with ethical and responsible conduct in research across cultures and nations, employing the "Mataatua Declaration on Cultural and Intellectual Property Rights of Indigenous People," "Principles for the Conduct of Research in the Arctic," and the "Guidelines for Respecting Cultural Knowledge" (Alaska Native Knowledge Network 2001).

Circumpolar Indigenous Initiatives

The University of the Arctic (UArctic) is a cooperative network of universities, colleges, and other organizations committed to higher education and research in the North. Members share resources, facilities, and expertise to build postsecondary education programs that are relevant and accessible to northern students. The overall goal is "to create a strong, sustainable circumpolar region by empowering northerners and northern communities through education and shared knowledge" (Kullerud 2005). Within the framework of the University of the Arctic there exist numerous networks, programs, and services directed toward this goal, including three PhD networks and the International PhD School for the Study of Arctic Societies, whose objectives are as follows:

- to promote the study of Arctic societies in the fields of history, culture and language;
- to explore new research trends in those fields and to develop coordinated and collaborative post-graduate teaching;
- to stimulate international networking and synergy between participating scientific institutions to foster partnerships between Arctic societies and participating scientific institutions; and,
- to encourage participation of and knowledge sharing with Arctic communities in its activities, so as to bring more students from Arctic societies to register at the PhD level (http://www.hum.ku.dk/ipssas/about.html).

With the UArctic infrastructure already in place, including a vice president for Indigenous Programs, it can serve as a close collaborator, particularly as it relates to support for Indigenous contributions to circumpolar education, research, and policy efforts. The potential of UArctic in this regard is noted by the Arctic Human Development Report:

> Many indigenous organizations see the potential of the University of the Arctic as an institution in which they may positively influence northern research and education. The opportunity to shape and develop the curriculum exists, as well as the possibilities for inclusion of traditional knowledge holders in teaching. This possibility would be a major shift from professionalized faculty to a more open classroom, which respects different forms and authority of knowing and teaching (Arctic Council 2004).

The international partnerships associated with this endeavor are essential to its success, particularly as it relates to gaining a deeper understanding of the relationship between Indigenous knowledge systems and Western science. The primary benefits of such collaboration on research related to Indigenous knowledge systems are the opportunities for scholars and graduate students to engage in cross-cultural comparison and analysis of data from diverse Indigenous settings to delineate what is particular to a given situation vs. what is generalizable across Indigenous populations and beyond. There are also considerable economies of scale and synergistic benefits to be gained from such collaborations, since many of the Indigenous populations are relatively small in number and thus are seldom able to engage in large-scale research endeavors on their own.

Conclusion

The success of these cross-institutional collaborations will be determined by the extent to which Indigenous people continue to provide leadership and guidance such that we can forge a reciprocal relationship that has relevance and meaning in the local Indigenous contexts, as well as in the broader social, political, and educational arenas involved. By focusing on an agenda led by Indigenous students and scholars, with interdisciplinary, cross-institutional, and cross-cultural research endeavors, we are well positioned to ensure that the community, institutional participants, and the infrastructure supporting them will move forward on a pathway to becoming self-reliant and sustainable well into the future.

References

Alaska Native Knowledge Network. (2001). *Guidelines for respecting cultural knowledge.* <http://www.ankn.uaf. edu/standards/knowledge.html> (accessed 24 May 2008).

Alaska Native Knowledge Network. (2007). *Indigenous higher education.* <http://www.ankn.uaf.edu/IEW/ihe.html> (accessed 24 May 2008).

Alaska Rural Systemic Initiative. (2005). *AKRSI annual report* (Fairbanks, AK: Alaska Native Knowledge Network, University of Alaska Fairbanks).

Arctic Council. (2004). *Arctic human development report* (Copenhagen: Arctic Council).

Barnhardt, R. and Kawagley, A.O. (2005). Indigenous knowledge systems and Alaska Native ways of knowing, *Anthropology and Education Quarterly* 36(1), 8-23.

Barnhardt, R. (2002). Domestication of the ivory tower: Institutional adaptation to cultural distance. *Anthropology and Education Quarterly* 33(2), 238-249.

Barnhardt, R. & Kawagley, A.O. (1999). *Education Indigenous to place: Western science meets Indigenous reality.* In G. Smith and D. Williams (eds.) *Ecological Education in Action*, New York: SUNY Press.

Battiste, M. (2002). *Indigenous knowledge and pedagogy in First Nations education: A literature review with recommendations.* Ottawa: Indian and Northern Affairs Canada.

Gutierrez, K. D. and Rogoff, B. (2003). Cultural ways of learning: Individual traits or repertoires of practice. *Educational Researcher* 32(5), 19-25.

Helander-Renvall, E. (2005). *Composite report on status and trends regarding the knowledge, innovations and practices of Indigenous and local communities, Arctic region.* Geneva: United Nations Environment Program.

James, K. (ed.) (2001). *Science and Native American communities.* Lincoln, NE: University of Nebraska Press.

Kawagley, A. O., Norris-Tull, D. and Norris-Tull, R. (1998). The Indigenous worldview of Yupiaq culture: It's scientific nature and relevance to the practice and teaching of science. *Journal of Research in Science Teaching* 35(2), 133-144.

Kawagley, O. (1995). *A Yupiaq world view: A pathway to*

ecology and spirit. Prospect Heights, IL: Waveland Press.

Krupnik, I. and Jolly, D. (eds.) (2001). *The earth is faster now: Indigenous observations of Arctic environmental change.* Fairbanks, AK: Arctic Research Consortium of the US

Kullerud, L. (2005). *UArctic strategic plan.* Copenhagen: University of the Arctic.

Pfirman, S., Bell, R., Turrin, M., & Mare, P. (2004). *Bridging the poles: Education linked with research.* Washington, D.C.: National Science Foundation, Office of Polar Programs.

Stephens, S. (2000). *Handbook for culturally responsive science curriculum.* Fairbanks, AK: Alaska Native Knowledge Network, University of Alaska Fairbanks.

Preparing Preservice Educators for Teaching in a Local Context: The Rural Practicum in Alaska

Ute Kaden and Phil Patterson

Abstract

Access to quality education for all Alaskans plays a critical role for sustaining healthy and vibrant communities in a fast-changing global context. A retainable effective teacher workforce with knowledge about culturally guided teaching and an appreciation of the Arctic environment is key for engaging students in meaningful learning. The purpose of this article is to review findings from a study designed to identify the effectiveness of a rural practicum as part of a teacher-education program in Alaska. A mixed-methods research approach was used to describe the impact of a rural practicum on preservice teachers' understanding of teaching and living in rural, small school communities with predominantly Indigenous cultures. Results suggest that participants felt better informed about teaching and living in rural communities. Furthermore, they gained a deeper understanding and appreciation for native knowledge and culture. Those findings have implications for teacher-education programs that prepare educators for working in rural and culturally diverse communities.

Keywords: rural practicum, preservice teachers, rural placements, teacher preparation, rural education

One constant between Alaska's schools of the past and those of today is the need for good teachers in rural communities. Alaska has historically suffered from shortages of teachers who are prepared to effectively work in areas that are sparsely populated and that are considerable distances away from more-populated communities, especially urban centers (U.S. Department of Education 2012; Castagno & Brayboy 2008; Slack, Bourne, & Gertler 2003). Such rural and remote communities are often populated by Indigenous people (Smithsonian.com 2007).

A common practice for preparing preservice teachers is allowing them to participate in authentic practicum experiences (Gurvitch & Metzler 2008). It is anticipated that university preservice teachers, through real-world experiences, will gain insight into professional practices, develop competencies through participation in actual classrooms, and learn to integrate into work environments (Ryan, Toohey, & Hughes 1996). For practicums in rural schools, it is additionally hoped that candidates will consider seeking future employment in such settings.

For purposes of this article *practicum* is defined as a temporary fieldwork experience that involves observations within an assigned classroom or classrooms and includes providing assistance to classroom teachers and conducting some actual lessons with students. This differs from *student teaching*, which is the culminating experience in a teacher-education program and typically involves having the preservice teacher assume most of the responsibilities of a supervising teacher over an extended period of time (Henry & Weber 2010). This article describes the findings from a study conducted to determine the effectiveness of preservice teachers' rural practicum experiences in Alaska.

The Alaska Context

Overall, Alaska's schools face many challenges that complicate the recruitment and retention of teachers: low salaries, the high cost of living, schools in corrective action, limited teacher housing in some areas, new policies related to teacher certification, the state's retirement system, and more lucrative career opportunities elsewhere (Lo, Madsen, & Snyder 2010). These problems are amplified even more for rural Alaskan schools (Monk 2007). Additionally, Alaska's public school system is currently facing multimillion-dollar budget cuts (Gara 2013). These challenges are suspected of being factors contributing to an ever-rotating series of teachers who are frequently learning on the job. Teachers who are new to rural Alaska generally learn about local cultures, lifestyles, and differentiating instruction for their students—often only to leave after a few years (Munsch & Boylan 2008; Lipka 1991). Because of low retention, students, parents, and teachers frequently don't have time to bond in order to develop strong working relationships (Hill & Taylor 2004). The inability to maintain a consistent teacher workforce may also play a role in the low academic achievement of Alaska's students (Roehl 2010) and in decreasing the importance of education in some rural areas (Benner & Mistry 2007).

Similar to population trends in other states, more Alaskans are moving to urban areas (Hunsinger, Howell, & Whitney 2012; U.S. Census Bureau 2012). Nevertheless, 25 percent of all Alaskans and 46 percent of Alaska Natives live in communities of fewer than 1,000 people. Nearly one-quarter of Alaskans live in communities accessible only by boat or aircraft (National

Rural Funders Collaborative 2010). Statewide public-school enrollment figures indicate that the two primary ethnic groups served in schools are Whites (51 percent) and Alaska Natives (22 percent) (Alaska Department of Education and Early Development 2011); however, approximately 90 percent of student enrollment in rural Alaska is composed of Alaska Native children (Hill, Kawagley, & Barnhardt 2006). Among the five states with the lowest populations, Alaska ranks first in teacher turnover even though it is the most populous of those five states (Alliance for Excellent Education 2005). Alaska employs approximately 8,000 public-school teachers. On average 985 teachers were hired annually due to attrition, retirement, and growth between 2008–2012 (Hill & Hirshberg 2013). There is a much higher turnover rate of teachers in rural areas (22 percent) when compared to those in urban areas (9 percent) (Hill & Hirshberg 2013).

One possible contributing factor related to the retention and effectiveness of teachers in rural Alaska pertains to teacher preparation. Alaska imports approximately 64 percent of its teaching workforce from other states (Hill & Hirshberg 2013). In other words, Alaska's colleges and universities only train less than half of the teachers needed within the state. Among teachers with less than ten years of experience, those who prepared to be teachers in Alaska have much lower turnover rates than those who prepared outside (Hill & Hirshberg 2013). This is of particular interest to policy makers, who wonder if training more teachers in the state would reduce turnover. The longevity of Alaska-trained teachers may be attributable to their training, which typically addresses place-based pedagogies, the cultural and linguistic diversity within the state, the impact of environmental conditions, and state-specific sociopolitical trends (Vinlove 2012). The in-state training also allows for authentic rural practicum experiences (Jones 2011; Munsch & Boylan 2008).

The Practicum Experience in Education

Practicum is derived from the term *practical experiences* (Smith & Lev-Ari 2005). These experiences are to provide trainees with opportunities to observe, analyze, and implement professional practices in real-world situations, typically under the supervision of a qualified professional and a college or university supervisor. Several professional fields, such as counseling, nursing, social work, and law, require practicum experiences. Other terminology may be used in place of *practicum*, such as *fieldwork, clinical practice, internship,* and *apprenticeship.* The duration and assumed responsibilities of practicum experiences can vary depending upon professional standards and program criteria established by individual colleges and universities. Practicum experiences are especially important in education because they allow trainees the opportunity to link theory to the realities of actual classrooms (Grundnoff 2011). It has been acknowledged that familiarity and mastery of teaching is best acquired and developed by actually teaching (Munby, Russell, & Martin 2001). In many teacher-education programs, practicums allow preservice teachers multiple opportunities to teach in multiple settings.

Internationally, practicum experiences are included in many teacher-education programs. Several studies have been conducted concerning the efficacy of these experiences using a variety of settings. For example, a study by Smith and Lev-Ari (2005) surveyed 486 student teachers from the largest teacher-education institution in Israel. The 68-item survey asked participants to evaluate a variety of components of the teacher-education program that they had completed. Survey respondents overwhelmingly indicated that the practicum experiences were the most important program components in their development as teachers.

The role and importance of practicum supervision is another variable that has been explored. Wyss, Siebert, and Dowling (2012) surveyed preservice teachers who participated in one of two preservice placement models. One preservice experience involved university faculty being on-site and available for consultation, while the other model had practicum participants without immediate university faculty supervision. Results indicated that those preservice teachers who had a university faculty member on-site had greater confidence in lesson planning and in dealing with student-to-student conflicts.

Alaska is not the only region where practicum experiences occur in remote and isolated rural areas. In a study by Kline, White, & Lock (2013) preservice teachers who had participated in practicum experiences in rural and remote communities and schools in Australia were surveyed. The survey queried participants about several possible components related to practicum experiences. Results of the survey identified two important factors associated with successful practicum experiences. These were: 1) placement in a community supportive of the school and preservice teacher and 2) access to knowledgeable teacher-educators as well as university support and resources. These factors contributed to preservice teachers' intent to seek employment in rural schools.

Although helpful, practicums may not provide a panacea for effectively preparing all teachers. Grudnoff (2011) reported findings from a qualitative study on a group of teachers in New Zealand who had completed their teacher-education programs the previous year. As preservice teachers, the participants had been placed in multiple practicum experiences. The teachers were interviewed about their experiences and how those experiences played in their development as first-year teachers. Results indicated that the participants considered the practicum experiences key to their preparation as teachers; however, they also felt that the experiences did not adequately prepare them for all of the challenges encountered as first-year teachers.

Practicums appear to be viable components to teacher-preparation programs. They may also aid in preparing teachers to effectively work in high-needs areas, such as rural communities. Practicums, particularly in rural settings, are intended to sensitize preservice teachers to instructional pedagogy, student characteristics and needs, culture, and community attributes (Kline, White, & Lock 2013; Jones 2011; Musch & Boylan 2008). Considering the time and expense in developing and implementing such experiences, it is important that teacher-education programs conduct ongoing assessments regarding practicum experiences and their efficacies. Therefore, the overriding research question for this study is: what is the value and efficacy of participating in practicums in rural Alaskan schools?

The Rural Practicum

The rural practicum for this study was a one-week educational immersion activity for preservice teachers enrolled in the secondary postbaccalaureate teacher-education program at the University of Alaska Fairbanks (UAF). The overall intent of the practicum was to experience teaching and learning in the context of Alaska's rural, remote, and Indigenous communities. Major objectives of the rural practicum were to:

- provide firsthand experience of the needs and expectations for teachers in remote, rural school settings and Native communities
- increase the knowledge and skills in delivering place-relevant education
- provide experiences in working with students whose cultural backgrounds are different from their own
- inform about alternative ways of knowing and learning in Indigenous cultures (Barnhardt 2005)
- give guidance from people who are grounded in educational methods that are different from those based on literate traditions, including experiential-based oral traditions of Alaska Native communities
- provide opportunities to network with rural teachers, experience rural community events and Native traditions, and to see the realities of living and teaching in remote areas
- increase informed interest in teaching and living in rural Alaska

The secondary postbaccalaureate program is a one- to two-year teacher-education program that prepares teacher candidates for teaching middle and high school grade levels. The practicum takes place in the spring semester before graduation. Participating in the rural practicum is optional but highly recommended. About 80 percent of the preservice teachers take advantage of the rural practicum. Those who participate are concurrently enrolled in a multicultural education course. The university funds the travel costs. The rural practicum preservice teachers travel in groups of two or three to selected small, remote, rural schools with predominantly Native student populations. Host schools are significant distances away from the university at fly-in (off the road system) Alaska village locations. Those collaborating schools serve a K–12 student population and have approximate enrollments between 10 and 200 students. A faculty member based at the university functions as the main person of contact for preservice teachers and participating school staff. The guidelines in Table 3 on page 66 were followed throughout the rural practicum.

Description and Methods of the Study

Multiple data collection methods were used for the study. The primary sources were pre- and post-survey data collected from 34 secondary-education preservice teachers participating in the rural practicum between 2010–2013, the transcriptions of participants' rural practicum blog sites, and the transcription of semi-structured interviews with participants before and after the rural practicum experience. Phenomenological perspectives, narrative inquiry, and ethnographic methods supported interpretation and understanding of the rural practicum experience (Creswell 2007; Moustakas 1994).

Instrumentation

The researchers developed a web-based pre-post survey intended to elicit information to evaluate the extent of effectiveness of the rural practicum experience. To establish content validity, two researchers with expertise in the fields of multicultural and Indigenous education reviewed the instrument, whereupon revisions were made. The pre-survey was given before preservice teachers traveled to the rural practicum sites and the post-survey was given immediately after returning from the experience. During the survey administration two subsequent follow-up reminders were sent to maximize the response rate (Dillman 2010). The surveys had a total of 24 items with Likert scale or categorical response options, and included four open-ended questions.

In addition, preservice teachers designed individual blogs, open to the public on the Internet, that described locations, sociocultural characteristics, and historical backgrounds of the rural practicum communities. The blog entries also reflected experiences during and after the rural practicum and summarized what was observed and learned. All preservice teachers had received instruction during a concurrent technology course, which addressed effective blogging, photography and photo editing, social media, and journal writing for the public. Internet connectivity in the rural and remote sites varied, resulting in some slightly delayed blog posts.

Two researchers read the blog postings (https://sites.google.com/a/alaska.edu/rural-practicum-2010/rural-practicum), developed a coding system, and documented emerging themes. Semi-structured interviews with a focus on place-relevant teaching, small rural schools, Native culture, and the rural practicum as a learning experience were conducted with each participant. These were then transcribed, and reoccurring themes were identified.

Participants

Thirty-four preservice teachers from the secondary postbaccalaureate teaching program at UAF completed the rural practicum between 2010 and 2013. The response rate for the surveys was 88 percent. The 30 students—20 female (67 percent) and 10 male (33 percent)—who returned both the pre- and post-surveys were the participants of this study. The average age of the participants was 26 years with 13 (43 percent) in the age group of 21–25 years, 11 (37 percent) in the age group of 26–30 years, and six (20 percent) with an age of greater than 30 years. The ethnicity was reported as three (10 percent) American Indian/Alaska Native, two (7 percent) Hispanic, one (3 percent) African American, and 24 (80 percent) White/Caucasian. About 40 percent of the participants were married. Only five (17 percent) of the participants had previously visited a Native rural community in Alaska that was not connected to the road system.

Data Analysis

A mixed-methods data approach was used to gather and analyze quantitative and qualitative data. Quantitative data were analyzed using descriptive statistical measures to discover patterns and to present findings. These data were used to create a narrative description of the rural practicum. Qualitative data were gathered by asking open-ended survey questions, transcribing blog entries, and semi-structured interviews with the participants. Thematic analysis was used to identify recurring themes and trends (Hatch 2002). Preservice teachers' rural practicum blogs were evaluated using the constant comparative method (Glaser & Strauss 1967) in which inductive coding and sorting allowed themes to emerge. Data from surveys, blog transcriptions, and conversions were triangulated to strengthen the validity of the results and discussion.

The study relied on self-report data and the postbaccalaureate secondary-education participant sample does not necessarily reflect preservice educators as a whole. It is noted that the authors of this study are involved in rural practicum organization and planning in various capacities. However, the authors feel that these experiences strengthen the accounts of the paper. Some of the findings may apply to a specific local context only. Participant statements reported in the results are illustrating the diversity of experiences and the internal fight between self-understanding and understanding others. Vignettes of unpacking thought-provoking moments are included to provide realistic representations of the rural experience as seen by preservice teachers. However, the overall results may have the potential to better understand and augment teacher-education field practices in regions with rural characteristics and Indigenous populations.

Results and Discussion

Overall, participants indicated in the post-survey that the rural practicum was a valuable experience in the teacher-preparation program. Twenty-eight (93 percent) participants reported an increase in knowledge and skills about teaching in a rural setting as well as a deeper understanding and appreciation for Native knowledge, culture, and community and school relations.

Face-to-face networking opportunities with rural teachers, observing of place-relevant teaching, experiencing differentiated instruction in multiage classrooms, and working with the community were cited by 28 (93 percent) of the participants as valuable rural practicum experiences in the post-survey. Overall, less than 14 (46 percent) of the participants considered (willing or strongly willing) teaching in rural areas of Alaska before the rural practicum. In the pre-post–survey comparison the willingness to teach in rural Alaska increased slightly to 19 (63 percent) participants (see Figure 1). Nonetheless, in follow-up interviews, participants indicated that they were more interested in rural employment for a limited portion of their careers. However, only seven (23 percent) of the participants were willing or strongly willing to spend most of their teacher careers in rural Alaska before they went to the rural practicum. This number decreased slightly in the post-survey to five (17 percent). Family considerations such as schooling prospects for their own children and employment opportunities for spouses may play an important role in decisions to teach in rural areas, as the results of the survey and interviews show. Those findings indicate that for the predominantly White and non-Native preservice teacher group the rural practicum alone is not the venue to ultimately increase the willingness to teach in rural settings. However, it may prepare preservice teachers for working with Native students in other settings (e.g., urban schools). Those findings are similar to other studies of rural practicum experiences (Kline, White, & Lock 2013; Munsch & Boylan 2008).

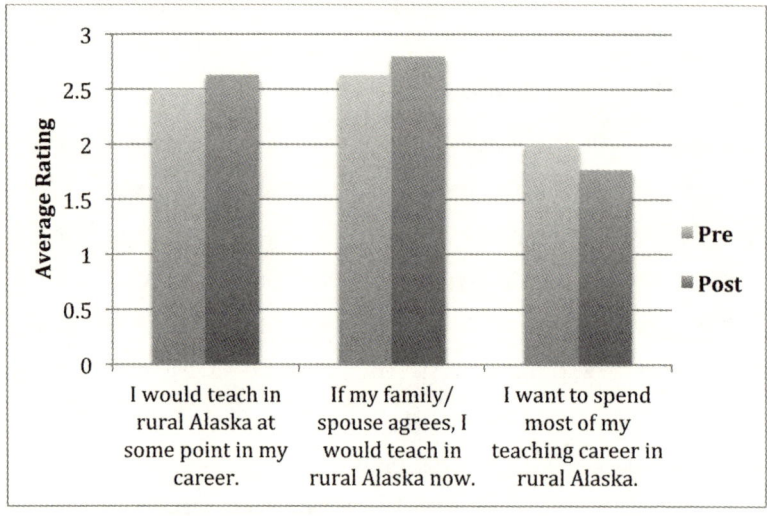

Figure 1 Willingness to teach in Rural Alaska Pre- and Post-Survey Average Rating Results; N=30 (Likert Scale 1 (Never), 2 (Undecided), 3 (Willing), 4 (Strongly Willing))

Responses to Likert scale survey items of the post-survey concerning teacher training for rural Alaska and the rural practicum are illustrated in Figure 2. Thirty (100 percent) of the participants agreed or strongly agreed that a rural practicum is needed to prepare teachers for teaching in rural Alaska. Twenty-seven (90 percent) of the participants stated that they felt better informed about teaching in rural Alaska and that a successful teacher in Alaska needs special training for teaching multiage and multigrade-level classrooms and in understanding Native cultures.

Eight (27 percent) of the participants indicated that they were more likely to apply for a rural teaching position after the rural practicum. One participant explained during the interview: "I am much more willing to teach in rural Alaska now; however, I am also more aware than before making that kind of commitment, I would want to know as much as possible about the village I would be going to."

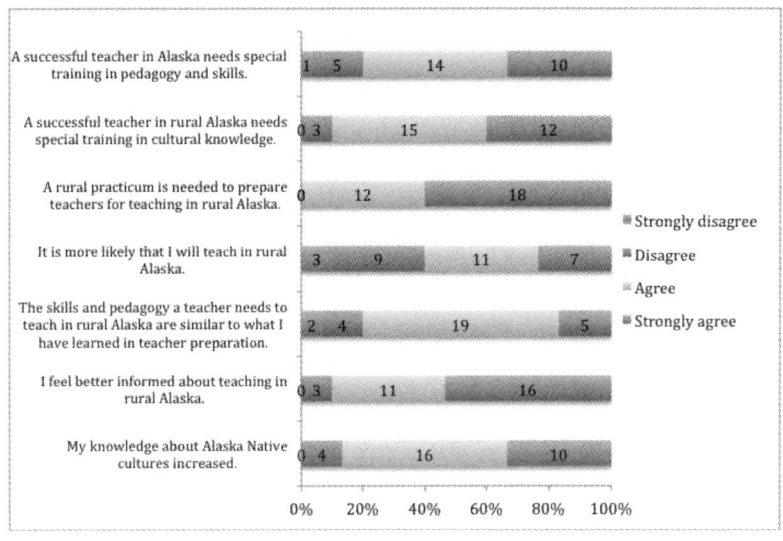

Figure 2 Likert Scale Survey Responses of Post-Survey Items; N=30

Responses to the open-ended questions from the survey, which concerned what was learned from the rural practicum that may enhance a professional career, are compiled in Table 1. Participants reflected on multiple topics around the emerging themes of teaching and learning, culture and community, and challenging issues.

	I learned ...
Teaching & Learning	Differentiation of teaching is important; Learn to teach multi-level classes and to be flexible; Holding back all judgments- one never knows what is going on behind the scenes; The need to be patient and flexible in my teaching is even more important in rural settings; Be respectful; I saw how teachers can really play a part in reconnecting students with their culture; Teaching in rural Alaska requires being creative and innovative; It's important that teachers incorporate the culture and art into the lessons/school work to make it relevant; Use local material as much as possible.
Culture and Community	Including culturally relevant materials to all students is important; Learned different teaching styles and techniques; First-hand experience with subsistence lifestyle; Provide chances to connect with the community and invite them into the learning environment; importance of bringing community resources into the classroom; Learn as much as you can about the community where you will teach and live in.
Challenging issues	Many of the problems in rural schools from 20-30 years ago are still occurring today; There is still negativity towards western education in rural villages and some of this is justified; There is a lot of tragedy at home in many places; The slow pace, the "laziness" as many teachers call it, and the seemingly inability to produce city-scale energy or enforce rules; Fun and friendly students but with limited sense of competition or school work ethic.

Table 1: Preservice Teachers' Responses to the Question of What They Had Learned from the Rural Practicum That May Enhance Their Professional Careers.

Responses to the open-ended survey question about culturally responsive teaching and classroom strategies that were observed are summarized under the themes of curriculum, culture, classroom management, students, and teachers (see Table 2). The long list of culturally rich activities under the active guidance and participation of Elders and community members demonstrates that education is a local, community-based enterprise (Corbett 2009; Howley & Howley 2005). The majority of participants indicated that they had never participated in Native activities, such as seal skinning, and that they deeply appreciated the invitation by the host communities and schools to participate in such activities. Flexibility of teachers, the need for knowledge across the curriculum in more than one subject area, networking and teacher peer support, appreciation of the natural Alaska environment, and community integration were frequently listed by participants as major factors for teacher effectiveness and retention in rural areas.

Reflections on Culturally Responsive Teaching and Classroom Strategies	
Curriculum	Native language and dances taught at school; assessment questions included Native topics and experiences from hunting trips; Moose, seal and whale hunting trips with Elders took place during the school year as part of the curriculum; Reading of Native literature; Place relevant teaching more visible in lower grades
Culture	Skinning a beaver; dissection of a seal and a Polar bear in class; demonstrations of sewing seal skins by Elders; Elder interview on importance of hunting seals and walruses to local culture and healthy communities; Writing essays on an Native activities; References to local landmarks and local historical events in class; School sponsored fishing trip; Yupik traditions on ice fishing discussed in social studies class; Wood shop projects were students make sleds for carrying food and other supplies; Practicing of songs and dances for potlatch; Students training for Native Olympics; Strong family, community and cultural relations
Classroom management	Elders had visible positive influence on students' behavior; Students showed great respect toward elders in the Yupik language classroom; Differentiation for multiage classrooms; Teachers seem to have a closer relationship with students; Slower pace, more informal class rooms with less rules; Student attendance was problematic
Students	Curious and friendly students; Kids are kids everywhere; Students are just as attached to their iPhones and electronic gadgets as students elsewhere; Older students are sleepy in class and more reserved toward outsiders
Teachers	Teachers must be super flexible; Positive student-teacher relationships are absolutely critical; Long days at school for teachers; Teachers need to be prepared for all types of situations; Networking and teacher peer support are essential; Knowing more than one subject area is critical; High number of different subject preparation; Knowledge about local customs and culture is a must; Patience and a none judgmental attitude are vital

Table 2

The majority of participants reflected upon Native languages in the open-ended survey questions. Twenty-seven (90 percent) of the participants reported that the Native language of the community was taught at the school. Delivery methods observed included Native language classes taught by a Native language teacher at the school, videoconferencing between schools, and instruction supported by technology, such as Native podcasts and vocabulary available on iTunes. An unexpected finding was that 19 (63 percent) of the participants had indicated in the pre-survey that they did not expect to observe Native languages being taught at the schools. One participant reported, "Native language was used more than I thought and students displayed great respect toward the Native teachers." They also indicated that students behaved very respectfully in those classes as illustrated in the following quote from one of the participants: "The students were most respectful during Yup'ik class, which was taught by Native teachers."

Participants in their survey responses and during interviews often noted the roles of rural schools. Participants frequently made reference to "the school as the center of the community" and "the school as the meeting place, sports arena, and place with Internet access and showers." The interconnection of community and school was recognized as a sign of healthy communities.

For 20 (67 percent) of the participants, the rural practicum provided the first opportunity to interact with Native students in a K–12 school setting as educators. Blog entries from the participants reflected that they appreciated the opportunity but also revealed that preservice teachers had little practical knowledge about teaching in a rural setting with a predominantly Native population. Blogs also revealed that participants had an appreciation for the "kindness" and sometimes-unexpected gestures of "welcome" by Native community members and students. It was the students at the school, the teachers, and community members whom they met that would be remembered most. Examples of preservice teachers' blog statements include: "All but one of the students at the school I visited were Alaska Native. I got a chance to talk with a lot of them, which was great" and, "They like the same music, the iPhone, and everything. The juniors and seniors were very self-motivated, which honestly kind of surprised me. It's as if they were taking responsibility for their own education, since they knew that the teacher had others to attend to in the multigrade classroom."

The need for special training in differentiation of curriculum and professional development for teaching multiple grade levels in one classroom was also a common theme in participant blogs. In addition, 25 (83 percent) of the participants noted in their blogs that a good relationship with students is essential for being successful as a teacher in a small school. Furthermore, participants commented on how the natural environmental (e.g., change to almost 24 hours of daylight in spring) and family factors visibly influenced students' behavior. Samples of the blog entries on relationships and environmental influences include:

"Teachers there had to really nurture students before they could get a lot of learning done. This has reminded me of the importance of building relationships with the students before any real learning can happen."

"They [kids] were more sleepy than normal, but that could have largely been due to the fact that the shades were closed and the lights were off in most classrooms, as rapidly increasing long daylight hours seem to be disrupting to human physiology."

"Having a good rapport with students is essential, as is knowing as much as possible about their backgrounds. The teachers I observed were very aware of their students' backgrounds and sensitive to their home lives."

As noted in the literature, one of the persistent problems in rural schools is teacher turnover (Kline, White, & Lock 2013; Munsh & Boylan 2008; White 2008). After only one week of observations it was cited by 13 (43 percent) of the participants that learning and school climate are influenced by the stability and effectiveness of the teaching workforce and leadership. An example of this insight is demonstrated in the following reflection:

"One of the main problems with the school was the teacher/administrator turnover. It led to much inconsistency and distrust."

Overall, blog entries reported the rural practicum was an effective field experience that provoked thought and the desire to learn more about Native culture, differentiated teaching strategies, methods, and community connections. One participant summarized the experience by writing:

"The rural practicum was a little different than I expected. Some conditions/situations in rural Alaska were worse than I expected but my desire to teach there is stronger. I'm glad the experience was real and not a candy-coated tour."

Recommendations

The extent of success of the rural practicum described in this article may, in part, be due to variables that concern the structure and organization of the experience (See Table 3). Thus, part of the participant surveys was the evaluation of rural practicum program structure and logistics to improve future implementation of rural practicum experiences. Recommendations that can guide a rural practicum experience are documented and are summarized in the following paragraph.

As the described rural practicum was only a week long, the researchers felt that it was critical to establish communication about responsibilities and expectations between the university and school partners. Suggestions for a successful experience included that the host school should identify a key staff member to coordinate efforts with the university contact person. Additionally, it was felt that university faculty and the host schools needed to thoroughly communicate what the preservice teachers were prepared for and expected to do during the practicum (e.g., teach lessons, tutor, support extracurricular activities, write a blog, participate in cultural and community events, observe classrooms including Native language, etc.). Furthermore, a written memorandum of understanding between the host school and the university may function as a guide and evaluation base for participants and stakeholders.

Other possible factors for the successful rural practicum identified in this study include: the long-term planning by university faculty, pre-practicum preparation of participants, and ongoing communication between all stakeholders. Hosting preservice teachers can be a rewarding but time-intensive activity for all involved. Being transplanted for a week into a completely different community and school culture can be overwhelming for preservice teachers. It was felt that ongoing support before and during the rural practicum was essential for preservice teachers and host school staff. Additionally, efforts were made to involve Native faculty and community elders in the process, thereby deepening preservice teachers' understanding of Indigenous culture, ways of knowing and learning, and community life. Overall, planning and organizing with the intent to develop long-term partnerships between the university, host schools, and the rural communities was a priority.

Another possible variable to the success of the rural practicum was the selection of schools and communities. The researchers felt that preservice teachers needed to be placed in authentic settings that possessed positive and welcoming climates. Just as with urban settings, there are problematic schools and communities. These were purposefully avoided in order to provide preservice teachers with supportive, successful models of teaching and living.

Recommendations for future rural practicum experiences include the ongoing need to establish and strengthen partnerships between rural districts and universities for the purpose of hosting preservice teachers. Optimally, such ongoing partnerships would build mentoring expertise and familiarity with goals and objectives of the rural practicum. Such strengthened partnerships would result in greater support to preservice teachers and as well as provide supervising teachers with greater expertise and leadership opportunities.

In this study, both preservice teachers and rural host-school faculty indicated that rural practicum experiences longer than a week would be beneficial for developing a deeper understanding of rural teaching, culture, and living in remote rural communities. This was especially suggested for those preservice teachers who planned to teach in such settings. Munsch and Boylan (2008), in their study on rural practicums, also supported extended experiences.

A final recommendation concerns the need for ongoing formative assessment. Such assessment can inform university personnel as to the quality of work done by the preservice teachers but can also alert university faculty to the quality of experiences that preservice teachers are encountering. Even though great care may be taken to appropriately place preservice teachers in rural settings, over time the characteristics of placements can alter. Teachers and principals at schools can transfer, educational priorities may switch, and the overall climates of schools and communities can change. What was once an effective placement site can become an inappropriate experience for preservice teachers. University faculty needs to be vigilant to such changes.

Guidelines for a comprehensive rural practicum in a remote rural community

Faculty	Preservice Teachers
Planning	
• Establish frequent communication between school administration, cooperating teachers, and student teachers (Memorandum of understanding)	• Research educational, socio-cultural, historical, and geographical data regarding destination school district, school, and community (community profile assignment)
• Set activities and goals for the visit	
• Work on logistics for the visit such as transportation, accommodation, and safety	• Read relevant literature inclusive of documents from Alaska Native authors
• Invite Native faculty and Elders to meet with preservice teachers before the travel for dialogue	• Start a blog site
	• Establish personal communication with rural school principals and collaborating teachers (e.g., e-mail, Skype)
• Provide a fact sheet, resources, and guidance on travel logistics and general terms of contact (e.g., FERPA rules photos, general behavior, dry villages)	• Prepare lesson to teach
	• Complete Pre-survey
Observation and activities during the visit	
	• Observe different classes and teachers
• Read and comment on preservice teachers' blog sites	• Participate in cultural and community events (touring the community)
• Provide logistics and support if needed	
	• Teach different classes
	• Provide instructional support (tutoring, individualized help)
	• Keep a reflective journal/blog
	• Network with teachers, staff, and community members
Reflection after the visit	
• Facilitate discussions/reflective writing	• Have a conversation with Native faculty members and Elders about experiences to raise questions, and understand context
• Invite Native faculty and Elders to the discussions	
• Incorporate preservice teachers' experience into other courses of the teacher preparation program	• Reflect in writing and group discussions about the experience
	• Post a summative blog
• Communication with all stakeholders for evaluation	• Write a thank you letter to the host school and collaborating teachers
• Data analysis from surveys, blogs, and discussions to guide future educational experiences	• Complete the post survey

Table 3

Conclusion

Teaching is a very local enterprise shaped by the sociohistorical, socioeconomic, and cultural values of each country, state, community, school, and classroom. Teacher-education programs have a responsibility to go beyond a generic multicultural mantra. Teacher-education programs need to offer teacher candidates authentic field-based settings to experience and appreciate local diversity.

Results of this study show that the rural practicum was successful in increasing participants' knowledge about teaching in rural and small school environments, Indigenous culture and place, and locally relevant teaching approaches. Offering such an expensive program in the light of financial constraints and educational cutbacks demonstrates a true commitment toward the education of teachers who have an understanding and respect for culture, location, and diversity. In addition, this study shows that there is great potential in utilizing social media, such as blogs, for reporting and sharing individual rural practicum understandings and field experiences in a teacher-training program. This study provides evidence that teacher-developed Web-based publications can enhance teachers' reflective practices and sharing of experiences with stakeholders, future preservice teachers, and educators who would like to learn more about teaching in rural settings.

Researching the long-term effects of a rural practicum on participants' teaching practices and dispositions toward culture, place consciousness, and retention after graduation from the teacher program may be needed. Alaska is part of a global world with strong local flavors and cultures, surrounded by magnificent nature. More research is also needed to explore the current state of access to education in rural Alaska to guide necessary changes in curriculum delivery and teaching that support living in the Arctic and celebrate and enhance culture in the Native communities. The findings of this study concur with those of other researchers in suggesting that the preservice teachers sensed the opportunities and dilemmas of those who choose to teach in rural, remote locations (Munsch & Boylan 2008). Overall, participants reflected that the rural practicum provided realistic experiences and left them a bit humbled, more thoughtful, interested, and open toward teaching in Alaska's Native rural communities. Preservice teachers' thoughtful reflections showed a realization toward the deeply human aspect of teaching in general. As one participant explained:

"Be flexible, be adaptive, be patient, don't judge. Let the students teach you how they learn. Thank you for providing us with such a great opportunity. It allowed me to create connections that I hope will continue into the future. The amount of community support I saw was amazing. Yes, schools can be really the center of a village."

References

Alaska Department of Education and Early Development (2011, October). *Total statewide enrollment by ethnicity, grade, and percent* (data file). Retrieved from http://education.alaska.gov/stats/StatewidebyEthnicity/2012St atewide_Gr_X_Ethnicity.pdf

Alliance for Excellent Education. (2005, August). Teacher attrition: A costly loss to the nation and to the states.

[Issue Brief]. Retrieved from: http://www.all4ed.org/
publication_material/straight_as/straight_public_
education_policy_and_progress_5_16

Barnhardt, R. & Kawagley, A. O. (2005). Indigenous
knowledge systems and Alaska Native Ways of
Knowing. *Anthropology & Education Quarterly, 36*(1),
8–23.

Benner, A. D., & Mistry, R. S. (2007). Congruence of mother
and teacher educational expectations and low--income
youth's academic competence. *Journal of Educational
Psychology,* 99(1), 140--153.

Castagno, A., & Brayboy, B. (2008). Culturally responsive
schooling for Indigenous youth: A review of the
literature. *Review of Educational Research, 78*(4), 941–
993.

Corbett, M. (2009). Rural schooling in mobile modernity:
Returning to the places I've been. *Journal of Research in
Rural Education (Online), 24*(7), 1–13.

Creswell, J. W. (2007). Qualitative inquiry and research
design: Choosing among five traditions (2nd Ed).
Thousand Oaks, CA: Sage.

Dillman, D.A. (2010). *Email and Internet surveys: The tailored
design method* (2nd ed.). New York, NY: Wiley.

Gara, L. (2013, March 8). Proposed cuts to school
shortages Alaska's children. *The Arctic Sounder.*
Retrieved from http://www.thearcticsounder.com/
article/1310proposed_cuts_to_schools_shortchange_
alaskas

Glaser, B.G. & Strauss, A.L. (1967). *The Discovery of Grounded*

Theory: Strategies for Qualitative Research. Chicago, IL: Aldine Pub. Co.

Grudnoff, L. (2011). Rethinking the practicum: Limitations and possibilities. *Asia-Pacific Journal of Teacher Education, 39*(3), 223-234.

Gurvitch, R. & Metzler, M. (2009). The effects of laboratory-based and field-based practicum experience on pre-service teachers' self-efficacy. *Teaching and Teacher Education, 25*(3), 437-443.

Hatch, Amos J. (2002). *Doing qualitative research in education settings.* Albany: State University of New York Press.

Henry, M.A., & Weber, A. (2010). *Supervising student teachers the professional way: A guide for cooperating teachers* (7th Ed.). Lanham, MD: Rowman & Littlefield Education.

Hill, A. & Hirshberg, D. (2013). Alaska teacher turnover, supply and demand: 2013 Highlights (Report summary). Anchorage, AK: UAA Center for Alaska Education Policy Research.

Hill, F., Kawagley, O., & Barnhardt, R. (2006). *Alaska rural systemic initiative* (Final report phase II). Arlington, VA: National Science Foundation.

Hill, N. E., & Taylor, L. C. (2004). Parental school involvement and children's academic achievement. *Current Directions in Psychological Science*, 13(4), 161-164.

Howley, A., & Howley, C. B. (2005). Rural Research Brief. Retrieved from http://www.ruraleducator.net/archive/26-2/26-2_Howley.pdf

Hunsinger, E., Howell, D., & Whitney, S. (2012, April).

Alaska Population Projections 2010-2035. Retrieved from http://www.census.gov/newsroom/releases/archives/2010_census/cb12-50.html

Jones, A. (2011). Teacher knowledge and student diversity: A rural Alaska practicum experience. Paper presented at 2011 annual meeting of the American Educational Research Association. Retrieved from the AERA Online Paper Repository.

Kline, J., Simone, W., & Lock, G. (2013). The rural practicum: Preparing a quality teacher workforce for rural and regional Australia. *Journal of Research in Rural Education, 28*(3), 1-13. Retrieved from http://jrre.psu.edu/articles/28-3.pdf

Lipka, J. (1991). Toward a culturally based pedagogy: A case study of one Yup'ik Eskimo teacher. *Anthropology & Education Quarterly, 22*(3), 203-223.

Lo, D., Madsen, E., & Snyder, M. (2010, November 12). *University of Alaska Teacher Education Plan: Deans' Report.* Retrieved from http://www.alaska.edu/files/research/TeachPrepPlan_101112.pdf

Monk, D. H. (2007). Recruiting and retaining high-quality teachers in rural areas. *The Future of Children, 17*(1), 155-174.

Moustakas, C. (1994). Phenomenological Research Methods. Thousand Oaks, CA: Sage.

Munby, H., Russell, T., & Martin, A. K. (2001). Teachers' knowledge and how it develops, in: V. Richardson (Ed.) *Handbook for research on teaching* (Washington, DC, American Educational Research Association),

877-904.

Munsch, T.R. & Boylan, C. R. (2008). Can a week make a difference? Changing perceptions about teaching and living in rural Alaska. *The Rural Educator, 29*(2), 14-23.

National Rural Funders Collaborative. (2010). Alaska rural community health strategies. Retrieved from http://www.nrfc.org/alaska.asp.

Roehl, R. F. (2010). *Correlation between teacher turnover rates in the state of Alaska and standardized test scores in the area of mathematics on standards based assessment/ high school qualifying exam* (Doctoral dissertation). Retrieved from ProQuest LLC, ISBN-978-1-1242-1428-3.

Ryan, G., Toohey, S. and Hughes, C. (1996) The purpose, value and structure of the placement in higher education: A literature review. *Higher Education*, 31(3), 355-377.

Slack, E., Bourne, L. S., & Gertler, M. S. (2003). *Small, rural, and remote communities:The anatomy of risk. A paper prepared for the role of government.* Retrieved from http://www.law-lib.utoronto.ca/investing/reports/rp18.pdf.

Smithsonian.com. (2007, November). Alaska: History and heritage. *Smithsonian.com.* Retrieved from http://www.smithsonianmag.com/travel/destination-hunter/north-america/united-states/west/alaska/alaska-history-heritage.html

Smith, K. & Lev-Ari, L. (2005). The place of the practicum

in pre-service teacher education: The voice of the students. *Asia-Pacific Journal of Teacher Education, 33*(3), 289-302. United States Census Bureau. (2012, March 26). Growth in Urban Population Outpaces Rest of Nation, Census Bureau Reports. *Newsroom.* Retrieved from http://www.census.gov/newsroom/releases/archives/2010_census/cb12-50.html

United States Department of Education (2012). Teacher Shortage Areas: Statewide Listing (Data set). Washington,D.C.: Author.

Vinlove, A. (2012) *Learning to teach where you are: Preparation for context-responsive teaching in Alaska's teacher certification programs* (Doctoral dissertation). Retrieved from http://www.ankn.uaf.edu/curriculum/PhD_Projects/AmyVinlove/Vinlove.pdf

White, S. (2008). Placing teachers? Sustaining rural schooling through place-consciousness in Teacher Education. *Journal of Research in Rural Education, 23*(7), 1-11.

Wyss, V. L., Siebert, C. J., & Dowling, K. A. (2012). Structuring effective practicum experiences for pre-service teachers. *Education, 132*(3), 600-606.

Who We Are and What We've Become: A Discussion from SLATE PhD Graduates Walkie Charles (UAF), April Counceller (UA-Kodiak), Theresa John (UAF), Patrick Marlow (UAF), Sabine Siekmann (UAF)

In 2007 a group of Alaska Native PhD students embarked on their doctoral journey through the Second Language Acquisition Teacher Education (SLATE) grant (US DoE #S356A060055). In this article three of these doctoral cohorts share their stories. First we describe the context and goals of the SLATE grant as well as the Guided Collaboratives Model at the center of our delivery model. Then the PhD students who have graduated to this date share their own stories. In the conclusion we reflect on how these past efforts are impacting ongoing projects.

Central Yup'ik is a highly endangered language traditionally spoken throughout southwestern Alaska. Roughly the size of Arizona, the "Yup'ik Region" consists of more than 60 villages and is home to approximately 23,000 Yup'ik Eskimos. Villages are not connected by roads, which means that transportation is limited to plane, boat, and snowmobile. According to Krauss (1997) only about one-quarter of all Yup'ik villages have large numbers of children growing up with Yup'ik as their first language.

Alaska Native Languages (http://www.uaf.edu/anlc/)

A broad range of Yup'ik language programs have developed within the more than 60 schools and nine school districts in the region. Programs include language and culture enrichment programs, transitional bilingual programs designed to facilitate acquisition of English by native speakers of Yup'ik, immersion programs designed to facilitate the (re)acquisition of Yup'ik as an ancestral language, and most recently dual-language development programs intended to foster the academic development of both Yup'ik and English. The goals of the SLATE grant discussed here included a) improving Yup'ik and English-language instruction, b) building capacity for local leadership in language programming, and c) conducting locally defined research. In order to meet the needs of the various Yup'ik and English programs, the grant supported 18 master's-level students pursuing either an MA in Applied Linguistics or an M.Ed. (for a discussion of the master's-level students, please refer to Marlow & Siekmann 2013(b)). The grant also supported four Alaska Native PhD students representing a number of different Alaska Native languages/cultures. The PhD students were an integral element in the GRC model, and their stories are the focus of this paper.

It has been well established in the literature that Indigenous students face many challenges in educational settings. Alaska Native students have high dropout rates in high school, only a small percentage of Indigenous students pursue higher education, and for those attending college, attrition rates are high (Faircloth & Tippeconnic 2010; DeVoe & Darling-Churchill 2008; Reyhner 1991; Aud, Fox, & Kewal Ramani 2010). Kawagley (1995) and others (Barnhardt & Kawagley 2005; Holmberg 2010) have suggested that this situation may be attributed, at least in part, to a mismatch between practices commonly found in mainstream education in both K–12 and postsecondary settings and Alaska Native cultural norms. Yup'ik society, for instance, is undergirded by a cooperative rather than competitive orientation toward goal completion (Siekmann & Charles 2011, Moses, personal conversation July 2010). In addition, instead of celebrating individual knowledge, Yup'ik society highly values a communal source of knowledge (Fienup-Riordan, Marie Meade & Reardon 2005). Educational practices that are organized around cooperation in joint activity are thus likely to be better suited to promoting the success and degree completion of Alaska Native students.

In an effort to foster collaborative teaching, learning, and researching within the SLATE grant, candidates were organized into four research cohorts called Graduate Research Collaboratives (GRCs). Each GRC focused on a general area of research (Language Pedagogy, Multiliteracies, Language Assessment, and Language Policy and Planning). One faculty member headed each GRC, and each GRC consisted of one Alaska Native PhD candidate and up to six master's candidates. Each GRC held regular meetings, which facilitated the development of individual and group research agendas as well as allowed for ongoing conversations and exchanges among peers, PhD students, and faculty members. Within this model, the PhD students acted as near-peer mentors to master's students as well as their non-Native academic advisors (see Webster & Siekmann 2013 for a more complete description of the mentoring approach with the GRC model).

Walkie Charles, April Counceller, Theresa John and Hishinlai' "Kathy R. Sikorski" started their coursework in the interdisciplinary PhD program at the University of Alaska Fairbanks in 2007 and enrolled in full-time coursework from spring 2007 until summer 2008. Given the context within which all PhD students worked and researched, the SLATE faculty developed two special-topics courses designed for SLATE PhD students: Sociocultural Theory and Second Language Learning and Critical Theory and Second Language Learning. These courses were offered as a yearlong sequence and laid the groundwork for a shared but not uncontested theoretical framework and also offered opportunities to discuss the role of Indigenous theories (see, for example, April Counceller below). Courses offered through the Indigenous Studies PhD program were also part of some of the candidates' graduate study plan.

With SLATE grant funding ending in August 2010 and most PhD candidates entering the final dissertation writing phase, Walkie Charles, April Counceller, and Theresa John were each awarded a Mellon Dissertation Completion Fellowship. It should also be mentioned that throughout their studies, all PhD students maintained partial employment and work duties. By summer 2011 Walkie Charles and April Counceller graduated with an interdisciplinary PhD housed in Applied Linguistics, and Theresa John graduated with an Indigenous Studies PhD. At the writing of the article, Kathy Sikorski is preparing for her dissertation defense.

Drs. Walkie Charles, April Counceller and Theresa John each prepared a reflective vignette about their PhD journey. They form the centerpiece of this paper.

Walkie Charles

I had the fortunate opportunity to speak my language as a child. In fact back then it was not considered a fortune; it was a standard practice and, most often, the only language of communication. Everyone in my community spoke Yugtun. Yugtun permeated every aspect of our living. Whether it was work, play, worship, or relaxation through evening stories told by parents and elders, we heard and spoke Yugtun. Although I grew up speaking both my father's and mother's dialects, and therefore chose when it was opportune to speak either, I felt safe expressing myself in the language of my own choosing—until I entered my public-school years through the auspices of the Bureau of Indian Affairs (BIA). English did not make any sense to my schoolmates and me, whose parents spoke exclusively

Yugtun at home and within the community. We learned rote English that we could not make any sense of, but since we were forced by our teachers to learn, we pretended to speak until we finally managed to utter English enough to satisfy them.

As children we learned the common rituals of reciting the Dick and Jane series (Gray 1951) accompanied by the Think-and-Do Book. As we learned English in school, we would revert to Yugtun upon leaving the school grounds.

Church Latin was exercised in the only organized church in my community. I remember hearing my mother chanting Latin hymns even though she did not know what they meant. Upon returning home, as English was left in the school, Latin was left in the church.

The community where I was born and raised was established when the evolution of the fishing industry and the availability of work to process fish brought people to my community. English quickly became the means of communication as the industry grew and more people from other parts of the region and the lower 48 established permanent homes in the community. People from the nearby smaller communities spoke Yugtun, but it was the outsiders who came into the community who brought English with them, and it became the lingua franca as a commercial language. Yugtun still was spoken within the community, but as the school became larger and more outsiders came to fill teaching positions and other borough jobs, the less the children began speaking Yugtun. There was a long period of time when students were sent out to boarding schools where Yugtun and other Native languages were prohibited, which led to the young people speaking more English than their heritage language (Lomawaima 1994; Adams 1995). Parents began to hear less Yugtun spoken among those students who returned home after being away from home for nine months in boarding schools. With the end of boarding schools came the beginning of small high schools in rural Alaska. English-only was taught exclusively with the advent of high schools, even though the schools were located in Yugtun-speaking villages.

Years later I entered the University of Alaska Fairbanks as a freshman. I pursued Elementary Education as my major. One of the first courses I took was ESK 101: Beginning Yup'ik Eskimo. I signed up for the class with apprehension, realizing that there was some element of dichotomy in that just a few years earlier I was forced out of speaking my heritage language. Here I was in a room full of eager colleagues—most of whom were of Yup'ik descent—wanting to claim the actual reading and writing of their ancestral language. Ironically it was taught by a Caucasian. I was rather impressed at the instructor's ability to make critical diagnosis of the Yup'ik language. I continued with the rest of the Yup'ik courses that were available in the early 1980s. The courses opened up my stronger appreciation for my language. I began involving myself in translating projects throughout the course of my undergraduate years.

Upon completion of my undergraduate coursework I became a primary school teacher with the Fairbanks North Star Borough School District. Within a few years I embarked on graduate work at the University of Massachusetts Amherst Graduate, School of Education in Reading and Writing. I completed my master's program as well as my PhD coursework. Unfortunately my father became severely ill which led to the expiration of the statute of limitation from UMass. It was difficult to have left such a great program at UMass, yet I never got the spirit to complete my PhD. I realized that that part of my academic life was over.

A few years later I was offered a position as instructor of Yup'ik. I never intended to teach Yup'ik at the university level, but I felt that the offer was an obligation to embrace every effort to regain my ability to speak and teach the language that was once altered by the early educational systems. I had the privilege of teaching with a mentor who was my first Yugtun instructor in the early years of my undergraduate studies. Most of my initial teaching was grammar-based as it had been taught since its inception. I quickly noticed the difference in the students who intended on taking Yugtun from the years that I began taking Yugtun courses. In the earlier years most of the students with whom I took the courses knew the language as I did, but wanted to learn to read and write the language. A new generation of learners evolved during my beginning years of teaching thirteen years before. The students rarely entered first-year Yugtun with the ability to speak the language. Most of the students wanted to learn their heritage language but I felt obligated to teach the courses as they had been traditionally taught. I felt that I could teach to accommodate the learners of Yugtun, but I felt that it was my duty to continue the tradition of teaching what had been taught by my mentor.

In 2007 I entered the SLATE doctoral program—with apprehension. Initially, cohort focus areas included language policy and planning, multi-literacies, pedagogy, and language assessment; however the only slot available at the time I applied was language assessment. I really didn't know anything about incorporating assessment into a second-language program, but I bit the bullet and embarked on a journey that would change my views about creating alternative and sociocultural directions of improving second-language learning and teaching. Attending national conferences that focused on dynamic assessment in second-language teaching and learning paved my way to a deeper understanding of the value of assessing from the learners' perspective. Naturally I was able to collect data for my study with the seven intermediate adult students in my third-semester Yugtun class. I grew to appreciate the ways by which incorporating dynamic assessment brought out the critical learning and teaching of Yugtun as a second language. I began to alter the grammar-based efforts of my predecessor as I began to learn to incorporate dynamic assessment as a process to make learning and teaching applicable to second-language acquisition.

Upon completion of my PhD with the University of Alaska Fairbanks, I applied for an assistant professor position in Yup'ik Eskimo. My mentor and predecessor had recently retired from teaching Yugtun after 36 years, one year before I completed my program. I want to express my gratitude to my mentor who taught me so much about the mechanics of my language. With the newer generation of Yup'ik students wanting to learn Yugtun, I felt that the time was right to accept the agency to make appropriate changes in teaching Yugtun so that the future students could gain the appropriate tools to gain access to the language of their ancestors.

Such a shift in the approach to organizing the content of the language courses, in addition to the shift toward dynamic assessment as a framework for teaching, may go a long way toward addressing another problem in the heritage language program: student attrition. The attrition rate for the university Yugtun classes is quite high, with as much as a 50 percent decrease in student numbers after the first semester of study. With a newer approach for learning and teaching, it provides students a stronger chance to continue with their dream of successfully gaining Yugtun proficiency as they engage in the Yugtun courses in the future.

Since the completion of my dissertation, I became the director of the Yugtun programs for both the UAF campus as well as the Bethel Kuskokwim Campus. I have also recently been appointed by the governor of the State of Alaska as chair of the Alaska Native Language Preservation and Advisory Council.

I want to express my gratitude to Drs. Marilee Coles-Ritchie, Sabine Siekmann, Patrick Marlow, and "Anaan" Joan Parker Webster for their unfathomable trust in seeing that all the students in SLATE received the highest quality of education, which undoubtedly has led all the participants in both the master's and PhD programs into leadership positions around second-language acquisition. Because of the guidance and trust, the former PhD students of SLATE are now faculty or associate faculty for a new generation of scholars who are beginning their pursuits in the summer of 2013 with the Alaska Native Education Computer Assisted Language Learning. What a trip it has been, and every effort worth its time. *Quyana cakneq.*

April Counceller
My journey in SLATE began a bit differently than the other

PhD students. Rather than being already employed by the University of Alaska Fairbanks at the start of the project, I was working as a language program manager at the Alutiiq Museum & Archaeological Repository in Kodiak. I also had not planned to seek my PhD so "early" in life, although I had hoped to get one eventually. When I found out that a single spot was still waiting to be filled in SLATE, and that the spot was for a student in Language Policy and Planning, I knew immediately that it was an opportunity I couldn't pass up. Minor issues like being seven months pregnant with my first child did not worry me in the least!

Patrick, who would later become my advisor, warned me that this endeavor would be extremely difficult, especially with a baby. Patrick would also go on to become my voice of reason throughout the doctoral process, but I did not feel that it would be too great a challenge. However, I was basing my judgment on my previous education, which was challenging at times but never stressed me to the point of crisis. I had earned my bachelor's in Anthropology and American Civilization at Brown University and my master's a few years after that in Rural Development through the University of Alaska Fairbanks, so I was confident in my academic abilities. I was accepted into the program but was little prepared for the whirlwind ahead of me as I sought to earn my PhD in two and a half years. Patrick was, of course, correct that it would be a difficult trial, but I am fortunate that he and the other SLATE faculty had confidence in my abilities and the commitment to guide me through my ambitious completion goals.

My first coursework began in the summer of 2007, two months after my daughter Emmy was born, and I graduated in December 2010, when I was pregnant with my second daughter. I walked in graduation the next spring with a four-year-old (Emmy) and a newborn infant (Laura) as well as a huge sense of relief and accomplishment. Looking back on those first weeks and months of the program, I recall flying to Fairbanks for the summer session, making my suitcase into a baby bed for Emmy, and bringing her to my daylong classes while she snoozed in the stroller. That winter, my husband, Jeremy, and I moved our family to Fairbanks for a year so I could complete the on-site coursework required for my degree.

I chose to do my research on the Kodiak Alutiiq New Words Council, after my committee recommended narrowing my focus from language revitalization in general. I was under a lot of self-inflicted pressure to directly apply what I was learning to help my home community, and I initially thought that solving the question of "how to achieve success" for all threatened language communities was the way I should contribute. Their guidance at this time was very important in reining in my too-broad research questions into something achievable, but it also helped me understand that by looking at one small thing (like the New Words Council) you can also gain insight into larger matters.

After a year of coursework and monthly research trips back to my home community, I returned home and continued working part-time at the Alutiiq Museum (made possible by a special arrangement between SLATE and my employer) while I completed my research and began drafting the first chapters of my dissertation. The next year and a half until I successfully defended in the summer of 2010 were tough, as my community and family commitments often interfered with forward-progress in my writing, and it seemed that I was stuck in an endless cycle of write, edit, revise, repeat. I had considered myself a good writer before entering the PhD program but realized that there was a whole additional level of achievement that would be expected of me in my dissertation.

My stubbornness did not help. I despised "theory," saying that it had little relevance to the on-the-ground realities in my community. Over time I found that there was Indigenous as well as non-Indigenous theory that was relevant and helpful but had not been applied in communities or written for a lay audience. I began to see that my research and writing could address some of these gaps, and I strove to make my writing theoretically informed but not alienating to members of my community. So I cranked out my chapters, page by agonizing page.

I also questioned why my committee members, and especially my advisor, Patrick Marlow, would not let good enough be "good enough." I had never experienced being challenged (intellectually, emotionally) at this level in my academic experience. There were times when I thought I was done with a particular section of the literature review, the analysis, or the discussion, only to be told to dig deeper and revise some more. In my weaker moments I remember wishing that I could be given an easier path. Later I realized that despite time and personal pressures everyone was experiencing, the SLATE faculty was holding us to the high academic standard that is signified by the PhD. My committee felt that I had the ability to improve my writing and therefore asked me to reach my higher potential. In the midst of the process, this was cold comfort, but I feel now that my degree means more to me because of it.

Since graduating I have had additional opportunities to continue and expand my work with language revitalization and Indigenous education. I was recruited to a new position at Kodiak College, a branch of the University of Alaska Anchorage, starting as a faculty member and project activity coordinator in January 2011. In this role I am helping develop an Alutiiq Studies Program and Native Student Support system at our community campus, while also maintaining close connections to the Alutiiq Museum as a member of the Alutiiq Heritage Foundation board. Along with another of my SLATE colleagues (Walkie Charles) I was selected in 2012 by the governor to sit on the newly formed Alaska Native Language Preservation and Advisory Council, recently formed by SB-130 in the Alaska Legislature. I have been told that once you get your PhD you are inundated with offers and requests. Experience shows me this is true, and an important skill for recent graduates to develop is how to limit your involvement to only the opportunities most important to you, where you can truly make a contribution.

Looking back, I could write so much more about the full experience of earning my PhD through SLATE—the safety net formed by the cohort structure and the ways we learned to incorporate Indigenous knowledge systems and research methods—but any in-depth discussion of those experiences will have to be saved for another time. In conclusion, I must say that although Patrick was correct when he warned me how difficult the process would be, I am glad I did not let that warning prevent me from seeking my PhD. If I had known the level of stress and pressure I would experience, I may never have taken the risk. As T. S. Elliot said, "Only those who will risk going too far can possibly find out how far one can go."

Theresa John

In the fall of 2006, the Second Language Acquisition Teacher Education (SLATE) faculty visited Bethel's Kuskokwim campus seeking prospective Alaska Native doctoral students. At this time, I was a tripartite tenure-track faculty for the Department of Alaska Native Studies and Rural Development (DANSRD) at the University of Alaska Fairbanks (UAF). The recruitment timing was perfect for my promotion and tenure clock. When I heard about this opportunity, I got very excited to apply to the graduate program knowing that it would be beneficial for my professional career.

I was first introduced to SLATE faculty members Dr. Patrick Marlow, Dr. Sabine Siekmann, and Dr. Joan Parker Webster by the Bethel campus administrator, Mary Pete. Before I met Patrick Marlow, I already had heard positive things about previous projects that he had collaborated on with the local Yugtun instructors, Sophie and Oscar Alexie. When I first met Patrick as a SLATE group-discussion facilitator, I was already familiar with his previous project in our region and had positive vibes about him due to his interest in our language. Because I have always been an advocate for maintaining, sustaining and revitalizing our Yugtun language, I felt privileged to be invited to apply to this new linguistic project.

After I had applied for SLATE, the stressful part of the application process was waiting to hear from the graduate office. I had to notify my landlord in advance that I was vacating my premises, as well as my director in DANSRD. The graduate program starting in the middle of the academic year also caused stress for me. As an assistant professor, I was already assigned to teach spring classes, and if I were accepted our department would have to hire adjuncts to teach the courses. Also, leaving my aging parents was one of the painful personal stresses for me because they relied upon me when they came to Bethel for medical purposes. On a personal note, leaving a rural location for an urban setting also caused me anxiety because the relocation would mean no more taking hot steam baths, speaking Yugtun on a daily basis, visiting local elders, Native dancing, and being able to eat fresh fish and game. The sacrifice was huge for me, but in my mind, the graduate commitment was the right choice at the right time.

The conversation at that first meeting concentrated on my profession as well as my research interests. After a few minutes of talking with the faculty, Patrick said that I would like meeting Joan because she and I had similar professional interests. He had the right inclination about us having matching interest areas and academic skills. When I was accepted as a graduate student, she was selected as my graduate cohort research advisor on the multi-literacies strand of the SLATE project.

After we got to know each other, we concluded that we were going to work together by utilizing our expertise in teaching, research, and scholarship. We both had been university professors for over a decade within the UAF system.

With this newfound knowledge, we decided to treat each other with professionalism and respect. We then reviewed and weighed our interests and expertise to balance our working relationship. In my years of teaching and during research, I had developed expertise in Yuuyaraq, Yup'ik epistemology, ontology, and cosmology and Native ways of knowing. Joan had expertise in Western academic knowledge systems, K–12 Yup'ik curriculum development, multi-literacies, and the promotion and tenure system.

Joan and I met on a weekly basis for advising and planning. My personal and professional goal was to finish my graduate program within the three-year time frame, based on the timeline of the SLATE program. In order to achieve this academic goal, I had to really stay focused on my academic plan. In order to stay on track, I ended up making a visual academic plan with specific due dates assigned for the required assignments, such as goals for submitting the Internal Review Board (IRB) protocol, dissertation chapters, qualifying exams, and defense dates. The monthly plan helped me to accomplish the required goals and objectives in a timely fashion. Having a calendar plan kept my motivation up as well as facilitated communication with my advisor.

The SLATE program definitely helped me through professional mentorship. It helped me in preparing and presenting at national and international conferences, conducting scholarship, and preparing publications. The SLATE program led me to achieve promotion and tenure. Joan and I ensured that our collaborative scholarship and publication would meet my graduate and promotion and tenure requirements. We coauthored several national articles and presented our work at international conferences. We also collaborated on teaching, research, and scholarship with other SLATE faculty and students.

I helped Joan advise the SLATE master's students. We developed a cohort advising plan to ensure that all their needs were met. Students would interview me in Yugtun on dance gestures and Yup'ik demonstrative movements, as well as understand Yugtun and Western knowledge systems. Student advising helped me to think about Indigenous methods that would work best for them. Knowing how relocation can cause stress and homesickness for the students, I occasionally cooked Native food for the students to eat and enjoy. I would cook in the evenings or early in the morning in my small apartment to ensure that the students were fed with Native food. Students and I also used lunch hours to process and discuss classroom discourse in an environment outside the university. The lunch hours also were used to speak only in Yugtun. Students expressed their appreciation for being able to get off campus to interact in a home setting. In spending time with them outside of the classroom, I learned about their worries, concerns, and needs by listening to their stories.

I proposed to write my dissertation in Yugtun to my graduate committee, as it would promote and enhance Yup'ik scholarship. Their response was that it would be beneficial to share my work with global audiences that use English as a research language. The committee members liked my idea to initiate Yugtun doctoral work, but the problem was that the university did not have the academic expertise to accept a

Yugtun thesis. The reality is that the faculty was not trained in Yugtun and there weren't that many Yugtun-speaking tenured faculty in place yet. Joan encouraged me to integrate Yugtun into my thesis with syntheses.

The dissertation collaborators were Yugtun speakers, so I conducted my interviews in Yugtun. I interviewed young adults, adults, and Elders in Yup'ik. I used video and audio recorders during the interviews. The Elders appreciated telling their stories in their language on the topic of Yuraryararput Kangiit-llu, our ways of dancing and their meanings. I transcribed and translated all of the recordings in Yugtun and English. Their contributions were immense and critical to my thesis. When I was done with the transcriptions, I conducted member checks in Yugtun to ensure that I represented their voices accurately. In the end, I made copies of their interviews and sent them DVD copies to reciprocate their generous contributions. I also deposited additional copies in the Nunakauiak Traditional Council Office in Toksook Bay.

Conclusion

Each PhD graduate has a powerful story to tell, and their journey is just beginning. It speaks to the strength of the Guided Collaboratives Model that of the four PhD students who started out in 2007, three had earned their PhDs by summer 2010, with the fourth expected to graduate in summer 2013. The persistence and graduation rates of the master's students are also noteworthy, as all 18 students who completed the initial summer session in 2007 finished their degrees by summer 2010.

As stated above, one of the goals of the SLATE grant was to build capacity for local leadership in language programming.

SLATE Cohorts (partial list)		ANE CALL Cohorts (partial list)	
Assessment	Dr. Marilee Coles-Ritchie **Walkie Charles** 3 master's students	Yugtun	**Dr. Walkie Charles** 1 Yup'ik Ph.D. student 4 master's students
Multiliteracies	Dr. Joan Parker Webster **Theresa John** 6 master's students	Yugtun	**Dr. Theresa John** 1 Yup'ik Ph.D. student 4 master's students

Figure 2: Cohorts, faculty, and students in SLATE and ANE CALL grants.

As the next step, UAF has been awarded another U.S. Department of Education grant to support computer-assisted language learning to improve Alaska Native education (US DoE # S356A120055). Drs. Charles and Theresa John are now heading their own cohorts (see Figure 2), placing Alaska Native PhDs in positions to mentor and advise Alaska Native PhD and master's students. More than this, as Yugtun speakers, Drs. Charles and Theresa John are in the unique position to teach at the graduate level using Yugtun as a medium of instruction.

References

Adams, D.W. (1995). *Education for Extinction: American Indians and the boarding school experience.* Lawrence, KS. University Press of Kansas.

Aud, S., M. Fox & KewalRamani, A. (2010). *Status and trends in the education of racial and ethnic Groups* (NCES 2010-015). U.S. Department of Education, National Center for Education Statistics. Washington, DC. U.S. Government Printing Office.

Barnhardt, R., & Kawagley, O.A. (2005). Indigenous knowledge systems and Alaska

Native ways of knowing. *Anthropology and Education Quarterly 36, 8-23.*

DeVoe, J.F. & Darling-Churchill, K.E. (2008). *Status and trends in the education of American Indians and Alaska Natives: 2008* (NCES 2008-084). National Center for Education Statistics, Institute of Education Sciences, U.S. Department of Education. Washington, DC.

Faircloth, S. C., & Tippeconnic, III, J.W. (2010). *The dropout/ graduation rate crisis among American Indian and Alaska Native students: Failure to respond places the future of Native peoples at risk. Los Angeles, CA: The Civil Rights Project/Proyecto Derechos Civiles at UCLA;* www.civil-rightsproject.ucla.edu.

Fienup-Riordan, A., M. Meade, & Rearden, A. (Eds.) (2005). *Yup'ik words of wisdom/ Yupiit qanruyutait. Lincoln, NE. University of Nebraska Press.*

Holmberg, A. (2010). Yup'ik funds of knowledge and science in a kindergarten classroom. Master's project. University of Alaska Fairbanks.

Kawagley, O. A. (1995). A Yupiaq worldview: A pathway to ecology and spirit.
Waveland Press. Prospect Heights, Ill.

Krauss, M. E. (1980). Alaska Native languages: Past, present, and future. Fairbanks, AK. Alaska Native Language Center.

Lomawaima, K.T. (1994). They called it prairie light: The story of Chilocco Indian
school. Lincoln, NE and London. University of Nebraska Press.

Marlow, P. & Siekmann, S., (2013a). Changing the Conversation: Promise and vulnerability in Alaska Native language revitalization. *Journal of American Indian Education, 51 (3), 46-69.*

Marlow, P. & Siekmann, S., (Eds.) (2013b). *Communities of Practice: An Alaska Native Model for Language Teaching and Learning. University of Arizona Press.*

Reyhner, J. (1991). Plans for dropout prevention and special school support services for American Indian and Alaska Native students. In *Indian Nations at Risk Task Force Commissioned Papers.* Washington, DC. U.S. Department of Education. ERIC Document Reproduction Service No. ED 343 762. Tucson: University of Arizona Press.

Siekmann, S., & Charles, W. (2011). Upingakuneng (when they are ready): Dynamic Assessment in a third semester Yugtun class. *Assessment in Education: Principles, Policy and Practice, 18 (2), 151–168.*

Webster, J. & Siekmann, S. (2013). Mentoring: Engaging Communities of Practice. In Patrick Marlow, & Siekmann, S., (Eds.). Communities of Practice: An Alaska Native Model for Language Teaching and Learning, pp. 46-76.

Indigenous Self-Determination in Education in Alaska: How Can Communities Get There?

Diane Hirshberg and Alexandra Hill

Background

Public education in the US has long been based on local control. Education is a state rather than a federal responsibility, with almost all states delegating control to local school boards. And 90 percent of those local boards oversee small districts with fewer than a dozen schools and enrollments under 5,000 (NCES 2011). Despite this nominal local control, members of diverse communities have often felt they lacked control of their children's schools and were disconnected from what their children were being taught. Indigenous students in particular were often forced to attend boarding schools far from their homes—schools that had the explicit goal of assimilating them into the majority culture and where they were sometimes abused (Hirshberg 2008).

Today the vast majority of Alaska Native students attend schools in their home communities. However, many of the schools are failing to educate these students. Alaska Native students today drop out at rates triple the national average, and most who attend college need remedial work (Martin and Hill 2009, McDiarmid and Hill 2010). While non-Native student achievement mirrors or even exceeds national averages, Alaska Native student achievement is generally poor, particularly in small villages. In 2011 Alaska Natives made up 22.5 percent of students in grades 7–12 but 41.2 percent of the dropouts from those grades. They had a dropout rate of 8.5 percent, compared with 4.7 percent for all students in those grades (EED 2012). The high school graduation rate for all Alaska students in 2011–2012 was 69.6 percent but just 53.9 percent among Alaska Native students—the lowest among all racial and ethnic groups in the state (EED 2012). In 2011 Alaska Natives had a dropout rate of 8.5 percent for students in grades 7–12, compared with 4.7 percent for all students in those grades (EED 2012).

There have been numerous efforts to improve schooling for Alaska Native children, including innovations in curricula, teacher professional development, education summits, systemic reforms, and programs aimed at getting students more interested in learning. But none of these efforts have had broad, sustained effects on students or communities. Successes have been intermittent, or only for relatively small groups of students.

Purpose of Paper

As non-Native education researchers who study issues of education policy in Alaska broadly, including challenges in and outcomes of formal schooling for Alaska Native students, we are interested in identifying what might lead to schools better meeting the needs of Alaska's Indigenous students. Recently, we looked at promising models of formal schooling for Indigenous students around the globe and found that self-determination and local control over education appear to be very important in helping improve education outcomes (Authors 2011, 2012). But in Alaska, many communities have not succeeded in exercising local control to create schools that reflect their aspirations for their children's education. In this paper we examine the historical, social, legal, and political factors that challenge efforts by Alaska Native communities to control their children's schools. We then discuss potential ways they could have more say in their children's education—as American communities typically do—and provide some examples where this is happening in Alaska.

The debate around self-determination in education in Alaska is not new; Indigenous peoples have been struggling to gain control over schools for years. Major shifts toward more local control of education in Alaska, from the building of rural high schools as a result of the *Tobeluk v. Lind* consent decree to the development of Regional Education Attendance Areas to creation of the Yupiit School District were the result of enormous and sustained efforts by Indigenous activists, educators, and policy makers (for more on these changes see Cotton 1984; Kawagley 1995; Ongtooguk 2003). However, there remain many barriers to Indigenous peoples in Alaska having genuine full control of their own schools; it is these that we address in this paper.

It is important to emphasize at the start that we are not making recommendations to Alaska Native people about the best courses of action around education. While we do research on and in Indigenous communities and schools therein, and collaborate with Alaska Native researchers, our roles remain those of allies and of outsiders who provide a different perspective. We bring both a Western academic perspective and strong advocacy for the rights of Indigenous communities. Thus, we hope the discussion in this paper provides a lens that is useful for Indigenous communities, policy makers, and education reformers as they make decisions about how best to provide formal schooling for their children.

Context for Self-Determination in Education

The United Nations has recognized self-determination in education as a human-rights issue. Article 14 of the United Nations Declaration on the Rights of Indigenous Peoples, adopted in 2007 and endorsed by the US in December 2010, says:

1. Indigenous peoples have the right to establish and control their educational systems and institutions providing education in their own languages, in a manner appropriate to their cultural methods of teaching and learning.

2. Indigenous individuals, particularly children, have the right to all levels and forms of education of the State without discrimination.

3. States shall, in conjunction with indigenous peoples, take effective measures, in order for indigenous individuals, particularly children, including those living outside their communities, to have access, when possible, to an education in their own culture and provided in their own language. (Article 14 of the U.N. Declaration on the Rights of Indigenous Peoples)

The Indigenous people of the Americas traditionally educated their children through family- and community-based practices, passing their knowledge, skills, and traditions forward to the next generation. But after European settlers arrived, Indigenous children began to attend formal schools. In the early 18th century, many tribes in the southeast (including

Cherokee, Choctaw, and others) had schools and high literacy rates. Those schools disappeared as tribes were forced from their lands, and no similar schools were restored for over a century and a half. In the 1960s the Navajo tribe worked with the Bureau of Indian Affairs (BIA), the US Office of Economic Opportunity, and a nonprofit group, Demonstration in Navajo Education, to establish a community-controlled school. They eventually established the Rough Rock Demonstration School in Rough Rock, Arizona, the first contemporary school with an all-Indigenous, locally elected governing board (Roessel Jr. 1968). Shortly after that, the first tribally controlled community college, Navajo Community College (now Diné College), was established in Many Farms, Arizona (Manuelito 2005).

In 1975 Congress passed the Indian Self-Determination and Education Assistance Act, (Public Law 93-638, 25 U.S.C. 450 et seq.), which formalized mechanisms for tribes to take responsibility for federally funded programs. This law gave tribes the option of applying to BIA-operated schools and amended the Johnson-O'Malley Act to create parent advisory boards in schools receiving federal funds for Indian education programs (1). The self-determination act has been amended a number of times. The first major amendments were in 1978, and the changes in some ways diminished the ability of tribes to fully control education, for example, by not allowing the inclusion of tribal-school funding in annual funding agreements but instead calling for annual appropriations approved by the secretary of the interior (1978 amendments to the code).

There are now more than 125 tribal schools serving over 28,000 students across the United States (Bordeaux 2011), but none are in Alaska. Recognition of the right to self-determination in education continues to be debated at the national level; for example, President Clinton recognized this right in 1998 (American Indian and Alaska Native Education Executive Order 13096), but President Bush overturned it in order to require tribes to meet the requirements of the No Child Left Behind Act of 2001 (American Indian and Alaska Native Education Executive Order 13336).

Current Situation in Alaska

The potential for more local control exists within Alaska statute and regulation. Both Regional Education Attendance Areas (REAAs) and school districts are governed by local school boards who make curriculum decisions and set graduation requirements within broad guidelines established by the state. In some places that potential is exercised, with charter schools, language-immersion programs, place-based education, and whole district reforms, as are described later in this paper. In other places, local communities are not as actively engaged in controlling their schools (Dinero 2004).

Almost all Alaska Native children, both in remote villages and in Anchorage and other urban areas, are educated in public schools that depend largely on state funding. There is one tribally operated charter home school with fewer than 20 students, one small K–12 private Inupiat immersion school, and a handful of private schools. The Bureau of Indian Education doesn't operate any schools in Alaska, but there are BIA-funded programs within public school districts—such as those operated under the Johnson-O'Malley Act, to provide support to Indian students in public schools. Rural (and urban) students also have the option of attending boarding schools. Mt. Edgecumbe in Sitka is the only state-operated regional high school. Three school districts also operate boarding schools, and a handful of students choose each year to leave Alaska and attend Chemawa Indian School in Oregon or to enroll in non-Native boarding schools.

Alaska's state government delegates responsibility for the daily operation of schools to either local or Regional Educational Attendance Area (REAA) school boards, which make policy affecting programs of local schools, within the confines of general state laws and regulations. The state currently supports schools in any community with at least ten students.

All organized boroughs and first-class cities outside boroughs are required to operate school districts. In areas without boroughs or first-class cities, Regional Educational Attendance Areas operate schools. Those REAAs vary considerably in size— one village/one school sites such as Kashunamiut in Chevak; small districts with a handful of schools, such as Yupiit; and large districts like the Lower Kuskokwim School District, which has 27 schools in 23 villages spread out over 22,000 square miles. No public schools are tribally operated.

As noted earlier, many Alaska schools, particularly small schools in remote villages, do not serve their Alaska Native students well. In the 30 rural districts enrolling predominantly Indigenous students, the 2012 graduation rates ranged from a low of 12.5 percent to 100 percent, with two-thirds graduating fewer than 70 percent of their students, including eight districts where fewer than 50 percent of students graduated (EED 2012 district report cards).

Rural and remote Alaska schools face many challenges, ranging from high teacher turnover to ever-increasing fuel costs that strain budgets. In many places there is also a disconnect between the community and the educators, who are overwhelmingly non-Native—only about 5 percent of certificated teachers are Indigenous people, and fewer yet are administrators. Most are also from outside Alaska; the University of Alaska system prepares about 20 percent of the teachers hired by districts each year (Hill, Hirshberg, et. al. 2013).

Across the state there have been concerted efforts to improve the education of Alaska Native students. In 2010 the Alaska State Board of Education adopted the Alaska Standards for Culturally Responsive Schools, which were developed by Alaska Native educators in collaboration with Indigenous elders and community members in the 1990s (Alaska Comprehensive Center 2012). The Alaska Federation of Natives in partnership with the University of Alaska Fairbanks operated the federally funded Rural Systemic Initiative for over a decade, in recognition of the need for Native communities to create their own approaches to improving school outcomes (Barnhardt 2012). And as noted before, in some districts and individual schools, parents and community members have created a different relationship with the schools—and the curriculum and pedagogy reflect the culture of the local people (2).

But overall, the public schools in rural areas are not culturally responsive. There is little parent and community involvement in many places, and indeed the lack of parental engagement is often cited by teachers and administrators as a cause of poor student achievement. At the same time, non-Native educators don't necessarily see Indigenous parents as partners in educating children, with valuable information to share, but rather as adults who need to support teachers by helping with classroom tasks (Dinero 2004 and Jester 2002). Schools operate on the traditional school calendar, which allows students easy participation in summer subsistence activities but not in spring and fall hunting and whaling. In the classroom, educators generally use Western ways of teaching. The curriculum is driven by state content standards and relies on curriculum packages developed outside Alaska.

National as well as state forces contribute to the current situation, from accountability requirements of the federal No Child Left Behind Act (NCLB) and how the state chooses to implement them, to the state's curriculum standards and grade-level expectations. This is not to say these standards are not in some ways helpful. The accountability mandates of NCLB revealed the big achievement gap between Native and non-Native students and allowed educators to track whether new initiatives were helping improve student learning. Still, accountability measures may also be having unintended consequences; when the state first opened secondary schools in villages in the late 1970s, attendance and graduation rates increased dramatically, but since the late 1990s dropout rates have risen (Goldsmith et. al. 2004; Martin and Hill 2009).

Self-determination alone won't remedy the situation described above. In an earlier paper (Hill, Hirshberg, and Argetsinger 2012), we describe how places such as Greenland that have achieved more self-determination still face challenges in improving student achievement—in part because of the legacy of the colonial school system. For example, Inuk teachers in Greenland who attended school under the Danish system struggle with adopting new ways of teaching and interacting with students—because of their background in the Danish system. They often have to go through what one Greenlandic scholar describes as "mental decolonization" (Lynge 2011). But Greenlanders now have control as they try to transform their education system, rather than having to simultaneously work for that control. In Alaska, the barriers to Indigenous control over education span multiple areas: legal, institutional, political, and internal.

Barriers to Local Control

The path toward Indigenous self-determination in education in Alaska is complex and multifaceted. We address the broad areas where there are individual types of barriers but do not intend this to suggest that the path toward change is somehow linear, or that all these areas have to be addressed before meaningful change can be achieved.

Legal and Institutional Issues

US Law. US law has mixed and complex mechanisms for Indigenous communities to run their own schools. The 1975 Indian Self-Determination and Education Assistance Act (Public Law 93–638) authorized funding for tribes to operate elementary and secondary schools as part of self-determination contracts, under the formula developed pursuant to section 1128 of the Education Amendments of 1978 (25 U.S.C. 2008) and the Tribally Controlled Community College Assistance Act of 1978 (25 U.S.C. 1801 et seq.). But that changed just three years later, when Congress passed the Education Amendments of 1978 (25 U.S.C. 2008) and the Tribally Controlled Colleges and Universities Assistance Act of 1978 (25 U.S.C. 1801 et seq.), which statutorily prohibited funding for elementary and secondary schools from being included in annual funding agreements (per 25 U.S.C. 458cc(b)(4)). This change meant that tribes do not have the same self-determination and self-governance rights in education as they do in health or other broad areas. (Congressional Research Service, personal communication via Office of Senator Mark Begich 2012).

Still, tribes have the authority to operate their own schools via annual appropriations from the secretary of the interior, and as noted earlier, there are over 125 tribally operated schools elsewhere in the United States, both on and off reservations. But there are no BIA-funded, tribally operated schools in Alaska. Alaska only had a few BIA-operated schools at the time the self-determination act was passed, and those were closed within a few years of when the law was implemented.

Moreover, in Alaska there is little "Indian country," as it is defined in other states—and where tribes have broad self-government powers on reservations—due to both the 1971 Alaska Native Claims Settlement Act and subsequent US Supreme Court rulings on this subject, such as *Alaska v. Native Village of Venetie Tribal Government* (US Supreme Court, No. 96-1577, decided Feb. 25, 1998) (3). It's difficult to interpret how this difference affects the ability of Alaska Native tribes to operate BIA-funded, tribally operated schools. Recently there was a proposal to increase the tribal authority in education by allowing tribes to operate Elementary and Secondary Education Act title programs within schools that are located on tribal lands. The proposal included a definition of tribal lands for Alaska that would potentially extend this authority to tribal governments within the state. However, neither this proposal nor ESEA authorization have moved forward (4).

Law in Alaska. The Alaska Constitution says, "The legislature shall by general law establish and maintain a system of public schools open to all children of the state . . ." (Article VII Section I Alaska Constitution). The state did not initially provide schooling to all Alaska Native students, but since the mid-1970s it has operated schools across the state; only communities with fewer than ten students don't have local schools. The legislature and governor determine school funding, and the state Board of Education sets broad policy, such as accountability and curriculum standards.

Governance of local schools is nominally in the hands of district or REAA school boards, though in practice many boards defer on key decisions to the superintendents they hire. Curriculum and hiring decisions are made at the district or school level. Communities within REAAs have local advisory school boards, but as their name indicates, their power is only advisory except as otherwise specified by the REAA regional school boards. This means that in many—but not all—villages there is no real local decision-making on key educational issues, including what is taught, how it is taught, and when it is taught. In some cases school districts or REAAs draw from single tribal areas, but in other cases they encompass multiple tribes, with multiple cultures and languages, and that complexity makes exercising tribal control through REAA school boards problematic.

Accountability Issues. Another institutional barrier is that of accountability requirements from the federal government, in the form of the No Child Left Behind (NCLB) Act of 2001. That act requires state education agencies to implement accountability measures, including standardized testing every year for students in grades 3–10; to report by school on standardized test results in predetermined disaggregated ways, as well as dropout and graduation rates; to define adequate yearly progress (AYP) on those measures; and to undertake remedies if schools do not make adequate progress.

The NCLB act is overdue for reauthorization or revision, but little has changed other than adding a process for states to apply for waivers from some of the act's provisions. Publicly funded tribal schools are still subject to NCLB mandates, and generally the AYP requirements are those of the state where the schools are located—although the school boards or tribal governing bodies may seek approval for a different measure (NCLB 2001) This means that while tribally controlled schools may have their own definitions of success for their students and their schools, they are also required to report on measures determined by their state education agency—no matter how different the definitions of achievement and measures of success may be.

Lack of Indigenous Educators. Only about 5 percent of certified teachers in Alaska are Alaska Native. This is a serious impediment to creating schools that are not only tribally controlled, but also based in local cultures, worldviews, and ways of teaching and learning. Non-Native teachers can, of course, successfully teach in Indigenous communities—and they can learn new pedagogy and content—but they need time to do this. They must make an intentional effort to develop the knowledge and expertise to connect with students from another culture and effectively implement materials and methods that are culturally relevant. Many non-Native educators are not in Alaska long enough to do this effectively.

Political and Social Barriers. There is broad political opposition to tribal sovereignty in Alaska. In 2001, for example, two leaders of the Alaska state legislature wrote the secretary of the interior asking the secretary to review the status of tribes in Alaska and potentially end recognition of Alaska Native villages as political entities with governmental authority (Cornell and Kalt 2003). Other issues involving sovereignty—in particular subsistence rights but also land access, tribal courts, and resource development—are all areas of significant political contention between the state government and tribal governments in Alaska.

The issue of tribal control of education has not been discussed broadly in Alaska (5). But there is consistent pressure to improve rural education by establishing regional secondary boarding schools that would once again force older children to leave their home communities to get high school diplomas. Cornell and Kalt (2003) note that advocates for regionalizing services for rural Alaska argue that it would increase the efficiency of service delivery and save money—arguments also made for regional boarding schools. But they found that for many residents of Alaska Native villages, regionalization under ANCSA via regional nonprofit corporations has not led to more effective delivery of services, and more important, that it may set back tribal self-determination and undermine federal recognition of tribes (Cornell and Kalt 2003).

Internal Barriers. All the barriers addressed above address issues external to Indigenous communities—federal and state laws, political issues involving policy makers or non-Natives, and issues of gaining fiscal control from external authorities.

But one barrier to self-determination may be internal, based in the mind-set of some Alaska Native people and communities, as Smith (2004) and Lynge (2011) found in their own national contexts of Aotearoa (New Zealand) and Greenland. As noted earlier, Indigenous communities do have ways of exercising more power over education under Alaska's current political and legal structures. If they acted on the legal powers they already have, Indigenous communities could create change—by having school boards that demand change, hiring superintendents who respond to their wishes and implement programs that meet their visions, and encouraging parents to be more active in parent councils. But the colonial legacy, including abuse, has left many Alaska Native parents simultaneously deferential to teachers and administrators and fundamentally distrustful of schools (Cottrell 2010).

Options for Moving Toward Self-Determination

Alaska Natives have a number of options for developing local control and self-determination in education. Some of these are steps they can take without changes in current legal, institutional, fiscal, or political structures; others would require changing the barriers identified above. But any actions require changes in the sense individuals and communities have about their power to effect change, and their confidence that they best know their children's educational needs.

Immediate Options. Communities have a number of options for creating locally driven schools—and some have already taken actions toward that goal. Those include developing charter schools, strengthening school boards, using home-schooling options, and creating private schools.

Charter Schools. Charter schools are publicly funded schools developed by educators, parents, and community members to provide an alternative to existing local schools. They operate subject to the approval of local school boards. There are three Alaska Native–focused charter schools in the state: Ayaprun Elitnaurvik Yupik Immersion School in Bethel, the Alaska Native Cultural Charter School in Anchorage, and the Effie Kokrine Early College Charter School in Fairbanks. These schools vary considerably from the focus on Yupik immersion in early grades at Ayaprun to the integration of traditional and contemporary knowledge at Effie Kokrine. But there are limits to what charter schools can do. Alaska has a "strong" charter school law, which means they don't have as much autonomy as in some other states. For example, decisions on standardized assessments are made by both the state and the district where charter schools are located, and professional-development offerings can be mandated by districts and in some cases the state; content standards are set at the state level. Still, charter schools are able to offer innovative programs that can reflect local cultures, knowledge, and Indigenous ways of teaching and learning.

Strengthening School Boards. Another option is to strengthen rural district school boards so that board members—who are generally Alaska Native—and the parents they represent can truly exercise the control of the districts that they nominally have. School boards are a potential source of real power if communities elect strong members who represent their interests, and if the board members exercise all their powers not only in hiring but directing superintendents to develop and implement policies and practices relevant for their communities.

A powerful example of such power is in the North Slope Borough School District, where the district has developed the Inupiaq Learning Framework and is now developing curriculum and pedagogical approaches to create an Inupiaq education system based fully in the Inupiaq culture but also preparing students to succeed in the Western education system. The school board has driven this reform and hired a superintendent who is implementing its vision. The reform effort is based on extensive work with elders, educators, and community members across all borough villages, to determine what children should know when they graduate.

Home Schooling and Private Schools. Another option is one Maori school reformers in New Zealand used in the 1980s: they walked away from the state-funded schools and created a parallel system without public funding, using only local resources (Smith 2003). In Alaska it is relatively easy to open private schools, with limited bureaucratic procedures. Private schools operate under few regulations other than basic safety requirements and minimal standardized-testing mandates (a national test must be given in grades 4, 6, and 8). Home schooling is also allowed and quite common. One community, Chickaloon, has developed the Ya Ne Dah Ah tribal school as a tribally supported entity, using a charter correspondence school model for the mainstream curriculum offerings and also offering Ahtna Athabascan history, language, music, and arts classes taught by community members.

Long-Term Options. To fully take control over their children's schooling, Alaska's Indigenous peoples need legal, structural, and fiscal changes that could take years to enact—as well as significant political will. We do not know all the changes that would be required, but here we discuss a few.

One step, which would be difficult to achieve but would be far-reaching, would be to make a major change in the Alaska Native Claims Settlement Act—to put into code a different definition of "Indian country" in Alaska to allow for tribally controlled schools under current Bureau of Indian Education rules. But it is also possible that such a complex change in the law would not be necessary. We are not sure whether under current law Alaska Native tribal governments could simply choose not to send their children to state-funded public schools and instead apply to have tribally operated schools, funded by the Bureau of Indian Affairs, in their communities. It is one possibility they could explore, though it would take congressional and presidential support to ensure sufficient funding within the BIE system to fully fund all the costs of such an effort.

Another broad change would be modifying P.L. 93-638 to allow compacting in education. Health care is the one area where Alaska Natives have attained broad sovereignty, via 1994 revisions to the self-determination act that allowed Alaska Native organizations to compact with the Indian Health Service to provide services. Could tribal health care be a model for a large-scale system of Indigenous control of social services? A potential barrier is that individual villages cannot contract to provide health-care services if they are within an area already served by an Alaska Native regional health entity. Would this restriction translate to education, meaning that individual villages wanting to run their own schools might not be allowed to do so if there was a regional Alaska Native education entity?

Discussion

In this brief, we have laid out some ideas for sovereignty in education for Indigenous communities and tribes to consider. There is, as we noted, significant change already happening in isolated parts of Alaska. But there isn't broad movement toward changing the structure of schooling for Indigenous students statewide. If changing Alaska's schools is a goal for Alaska Native parents, policy makers, and communities, wider and deeper reforms are needed.

Only the Alaska Native communities themselves can define the best way forward. But true Indigenous community control will require an attitude shift among individuals and communities. Whether this requires the sort of "mental decolonization" work being done in Greenland (Lynge 2011), or whether people simply need reminding that they have this power and can use it, is something we can't determine. Tribal governments have legal powers to negotiate as sovereign nations with the state and federal governments, despite the refusal of Alaska's state government to recognize these rights.

The issue of fiscal resources will be important, because state and federal funding for public schools comes with requirements, such as curricular and accountability mandates. Consideration of these issues is beyond the scope of this paper. Many communities in rural Alaska do not contribute funds to schooling but depend entirely on state and federal government resources. But some people have asked: what should the role of ANCSA corporations be? Some of the corporations are successful financially, and others are less so. Could the wealthier corporations, or their affiliated not-for-profit foundations, provide sufficient support to create independent schooling options? Would these schools be sustainable? The privately funded Kamehameha Schools in Hawaii, free from the fiscal constraints of either the state or the Bureau of Indian Affairs, have a significant ability to set their own agenda. Can Alaska communities marshal sufficient resources to do something similar without relying on the BIA, the state, or even the corporations? Should they have to? That is something we cannot answer at present.

It is important to point out that the examples of educational change we have presented are only from rural and remote Indigenous parts of Alaska and do not address the urban communities of Anchorage, Fairbanks, or Juneau. Different questions have to be addressed in diverse, multicultural communities: should Indigenous people in urban Alaska create their own schools within the boundaries of urban districts, or perhaps consider the way the Aboriginal Enhancement

Agreements work in British Columbia? Those agreements provide extra support to aboriginal students attending schools that may be majority non-Native. Can self-determination be achieved when the population in urban areas includes Indigenous peoples from many different tribes and different cultural and linguistic heritages? This is an important issue that needs more exploration.

That said, we believe the barriers to change described in this paper are not insurmountable. Creating Indigenous schools will not be easy, but it is possible so long as people believe they can do it. Indeed, as the Maori in New Zealand have shown, it may be that people need to "just do it," regardless of resources, and once they start, the way forward will become increasingly clear.

Endnotes

i. The Bureau of Indian Education, formerly the Office of Indian Education Programs, sits within the Bureau of Indian Affairs. It was renamed in 2006. Prior to 2006, federally funded schools in Alaska were commonly called "BIA Schools."

ii. Some examples include the Effie Kokrine Charter School in Fairbanks, the Ayaprun Elitnaurvik Yup'ik Immersion School in Bethel, the Alaska Native Cultural Charter School in Anchorage, as well as the Math in a Cultural Context curriculum-development initiative and teacher-preparation programs for rural and Indigenous schools, such as Cross Cultural Educator Development program known as XCED and PITAAS (Preparing Indigenous Teachers and Administrators for Alaska's Schools).

iii. Alaska does have one reservation, Metlakatla, but the education there is provided through state-funded public schools.

iv. Tribal Education Departments National Assembly. "Tribal Education Departments National Assembly Proposed Statutory Language for the Reauthorization of the Elementary and Secondary Education Act." May 6, 2011. Boulder, CO: Author. Retrieved from http://www.tedna. org/proposed_esea_language_5-6-11.pdf Along side this proposal, there was a discussion of using the Definition of Indian land from the Impact Aid code (20 U.S.C. Title 20 Education Chapter 70 Strengthening and Improvement of Elementary and Secondary Schools Subhapter VIII-Impact Aid Sec 7713-Definitions) to define how tribes could operate their own schools even in Alaska. That tribal land definition is as follows: (I) held in trust by the United States for individual Indians or Indian tribes; (II) held by individual Indians or Indian tribes subject to restrictions on alienation imposed by the United States; (III) conveyed at any time under the Alaska Native Claims Settlement Act [43 U.S.C. 1601 et seq.] to a Native individual, Native group, or village or regional corporation; (IV) public land owned by the United States that is designated for the sole use and benefit of individual Indians or Indian tribes.

v. A group of Indigenous and non-Native educators and advocates, including the first author of this paper, have engaged in work around this topic supported by a Harvard University Nation Building project.

References

Alaska v. Native Village of Venetie Tribal Government, 522 U.S. 520 (1998).

Alaska Comprehensive Center, Alaska Native Educators and Education Northwest in collaboration with the Alaska Department of Education & Early Development. (2012). *Guide to implementing the Alaska cultural standards for educators.* Juneau, AK: Alaska Department of Education & Early Development. Retrieved from http://education.alaska.gov/standards/pdf/cultural_standards.pdf

Alaska Department of Education and Early Development (EED). (2012). 2011-2012 Report Card to the Public. Retrieved from http://education.alaska.gov/reportcard/2011-2012/reportcard2011-12.pdf

Alaska Department of Education & Early Development (EED) (2012) Alaska School and district report cards to the public from 2009-2012. Retrieved from http://education.alaska.gov/reportcardtothepublic/

American Indian and Alaska Native Education Exec. Order No. 13096, Aug. 6, 1998, 63 F.R. 42681.

American Indian and Alaska Native Education Exec. Order No. 13336, Apr. 30, 2004, 69 F.R. 25295

Barnhardt, R. (2012). Indigenous education renewal in rural Alaska. *NABE Perspectives, 34* (July-August), 16-20.

Cornell S., and Kalt, J.P. (2003). Alaska Native Self-Government and Service Delivery: What Works? Joint Occasional Papers on Native Affairs No. 2003-01. Cambridge, MA: The Harvard Project on American

Indian Economic Development

Cotton, S. E. (1984). Alaska's "Molly Hootch Case": High schools and the village voice. *Education Research Quarterly, 8* (4), 30-43.

Cottrell, M. (2010). Indigenous Education in Comparative Perspective: Global Opportunities for Reimagining Schools. International Journal for Cross-Disciplinary Subjects in Education (IJCDSE), 1 (4), 223-227.

Dinero, S. (2004). The politics of education provision in rural Native Alaska: the case of Yukon Village. Race Ethnicity and Education, 7(4), 401-419.

Fuhrman, S. H. Goertz, M. E. & Weinbaum, E. H. (2007). Educational governance in the United States: Where are we? How did we get here? Why should we care? In Fuhrman, S. H., Cohen, D. K., & Mosher, F. (Eds.), The state of education policy research. Mahwah, NJ: Lawrence Erlbaum Associates, pp. 41-61.

Goldsmith, S. Angvik, J., Howe, L., Hill, A. & Leask, L. (2004). *The Status of Alaska Natives Report 2004*. Anchorage, AK: Institute of Social & Economic Research

Hill, A., Hirshberg, D., Lo, D., McLain, E., and Morotti, A. (2013). Alaska's University for Alaska's Schools 2013. Fairbanks, AK: University of Alaska Office of Academic Affairs.

Hirshberg, D. (2008) "It was bad or it was good: Alaska Natives in past Boarding Schools." Journal of American Indian Education. (47) 3, 5-30.

Hirshberg, D & Hill, A. (2011). Formal Schooling of

Indigenous Peoples in Remote and Rural Regions: Promising Models. Paper presented at the International Congress of Arctic Social Sciences, Akureyri, Iceland, June 2011.

Indian Self-Determination and Education Assistance Act, Pub. L. No. 93-638, 25 U.S.C. 450 et seq. (1975).

Iseke-Barnes, J. (2008). Pedagogies for Decolonizing. Canadian Journal of Native Education, 31(1), 123-148, 320.

Jester, T. (2002). Healing the "Unhealthy Native" Encounters with standards-based education in rural Alaska. Journal of American Indian Education. 41(3), 1-21.

Kawagley, A. O. (1995). *A Yupiaq Worldview: A Pathway to Ecology and Spirit*. Prospect Heights, IL: Waveland Press, Inc.

Lomawaima, K. T. has a chapter "Tribal Sovereigns: Reframing Research in American Indian Education" in a volume entitled *Indigenous Knowledge and Education: Sites of Struggle, Strength, and Survivance*. Edited by Villegas, Malia; Neugebauer, Sabina Rak & Venegas, Kerry R. Cambridge, MA: Harvard Education Press.

Lynge, Aviaja Egede. (2011). *Mental Decolonization in Greenland and Alaska: Comparing Issues*. A talk at the Elders and Youth Conference, Anchorage, Alaska, October 2011.

Manuelito, K. (2005). The role of education in American Indian self-determination: Lessons from the Ramah Navajo Community School. *Anthropology and Education Quarterly, (36)*, pp. 73-87.

Martin S. and Hill, A. (2009). The Changing Economic Status of Alaska Natives, 1970-2007. Web Note No. 5. Anchorage, AK: Institute of Social and Economic Research. Retrieved June 15, 2011 from: http://www. iser.uaa.alaska.edu/Publications/webnote/WebNote5. pdf.

McDiarmid, G and Hill, A. (2010) Alignment of Alaska's Educational Programs from Pre-School through Graduate Study: A First Look. ISER Working Paper 2010.1. Anchorage, AK. Institute of Social and Economic Research. Retrieved June 15, 2011 from: http://www.iser.uaa.alaska.edu/Publications/ alignmentmemo.pdf.

Morehouse, T. A. (1992). The Dual political status of Alaska Natives under US policy . Anchorage: Institute of Social and Economic Research, University of Alaska Anchorage.

No Child Left Behind Act of 2001 (NCLB). Public Law 107-110, 115 Stat. 1425, § 30.104 retrieved from http:// www.gpo.gov/fdsys/pkg/CFR-2010-title25-vol1/xml/ CFR-2010-title25-vol1-part30.xml#seqnum30.102

Ongtooguk, P. (2003). *Education and Cultural Self-Determination*. Presentation to the 2003 AFN Youth and Elders Convention, Anchorage, Alaska. Retrieved from http://www.alaskool.org/native_ed/articles/ ongtooguk/Youth&ElderAFn2003Self-Determination. htm.

Roessel, Jr., R. A. (1968). An overview of the Rough Rock Demonstration School. *Journal of American Indian*

Education, 7 (3), 2-14.

Smith, G. (2003). Indigenous struggle for the transformation of education and schooling. Keynote address to the Alaska Federation of Natives, Anchorage, AK, Oct 2003.

Smith, G. (2004). Mai i te Maramatanga, ki te Putanga Mai o te Tahuritanga: From Conscientization to Transformation. Educational Perspectives, 37(1), 46-52.

Cup'ik Dreams: Chevak Teacher Education Initiative

Nancy Boxler

The College of Education at the University of Alaska Anchorage is working in partnership with the Kashunamiut School District, which is the school for the Cup'ik village and community of Chevak, Alaska. Chevak is located on the Bering Sea coast of Alaska and, like most villages in this region, is a traditional Indigenous community.

This unique partnership involves the local school, university, and community in supporting 12 paraprofessionals in becoming certified teachers in elementary education. The 12 community members are from Chevak and speak the local language, which is Cup'ik. They have been teachers' aides, and the partnership, known as Cup'ik Dreams, embraces the concepts of inclusivity and culturally relevant teaching. The university courses reflect both Western and Cup'ik cultures and philosophies.

By December 2013 it is expected that about half of the group will have earned their associate's degrees. This initiative is providing important insights about the power of collaboration as an Indigenous community, school, and university come together to create a space that supports cultural and language revitalization.

During the April 2013 Alaska Native Studies Conference, a panel consisting of myself, John Atchak (chairman of the Kashunamiut School District), Larry Parker (superintendent of the Kashunamiut School District), and members of the Chevak cohort (Laura Atcharian, Elsie Ayuluk, Cora Charles, Twila Chayalkun, Susie Friday-Tall, Catherine Joe, Jacquelyn Kashatok, Priscilla Matchian, Mary Matchian, Neva Mathias,

Pauline Miles, Liana Pingayak, Darlene Ulroan, and Lisa Unin), along with faculty from the UAA College of Education (Claudia Dybdahl, Irasema Ortega, and Cathy Coulter) had the opportunity to share their experiences. The panel discussed what it means to be part of this partnership and provided an opportunity to hear the voices of Indigenous students, university faculty, and community leaders as they reflected on the importance of partnership as they continue to work and learn on behalf of each other to create a partnership to support language and culture revitalization. (i)

Cathy Coulter, who is one of the University of Alaska Anchorage professors involved in this endeavor also provides her experience in this project below.

Photo Credit: Rob Stapleton

Figure 1: Susie Friday-Tall, one of the students in the
Cup'ik Dreams program.

Photo Credit: Rob Stapleton

Twila Chayalkun, a student in the Cup'ik Dreams program.

Figure 3: Cora Charles of the Cup'ik Dreams cohort.

Photo Credit: Rob Stapleton

Pauline Miles of the Cup'ik Dreams cohort.

Photo Credit: Rob Stapleton
John Atchak, chairman of the Kashunamiut School District.

Cumikluten

Cathy Coulter

One of the many things my friends in Chevak have taught me is this: *cumikluten.* Pay attention. Be aware. (ii)

Dr. Irasema Ortega and I spent a week in Chevak with the curriculum-writing team last July. The first three days we spent listening and learning, because our Cup'ik partners knew it was necessary. We learned *cumikluten.* We learned about Cup'ik stories of origin, about Cup'ik cultural values, about the importance of the collective, of taking care of one another and of the abundant subsistence the tundra offers. We learned about the importance of gratitude for the gifts of those that give themselves—the seal, caribou, moose, fox, and ermine—and of the profound gratitude of "taking care" of those gifts properly.

We learned about the different healing qualities of tundra grass, roots, berries, willow bark. When we asked: How do you know when the tundra greens are ready? How do you know when it's time to pick the berries? How do you know when the salmon will run? We were told: We just *know*. We *feel* it.

Cumikluten. Pay attention.

Three decades ago the elders in Chevak were paying attention. They knew that it was time to begin the process of change in Chevak School. And they did. Chevak became an independent school district and hired superintendents who understood the importance of language and culture revitalization. They hosted culture weeks. They forged partnerships. They started a K–12 language-immersion school so that the children could learn Cup'ik alongside Cup'ik cultural values and subsistence. The children would learn math, science, social studies, and language arts through cultural knowledge in a rich environment that taught them to flourish and succeed in two worlds.

Three years ago, a few decades into this endeavor, I found myself in Chevak at a talking circle with the elders and the cohort. The generosity of an anonymous donor had provided embodiment to a profound solution: bring a teacher-certification program to Chevak School's many Cup'ik-speaking paraprofessionals. Cup'ik people who speak Cup'ik and who have the cultural knowledge necessary to provide the Cup'ik children. Certified, highly qualified teachers who stay in Chevak.

At that talking circle David Boyscout and John Pingayyak spoke about our partnership. We are two rivers, Cup'ik and Western, flowing together, becoming one.

A Western "elder", Ford Motor Company taught us a while ago that we could build things more efficiently by using the factory model. Each worker would be given a specific task to fulfill on every vehicle, and cars could be made in a quicker, cheaper fashion. The wider public quickly picked up this concept and applied it to everything you can imagine, including our schools. We could prepare children more efficiently by modeling our schools after factories. This model still prevails in schools today. Our children are rendered into products. Each grade-level teacher does specific tasks so that the outcome is a standard model of a graduate. A "standardized" child.

The Cup'ik ancestors knew that in order to survive, the people would need to be able to adapt to changes. They knew that the people needed to understand their roles in the vast and dynamic ecosystem they lived in. They knew that a "standardized" village would not survive.

Computers, when they start getting close to storage capacity, segment data in order to store it in various places on the drive. Every once in a while, a computer user will have to run a "defrag" to bring those pieces of data back together. The cohort and our other Cup'ik partners have taught us at the College of Education that we have to defrag our system. Our institutionalized policies may make sense in a factory model, a standardized system, but they don't always make sense for our individual, human students. In order for us to survive as a college, as an institution, as a society, we need to understand our roles in the vast and dynamic systems we inhabit. Cup'ik Elders know this, even predicting that a time will come when the Cup'ik people will go back to the old ways. We simply can't survive on a factory model. A standardized society by definition cannot survive.

Cumikluten. Pay attention.

Because my Cup'ik friends have taught me *cumikluten,* I have learned to defrag myself as a teacher educator, as a researcher, as a mother. I have learned that that in order to survive—no, in order to flourish—we have to work as a collective. Not in a fragmented way, but each a dynamic and changing part of a whole. My role is one of many. It is necessary, it is functional, and it is beautiful because it is a part of a dynamic system.

Three decades ago, the Elders began building a new way. And *cumikluten* is telling me something very important.

Look around this very room. We have a member of the school board here as well as the superintendent, and our heroes - the cohort. We have university members, at least one member of the media, and others who know *cumikluten* and so are here. We *know.* We *feel* it. The berries are ripe, the salmon are running. It is time for us to hunt and to harvest and to take care of the abundance around us. It is time for us to work together, each a part of the whole, and show the state what effective education really looks like. Because the Elders understood what I am just coming to understand: This endeavor is about more than the precious Cup'ik children, although they are enough. It's about more than the revitalization of Cup'ik language and culture, although that, too, is enough. It's about sustaining *all* of Alaska's children. It's about transforming our Western institutions of education that have become hopelessly fragmented, standardized, and ineffective. Not to mention the role they play in marginalizing Indigenous peoples. The imperative is clear, and the effects of our work together are far-reaching. As we tell our stories, we show others—other communities, institutions, and policy makers—that the transformation of education in our state can be done. Schools can be used as a mechanism for language and culture revitalization through which children achieve a high level of academic performance. We just have to continue to do what we are doing and show them the evidence of what we know and what we feel. And *cumikluten*.

Quyana to my Cup'ik friends for your patience and for teaching me *cumikluten*.

Endnotes

i. A podcast of the presentation is at: http://greenandgold.uaa. alaska.edu/podcasts/index.php?id=794

ii. This is in the Cup'ik language and is the local language spoken in the community of Chevak, Alaska.

Photo Credit: Beth Leonard

Gordon Pullar accepting the Oscar Kawagley Award at
the Alaska Native Studies Banquet. L–R: Gordon Pullar,
Ray Barnhardt, and Maria Williams.

Photo Credit: Rob Stapleton

Alvin Amason, Sugpiaq artist and UAA faculty
member and Lawrence Ahvakana, Inupiaq artist at the
roundtable discussion during the pre-conference
on Alaska Native art.

Photo Credit: Rob Stapleton

Da-Ka-Xeen Mehner of the University of Alaska Fairbanks Native Art Program listening to keynote address by Graham Smith at the opening session of the April 2013 conference.

Photo Credit: Rob Stapleton

Maria Williams at the opening session of the April 2013 conference.

Photo Credit: Rob Stapleton

Ethan Petticrew, Unangan educator and traditional
performer, at the pre-conference entitled
The Things We Make.

Photo Credit: Rob Stapleton

Heidi Senungetuk at The Things We Make pre-
conference, which focused on Alaska Native
art and artists.

Photo Credit: Rob Stapleton

Panel presentation at The Things We Make pre-conference. L–R: Ishmael Hope, Susie Bevins-Ericsen, Alison Warden, Ethan Petticrew, and Jack Dalton.

Photo Credit: Rob Stapleton

Meda Schleifman and Da-ka Xeen Mehner at The Things We Make pre-conference.

Photo Credit: Rob Stapleton

Nathan Jackson, Tlingit carver, and Perry Eaton Sugpiaq, artist, at The Things We Make pre-conference.

Photo Credit: Rob Stapleton

Joel Isaaks, Benjamin Schleifman, and Nicholas Galanin at the pre-conference.

Photo Credit: Rob Stapleton

Haida artist Delores Churchill in foreground and Inupiaq artist and professor emeritus (UAF) Ron Senungetuk in the background at the pre-conference symposium.

Photo Credit: Rob Stapleton

Dalee Sambo Dorough (UAA) moderating a panel during the main conference in 2013.

Photo Credit: Rob Stapleton

Edgar Blatchford (UAA) presenting during the
Alaska Native Studies Conference 2013.

Photo Credit: Rob Stapleton

Emil Notti during one of the panel discussions.

Photo Credit: Rob Stapleton

Kimberly Martis, one of the presenters during the
April 2013 conference.

Photo Credit: Rob Stapleton

Kristina Woolston presenting during the
ANCSA I panel.

Photo Credit: Rob Stapleton

Sharon Lind (UAA) presenting during the
ANCSA I panel.

Photo Credit: Rob Stapleton

Ishmael Hope, Tlingit writer, addresses his new work
based on the Alaska Native Brotherhood.

PART III
INDIGENOUS WORLDVIEW, LANGUAGE, AND THE ARTS

Poetry

THREE POEMS
Anna Smith-Chiburis

Cow Town
After they left the powwow,
they drove for miles
past endless acres of hot humid farmland,
when the sky turned slate smoke,
electric with thunder
and a heavy rain
tumbled down upon the landscape;
they had to leave the road,
outside of Edmonton.

A bright, blue neon sign
sizzled ultraviolet across the worn walls
of their dive motel room.
Cable TV was a parallel world
that played out in noir shadows
across their motel window.

After the thunder and lightning stopped,
he went outside, under the porch
and lit up a cigarette he shared with her,
they both looked up at the black sky,
there were no stars or moon,
only a windswept road
that coiled far away from Eden

when they stepped out into the rain,
into the dark fields
that unfolded, one past the other;
a mist ascended from the
bright lines of the road
and the earth smoked
where the land
once burned their feet,
but now they walked on water.

Ursa Major Star Formation

From the shores of the Chilkat River,
you can sometimes look up,
at a clear, night sky
and see a bear
running across the universe,
some say he searches
for a woman who built a fire
on the river's edge,
that he runs to her, past the stars,
past the mountains and woods,
past the moonlit sea,
where the fishing boats
sway on the water,
they say he follows the sparks
from her fire,
which have scattered up, into the night
and the bear,
he keeps running after them,
pounding, breathless through the brush
because he thinks he is on the river,
but he is not.

Wildfire

Everything is on fire.
Smoke smolders on rural roads,
as a nearby forest crackles with sparks;
miles away, neat sun-dried lawns
are parched yellow and orange.
Even the city has a haze of smoke
that looks like a halo.
Where is the rain?
The other morning,
I read that Amazon Indians in Brazil
performed sacred ceremonies to bring rain.

Most of the garden flowers wilt
And the air is thick with a scorching heat
and I wonder how long it has been like this
and how long it will last. One day,
I see a sign that says in case of fire
call the brigade, but they have no water.

The TV news said that in Brazil,
crops and cattle are parched
due to drought and that jaguars
wander ghostlike between two worlds,
in their search for water.
They said some Amazon Indian tribes
beat the walls of their house to exorcise evil spirits.

In Arizona, exhausted firefighting crews

battle a wildfire that has burned through acres
of pinyon, juniper and ponderosa pines.
While in Brazil, flames surround the Indians.

Last night, I read Brazilian Indians
chant and pray for rain. They fear apocalypse,
as the world burns around them.
And yet, they said some things
survive even fire and though much is gone,
there is something new and
something that remains of the old.
The sky tells them this.

Alaska Native Language Revitalization: Transforming the Fabric of Our People

Lance X̱'unei Twitchell

Haa léelk'u hás jeeyís áyá,	For our grandparents,
haa nák̲ has woo.aadí aa.	they walked away from us.
Haa toowú yéi has yatee yeedát,	They are inside us now,
tlél aadé has du kát seigax̲tux'áagu ye.	there is no way we will forget them.

Ax̲ káak Keihéenak'w x̲'éidáx̲ áyá yáat'aa:	This one is from my uncle John Martin's mouth:
ax̲ tuwáa sigóo ch'a yéi gugéink' haa	"I want to make a little bit of our
léelk'u has yoo x̲'atángi x̲waliyéx̲i	grandparents' language."

Ldakát yeewháan.	Everyone.
Ch'a ldakát yeewháan.	All of you.
K'idéin ax̲ x̲'éit yisa.áx̲.	Listen carefully to me.
X'éigaa át áyá yeedát.	It is a true thing now.
Yisa.áx̲. yisa.áx̲.	Listen.

Yaa nanáan haa yoo x̲'atánkx'i.	Our languages are dying.

Ách áwé uháan tsu,	Because of that, us as well,
k̲únáx̲ haa toowú hóochk' liyéíx̲.	our spirits are being destroyed

147

Yá hóoch'i aayí.

This is the last thing.

Shéiyi xaat yáx yatee haa yoo x'atángi.

Our languages are like tree roots.

Ch'a aan haa géit ayawditeeyí,

Even though the storm blows against us,

woosh jín gaxtoolasháat,

we are still holding each others' hands,

uháan ka haa shagóoni.

those of us here and our ancestors.

Tlél aadé dleit kaa yoo x'atángi tóonáx

There is no way we can do these things in

gaxtoodlaagi yé.

English.

Ch'as haa Lingít tundatáani tóonáx

We need our Tlingit ways of thinking

gaxtoodlaak

in order to succeed.

Sh yaa awoodinéix'i.

Self-respecting people.

Yadáli át áyá yáat'aa,

This one is heavy.

Yá Lingít yoo x'atángi daat yéi jitunéiyi

We were born to work with our languages.

káx áyá koowtudzitee.

A ku.aa tlél ch'as uháan áyá.

But it is not just us.

Wé x'aháat tóonáx has woo.aat.

They have walked through the door.

Haa Tlagu Kwáanx'i Yán.

Our Ancient Ones.

Haa Shagóon.

Our Ancestors.

Haa Shuká. Haa dachxánx'i yán, haa yátx'i.

All of Those Who Have Come and Are Yet to Come.

148

Haa xoot has yatee ḵúnáx.	They really are among us.
Haa yátx'i yán yís á, kakḵwa.áaḵw.	For our children, I am going to try.
Haa dachxánx'i yán yís á, has x'akḵwatée.	For our grandchildren, I am going to imitate them.
Has du latseení eetéenáx haa yatee.	We need all of their strength.
Át wulihásh haa yaakw tleiní.	Our giant canoe is adrift.
Ch'u uwayáa ḵáajaa xoox wutulihásh.	It is as if we are floating among the kelp islands.

Haa yoo x'atánkx'i wool'éex'.	Our languages are broken.
Sh tóo yaa ntudijáḵ.	We are killing ourselves.
Aadáx yaa ntu.aat yeedát.	We are walking away from it now.
Tlél a yáx áwé.	This is not right.

Haa toowú sh kagaxtus'éet	We will bandage our spirits.
Haa aat neili ḵuxdé gaxtoo.áat	We will walk back to the house of our aunties.
Has du eet gaxtooshée, haa léelk'u hás.	We will help them, our grandparents.
Ch'as woosh tín gunéi yoo x'ayla.á!	Just begin speaking with each other!
Sh tóo gaxtool.tóow	We will learn it together

Haa tuwunáagu áyá haa yoo x'atángi.	Our languages are spirit medicine.

149

Ch'as yoo x̱'ayla.á!	Just speak!
Has du tuwáa sigóo s yee seiwa.aax̱í.	They want to hear your voice.
Ch'a has du x̱'éit gax̱toosa.áax̱.	Let us listen to them.
Ch'as haa yoo x̱'atángi k'idéin has	They really understand our language, not
aya.áx̱ch, tlél dleit k̲aa x̱'eináx̱.	English.

Haa léelk'w gaysax̱án!	Love our grandparents!
Yee gu.aa yáx̱ x'wán!	Have strength and courage!
Yadáli át áyá	This one is heavy.
A gaawú áyá yá yeedát,	This is the time now
haa dachx̱ánx'i yán yís yéi jigax̱toonéi.	for us to work for our grandchildren.
A gaawú áyá yeedát,	This is the time now
haa léelk'u hás du jiyís yéi gax̱toosaneix̱.	for us to heal it for our grandparents.

Haa saneix̱í áyá haa yoo x̱'atángi.	Our languages are our salvation.
Haa daséigux̱ sitee haa yoo x̱'atángi.	Our languages are our life breath.
Lingítx̱ haa sateeyí,	Our Tlingit identity,
Deikeenaax̱ haa sateeyí,	Our Haida identity,
Ts'ootsxánx̱ haa sateeyí	Our Tsimshian identity,
ldakát uháan a tóonáx̱ haa k̲ukgastee.	we will be born through all these things.

Yoo x̱'ayla.á	Speak!
Yoo x̱'ayla.á	Speak!

Gunalchéesh, Háw'aa, Dyok'shm.	Thank you.

150

Abstract

This paper examines the many factors surrounding attempts at language revitalization in Alaska, seeing it as two equal and deadly parts: 1) internal disconnect with cultural identity and values, and 2) living within a society that does not value what it cannot financially exploit. Pulling from a wide variety of sources, the issues of Alaska Native language survival are viewed in terms of language death, murder, and suicide. Some of the practical and theoretical methods for a true revitalization movement in Alaska are explored while keeping in mind similar struggles for Indigenous language stabilization worldwide. We have not yet created the change we need in order to ensure that future generations will be able to communicate with their ancestors, the vast majority of whom did not speak English. It will take a massive coordinated effort to succeed in monolingual America, but it can and will be done.

Alaska Native people have been tied to specific places by their evolving and complex languages for over 10,000 years. Within Alaska's languages we see an incredible and rich history that involved learning of place, belonging, adaptation, and identity. The imperialistic attacks on Alaska Native people over the last several hundred years have left their languages in great peril, which has led to some of the highest rates of destruction and self-destruction in recent history. If anything is going to assist the current emotional and spiritual state of Alaska's Indigenous people, it is going to be revitalization. That is a difficult task to truly undertake, though, as every part of Alaska continues to undergo a language shift that is genocidal in its origins and results. Still, the hope is bright; it will just take a complete redefinition of who we are, what we are doing, and what is important to Alaska.

During a recent visit to an intermediate Tlingit class at the University of Alaska Southeast, elder George Ramos (2013) looked at everyone in the classroom and said the following: "All of the big leaders across the United States. What did they fight for? Cochise, Geronimo, Red Cloud, Crazy Horse, Sitting Bull. They were fighting for their way of life, as you are doing right here." At the heart of language revitalization, at this point in history, we see change and revolution; we see a need for rising up and speaking back at a system that tried to destroy us as people and nations. It was at that moment I realized that speaking your Alaska Native language is the single greatest act of sovereignty. It is one of the final ways we have left to stand up and say, "We are still here." It is the only thing that can never be taken away, unless we continue to give it up.

The focus of my work is in southeast Alaska. I have attempted to compile numbers on Alaska Native languages, populations, and speakers but will leave the publication of those numbers up to individuals and organizations working within those languages to avoid generalizations about languages and cultures outside of my area of expertise. In southeast Alaska, however, informal surveys of individuals and organizations working within our languages have led me to the following statistics, which will be one of the first points in this discussion on Alaska Native language revitalization.

Tlingit is the largest group in southeast Alaska, with a global population of approximately 16,000 located mostly in southeast Alaska, northwestern British Columbia, and southwestern Yukon (Pritzker 2000, p. 286–287). There are about 200 known speakers of the language, which is 1.25 percent of the population. This means that 98.75 percent of the Tlingit people cannot speak their own language, which is more troubling when considering that the vast majority of speakers are over 60 years old. The second-largest group is Tsimshian, which may be around 10,000, which would include Coast Tsimshian, Southern Tsimshian, Nisga'a, and Gitksan people. Coast Tsimshian is the group in Alaska, and informal inquiries suggest fewer than twenty speakers out of a population of about 1,300 (1.5 percent), which are almost all over 70 years old. The smallest of the three is Haida, with approximately 1,700 people, 600 of whom are in Alaska and the majority of the remaining on Haida Gwaii. There are probably 30 speakers worldwide (1.8 percent), and perhaps five or six of those reside in Alaska (Holton, 2010).

An analysis of the basic numbers is always a bit of a guessing game because of population relocations, disagreements over what constitutes a speaker, and the geographical spreading of people from rural to urban locations, which includes places outside of the traditional territory of the southeast Alaska Native peoples. But these types of analyses are necessary at this phase of language revitalization, which in southeast Alaska is a race against time, an attempt to add to the number of speakers instead of stand aside and watch a steady progression toward zero (language death). For revitalization to occur, it is helpful to know what you have to work with, who is ready for which phases of language acquisition, and which communities still have speakers living there.

One of our main hurdles today is the way we value languages. If 98 percent of your population does not speak the language, then it is safe to say that they do not value the language. This is not to say that people do not care, but it is saying that perhaps we have lost the ability to see why speaking our language matters. To engage in this discussion, we will examine the words of Richard Littlebear (1997):

> But why save our languages since they now seem to have no political, economic, or global relevance? That they seem not to have this relevance is exactly the reason why we should save our languages because it is the spiritual relevance that is deeply embedded in our own languages that is important. The embeddedness of this spirituality is what makes them relevant to us as American Indians.

What we have here is a failure to adhere to the values that made us. One of the goals of cultural genocide and assimilation is switching the value system of a people. By embracing the monolingual English world of America, we cannot help but speak the same vocabulary of a worldview that values the world according to economic principles. The primary question is no longer how we fit into the systems that surround us, but instead how can we ascend within the system that confines us.

There is not a lot of money in our languages. One of the common arguments against languages is that we need to prepare our children for the world they live in, which is often referred to with supremacist terminology like the "real" or "modern" world. These modes of thinking attempt to freeze our traditional languages and modes of thinking into being primitive and outdated, simplistic and otherwise fictionalized in the Euro-American mode of othering Indigenous knowledge systems.

The reality is that when you remove the value system of a culture, the people begin not only to fail to see the value in their own languages, but they fail to see the value of themselves. Our languages have long since tied us to specific places, names, events, and ancestors, and when we enter the disconnected, monolinguistic world of Euro-America, we find failure in nearly every direction we turn.

Our languages in southeast Alaska are trapped in a downward spiral, which we can map out here as an adaptation of a model used by Schmidt mapping Australian Aboriginal languages and Perley (2011, p. 56) doing the same for Maliseet:

• Limited language use
• Limited exposure to the language
• Reduced language knowledge and fluency
• Lack of confidence in using the language
• Increasing reliance on English
• Limited Alaska Native language use
• CYCLE REPEATS

In order to have an honest discussion about language revitalization, we need to know where we are with things, so we must engage in frightening conversations about where our languages are currently and what factors are contributing to their ongoing death. This is not to say, by any means, that language loss is a foregone conclusion, but we need to know what we are facing. We must document the actual state of our languages in order to awaken a sense of urgency and responsibility in our people, neighborhoods, villages, cities, and regions. This has yet to happen in a percentage of the population large enough to reverse language shift.

In southeast Alaska, we have language programs that produce students with knowledge of language but that do not create enough speakers of the language. It is not enough to know about the language and how it functions, because we need our people to think in the same ways as our ancestors in order to process survival in a world that tried to destroy them. For many of our students, this means always looking for the next challenge in becoming a speaker and thinker of our languages, someone who will be there for the next generation of learners, who will experience language in a way radically different than any of us who are studying today.

The next step in analyzing our situation is categorizing our languages. The following list is a combination and simplification of other systems of categorizing language endangerment, based upon the works of Krauss, Fishman, Dixon, Hudson and McConvell, Schmidt, Wurm, and others (Tsunoda 2005, p. 9–13):

Stage One—safe
- The first language of entire communities
- Used in every aspect of daily life

Stage two—endangered
- The first language for some, second language for most
- Use limited by availability and comfort of speakers

Stage three—moribund

- First language for only a few people
  with small groups of learners
- Used mostly for ceremonial or self-
  identification purposes

Stage four—dying

- No living birth speakers
- Very few speak, often with simplified
  grammar, content, and function
- Language is symbolic only, conversations
  in the language are nonexistent.

Stage five—extinct

- No remaining speakers
- Students study texts or recordings
- All cultural concepts are translations

Those in southeast Alaska find themselves in stage three. In reality, all languages in Alaska except for Yup'ik languages probably find themselves in stage three or four. That is not to say that there is no going up the ladder, but it does mean that there needs to be more and more awareness of the situation and the work required to move away from extinction.

This leads us to the following question: what are we doing with our languages? The goal should depend upon the situation. Every language in Alaska is undergoing language shift, which we can understand as the movement from multilingualism to monolingualism: from Alaska Native languages to English only. If language shift is going in that direction, then most of our goals should center around reversing language shift, which means a move back toward multilingualism. For languages that are *safe,* that means the goal is **Ending Language Shift**: keeping communities, homes, families, and institutions bilingual. For all *endangered, moribund,* and *dying* languages, it means **Language Revitalization**: creating language use in homes, families, and institutions with the goal of making those realms bilingual. For *extinct* languages that are no longer spoken, it means **Language Revival**: bringing the language back to life and then revitalizing it.

The techniques for each of these may vary a bit, but we can simplify the desired outcome as this: people who use the language everywhere, for anything, and to anyone. One of the most oppressive outcomes of American colonialism is the extinguishment of Indigenous language use. The most racist assumption in Alaska is the assumption that English should be the default language in education, commerce, and daily communication.

At this point in language loss, it is an absolute necessity that we understand the need for our own people to take control of the situation. Many of our people fall victim to the waiting game: waiting for an organization to take care of the situation. In turn, many of our organizations fall victim to the responsibility game: waiting for some other organization to step forward and claim responsibility for and take care of the situation. While there is a clear path of responsibility that ties language loss to state and federal governments, as well as religious organizations, we cannot wait for those organizations to undo the situation because the consciousness that created them in the land of our ancestors wanted our way of thinking gone.

Someday there may be a place for an Alaska Native Language Claims Settlement. ANCSA was a land agreement, so it makes sense that there may be room for lawsuits against governments and the churches that ran Alaska's schools. Still, we cannot ever afford to wait for someone else to take care of things for us. When we subscribe to external value systems, we will never value our ancestors, our children, or ourselves. This is a critical factor in language revitalization: the current mode of consciousness, that found within American English societies, will not truly value Indigenous languages. Not yet.

This concepts is summarized brilliantly by the late Oscar Kawagley, who stated the following at a language conference in Arizona:

> Many Americans are intolerant of diversity, be it cultural with its concomitant languages, or biodiversity in an ecological system. Instead, we see notions of human and cultural superiority with designs for a monolingual and monocultural society in which the English language and its associated culture presumes to become the language and culture of the world . . . We use English predominately in our everyday lives today. We don't realize that English is a language contrived by the clever rational mind of the human being. The letters were derived by the human mind. The words are a product of a mind-set that is given to individualism and materialism in a techno-mechanistic world. For us to think that we can reconstruct a new world by using English and its ways will not work. We need to return

to a language that is given to health and healing. To try to make a paradigmatic shift by using the consciousness that constructed this modern world is bound for failure. Albert Einstein stated something to the effect that "you cannot make change in a system using the same consciousness used to construct it." This should be very clear to us as a Native people.

Therefore, language revitalization is more than deciding to speak a different language. It is more than saying the same thing a different way. Instead, it is a rebirth of an ancient way of thinking that has kept our people alive for countless generations, through countless phenomena that threatened us physically, spiritually, emotionally, and mentally.

It is important to keep a positive mind-set while engaging in discussions on language revitalization. We are up against everything here: the world's most successful and least discussed genocide, the mass murder of hundreds of languages and the cultures that are delicately tied to them. The people doing actual day-to-day work in language revitalization are standing up to the most powerful force in the world and saying: We are still here. We have withstood everything and still see our true selves. We are going to stand back up and build a better world for our descendants.

In any region of the world where endangered languages have attempted to revitalize, we can see common mistakes and learn how to avoid them. Tsunoda (2005, p. 180–195) lists a summary of common mistakes and ways to avoid them, which are gathered from a wide variety of sources. These are also important to understand to make sure your goal is language use by the majority of your people for everything in their daily lives. So often we are stuck in the same circles, where the new expert comes into our community with the new technique that creates new posters and games but does not create speakers. That list of common difficulties is consolidated below.

- Language programs are of low quality and offered just as a token
- Insufficient hours are allocated to teaching of the language
- Shortage of adequate language resources and language learning materials
- Lack of human resources, especially trained teachers and native speakers as co-teachers
- Unstructured programs and curricula, which are confined to the teaching of isolated vocabulary, rather than overall language ability, including communicative skills
- The illusion that a given language-revitalization program is a success only because its associated cultural activities, such as dance groups and cultural gatherings, are enjoying popularity

Most of them are the result of inadequate funding, planning, and commitment. Sometimes organizations might respond to requests for language revitalization but do not change the culture of their organization. What we find is a department within an organization that conducts its business entirely in English and does not expect or require its employees, council members, or citizens to follow the doctrine of language revitalization. Instead, a minority practices language use on its own, or worse, experts are brought in who have no knowledge of the language but have external credentials that make them experts in the field of education, language learning, and anthropology. Sometimes we fall victim to the myth that someone is going to come in and save us, and save our languages, but it is our turn to take the stand and rediscover ourselves.

This is not to say that people from outside our cultural groups are of no value, but learning languages and instigating true movements of revitalization and language sovereignty takes an internal change. In fact, the internal and external should not be ethnically or even culturally based terms, nor should they be locked into rigid definitions of people as binary logic often does. For our language-revitalization movements, *internal* means those who are committed to speaking and hearing our languages. As one of my colleagues, Roy Mitchell, has said, in order to learn a language you have to make it one of the top three things in your life. That does not mean all languages or the concept of language revitalization, but that means committed to learning a language and using it at an elevated ability. And *external* are those that do not. In no way does that mean they should always be considered outsiders, but rather are the ones we have to strategize differently for, the ones who may need more convincing and encouragement. I think of part of a speech by Íxtik' Éesh (A.P. Johnson), "Ḵaa yoo x̱'atángi héen yíx̱ kei nagut ḵáa yáx̱ yatee, k'éx̱'aa teen—Public speaking is like a man walking up along a river with a gaff hook" (Dauenhauer & Dauenhauer 2000, p. 156–157). We need that gaff hook dragging in the water, bringing more people out into the movement.

Some of the problems in language revitalization stem from the terminology that we use to talk about language death. Sometimes we call it *language loss*, which makes it sound like the language was misplaced somehow, like keys you might find beneath a couch cushion and be fine. Other times, we call it *language death*, which has more urgency but might lead to the belief that languages die like pets, plants, and people. This contributes to a false belief that Alaska Native languages have just fallen behind as the world had no more use for them: an evolution so to say. In fact, the term we should be using for historical language shift in Alaska is *language murder*. There were powerful people and groups who sought to eliminate Alaska Native languages, and we are seeing the success of such efforts. Even more important than that term is what Perley (2011, p. 121–148) and others have been stressing, and that is *language suicide*. I have heard story after story of violent and cunning forms of abuse to keep our older generations from speaking while they were in school. I heard kids in school while growing up who would make fun of Alaska Natives by imitating Alaska Native accents, diminishing the intelligence and humanity of our people while doing so. But here is an important fact: No one is stopping us now. We are choosing to walk away from our languages.

We are leaving our ancestors behind, our children behind, and ourselves behind. This message is not intended to dismiss the racism, genocide, and overall loss that Alaska Native people have felt. But we are still here. No teacher will wash your mouth out. No religious leader will smack your hand or face. No one is going to lock you in a closet over the weekend without food or light. No one will be elevated above you because they speak English more than you choose to. We stand in the shadows of the terrible actions of spiritual, cultural, and intellectual genocide, but we are still here and can still speak..

It is time to take control of the impulses that tell us that such acts are still in existence. Language revitalization often means looking right at those things and figuring out what to do. I have students whose parents decided not to teach them their language, and they struggle to forgive them for making those decisions. This leads us back to Kawagley, who correctly pointed out that the healing must take place within our languages. English does not have the tools necessary for us to understand there is a void where our language used to be.

A Tlingit elder, Walter Austin, once told me that there is a place in your mind called the subconscious. Our people always knew about this place, he said. They have left things for you there, and when you learn your language it is like you are opening a door to the attic in your mind and finding these things. That is revitalization. That is a place where we can protect our children, our elders, and ourselves.

The key to the whole puzzle is a generation of learners who are gaining language acquisition from birth. The simple answer is this: Speak the language and it lives. Don't and it dies. Put it in your homes and use it as much or more than English. Put it in your schools and use it as much or more than English. Speak. We have been waiting for so long for something to happen, when all this time we just needed to make things happen. Living in an English-only world is killing us, and a long time ago when something was killing us we just got rid of it. It took epic levels of effort and battle, but we did it before and we will do it again. Our Alaska Native organizations can help by making languages a viable part of their organizational culture. Answer the phone in the language; give employees time and incentives to learn the language. Make knowledge of language a measurable quality in elections, job placements, and promotions. We can make our languages the core of our organizational identity and dismiss the idea that we sold our land for corporate identity and are just another entity focused on the bottom line. We live for identity, and not just economics. The Euro-American world will not value our languages the way we should, so we must internalize our values in ways that make sense and are sustainable.

Our leaders can push for room at education tables for Alaska Native languages. If we are going to have standardized tests and higher education requirements, then Alaska Native languages need to be included and not excluded. As it stands, English is seen as the natural default, which is a concept born out of the lie of racial superiority. We need these items on the table because this is not our problem alone. Everyone who is in Alaska is in the aftermath of a great and terrible attack on entire cultures. You cannot be born into the scene of a mass murder and think that everything should just carry on as planned.

Alaska Native languages are the key to sovereignty. I have no illusions that if we all spoke our languages then there would be no problems. But as Tsunoda and others point out, we will give our future generations intellectual advantages by building a multilingual Alaska. Tsunoda states that, "Unlike monolinguals, bilinguals will be aware that the same thought may be expressed in more than one way, with different words and sentences in different languages, and that some words and expressions may have no exact equivalent in another language" (Tsunoda 2005, p. 200). They will be able to look at the complex range of problems that are resulting in preposterous rates of suicide, homicide, diabetes, educational failure, economic failure, and more with multiple simultaneous thought worlds.

If we are wondering how to revitalize languages in Alaska, then I would offer the following suggestions, which are based on the world's most successful language-revitalization programs, namely Maori, Hawaiian, Mohawk, Celtic, and Hebrew. For more specifics on these programs, see Tsunoda and Grenoble & Whaley.

- Create schools that are committed to teaching entirely within the language and fill it with as many children as we can find.
- Identify families who are committed to multilingual households and then link them with the schools that you have built.
- Create a culture of revitalization. Make language learning the standard and find ways to include everyone. Our differences and squabbles are insignificant compared to being killed off.
- Put the language back on the land. Reintroduce native place names and make them the standardized way of referring to places. This will add value to the land and make knowledge of the language common in the community.

- Do not be afraid to fail or make mistakes. Allow your people and yourself to be students within our languages. Have fun, but always protect the self-esteem and the right to belong for everyone.
- Be selfless. One of the most damaging things from the Euro-American mode of thinking is the concept that everything is somehow about me. Find ways to help others, to give your time and energy, and to understand that isolation often leads to monolingualism.
- Stop waiting. No one is going to do this for you, and people in high political places are not likely to say it is a great idea to make Alaska Native languages an actual equal part of Alaska. You do not need permission, and you do not need to meet any external standards.

We have seen this world fail us over and over again, so it is time to step up and build a world that bridges the one our ancient people knew and then one we are preparing for the future. There is no way we can begin putting an end to suicide and murder, the rape of our women, the destruction of our land, the mass murder of our ancestors, unless we force English to release its grip on our consciousness. If we think back just a few generations, we have ancestors who did not understand English and probably would not want to. Just because they are dead does not mean that they are gone. If we do not embrace our languages and live with them, then we are ignoring the ones who made us who we are. If we do not stop language shift right now and begin reversing it, then we are saying that the concept of "killing the Indian and saving the man" (George Mason University, n.d.) is the right move after all.

There is a real need for language centers in our communities. I have been in Alaska cities and villages and seen people often wandering without purpose. Maybe we can do the same thing each day: commute, shop, work, eat, sleep. But maybe there is something more. Maybe there can be a place in our community where I can stop on the way home, or call someone and meet them there. It is a place where everyone is welcome, but once you step in the door you switch to the language of that place.

Our speakers are often lonesome, and language-revitalization work has too much time where you are with the same small group of people hoping for some real change. To our leaders, it is time to realize that the future is in your hands. You do not want to be remembered as the ones who were at the helm when we allowed our languages to be killed off. For our people, we need to know that we are every bit as capable, brilliant, and strong as we need to be. We have been embracing the wrong modes of thinking and the wrong concepts of what it will take to create meaningful change. Sometimes changing the world is as simple as saying no to something that seems to exist everywhere at all times. When we embrace our languages, we will see that invisibility is just a curtain, and an entire world of knowing, healing, and existing is waiting for us. When English forcefully replaced our languages, it instantly taught us to hate ourselves. It was full of racial slurs and undertones that hinted at a superiority that is simply not there. So stand up, shake it off. This is a world of unity and purpose: we were born for this fight and are about to make language death a distant memory.

References

Dauenhauer, Nora Marks and Richard Dauenhauer. (2000) *haa tuwunáagu yís: for our healing spirit—Tlingit oratory.* Seattle: University of Washington Press.

George Mason University. (n.d.) "'Kill the Indian, and save the man': Capt. Richard H. Pratt on the education of Native Americans." *History matters: The U.S. survey course on the web.* Retrieved from http://historymatters. gmu.edu/d/4929/

Grenoble, Lenore A. & Lindsay J. Whaley. (2006). *Saving languages: An introduction to language revitalization.* Cambridge: Cambridge University Press.

Holton, Gary. (2010, October 19). "Guide to the Tsimshian language collection." *Alaska Native Language* Archive. University of Alaska Fairbanks. Retrieved from https:// www.uaf.edu/anla/collections/tsimshian

Kawagley, Angayuqaq Oscar. (2003) "Nurturing Native Languages." *Nurturing Native Langauges.* Northern Arizona University. Retrieved from. http://jan.ucc.nau. edu/~jar/NNL/NNL_Kawagley.pdf

Littlebear, Richard. (1997, May 2) "Some Rare and Radical Ideas for Keeping Indigenous Languages Alive." *Revitalizing Indigenous Languages.* Northern Arizona University. Retrieved from http://www2.nau.edu/~jar/ RIL_1.html

Perley, Bernard C. (2011). *Defying Maliseet Language Death: Emerging Vitalities of Language, Culture, & Identity in Eastern Canada.* Lincoln: University of Nebraska Press.

Pritzker, Barry M. (2000). *A Native American Encyclopedia: History, Culture, and Peoples.* Oxford: Oxford University Press.

Ramos, Geroge. (2013, March 27) "Wooshji<u>x</u>oo Éesh — Tlingit Language Class Visit." Trans. Lance A. Twitchell. University of Alaska Southeast. Retrieved from http://youtu.be/QLXfGUP2018

Tsunoda, Tasaku. (2005). *Language Endangerment and Language Revitalization: An Introduction.* Berlin: Mouton de Gruyter.

From the Practical to the Spiritual and Back: A Model for the Interaction of European and Native Societies

Tony Kaliss

Abstract

This paper is an exploration of why European and Native societies act as they have toward each other. Key is an examination of the deep interaction of practical and spiritual issues. It is necessary to go beyond what happened or how it happened to the roots of a still-ongoing complex interaction. The purpose is a deeper understanding by both Natives and non-Natives with the goal of developing strategies to strengthen Native societies and to clarify the place of Native societies and Indigenous worldviews as active and essential contributors to the resolution of basic issues affecting all peoples in the modern world. The motivation for this paper is 46 years of involvement by the author with issues between Native and non-Native societies in which the need to reach deeper understanding arises from the everyday challenges of practical realities. Specific examples are drawn from Alaska and the Russian Far East (Chukotka).

Introduction

The purpose of this paper is to share a model for understanding the dynamics of the Native/European interaction. Forty-eight years' work with issues between Native and non-Native, primarily European-based, societies make clear the need for answers to several basic questions: Why have Europeans behaved as they do toward Native peoples? Why has much of that behavior had such negative effects on Native societies? And why have Native peoples responded as they have?

In recent years, as Indigenous people worldwide have strongly reasserted themselves, the need for an in-depth model is all the more obvious and useful.

In its present form this model goes back about ten years and is a work whose continuous progress and refinement is aided and abetted by responses, which are most welcome.

The Model

The model is as follows:

Native		**European**
Sharing	←vs.→	Taking Without Giving
↕		↕
Connection	←vs.→	Disconnection
↕		↕
Harmony	←vs.→	Disharmony

I wanted a model that can be put briefly and clearly. At the same time it must be a model that once put in motion can fully spin out the interactions of the Native-European encounter.

I also deliberately chose terms that combine the practical and the spiritual. That is, each term is practical in that it can be studied and documented, spiritual in that each term embodies a spiritual outlook on how life should be lived. For example, the process of sharing can be documented, but sharing is also a spiritual expression of a way of life.

My life's work made clear to me that the practical and spiritual are directly and deeply related. Working with Native communities taught me the importance and centrality of the spiritual factor, something not consciously present in my own upbringing.

The model presented is my own. From Christopher Columbus, an Italian, in 1492, to Linda Tuawai Smith, a Maori, in 2012, Europeans and Native peoples have been remarking on the differences between their societies. They have done so because the differences are, indeed, remarkable. However, I am not aware of any model with the explanatory content presented here. Of course, I am much indebted to many works studied and people talked with that shaped and informed my thinking; more on this below. The format—the interacting contrasts—was suggested to me by several one-page parallel lists of what are often labeled Native versus Western cultures or thinking.

Two quick disclaimers: First, the two sides of the model absolutely are not meant to represent a case of noble Natives sharing everything and savage Europeans taking everything. Native teaching stories make clear the presence of good and evil in their own societies long before any Europeans entered the picture, and within European societies there has always been a strong resistance to taking without giving.

Second, Europeans have no monopoly on conflicts with Native societies. I focus on Europeans because that's whom I've been working with and, also, Europeans have interacted with more Indigenous peoples worldwide than anyone else. By

European I mean Euro-American, Euro–New Zealand, English, French, Russian, etc.

Beware—Those Terms Are Loaded

Long ago I realized that the terms used in the discussion of Native-European interactions are thoroughly loaded with built-in assumptions about both sides of the model and can determine the direction of the analysis before it begins. Sometimes these assumptions are clear and up front. More often they are half-hidden and unconscious.

A good example is that there is no agreement on terms to use to describe what the two sides of the model represent. To be specific, I believe they represent two different and opposed social-economic systems: communal and capitalist.

No one denies that something came out of Europe that had a tremendous impact on Indigenous peoples all over the world. Nor can it be doubted that the general Indigenous reaction is to remain as distinct peoples in spite of great European pressures to change.

But what name to give the something from Europe? I have assembled a list of around 35 different words or phrases. One must ask what it signifies when one side of an important worldwide interaction is described by 35 different words.

The list of terms to describe the Native side is somewhat shorter but also represents a range of assumptions behind words ranging from *savage* to *autochthonous*. I generally use the term *Native*, which has the original meaning of being born here and because it is a term in common use, as in "Alaska Natives."

It is true that *Native* only specifies being born here and says nothing of origin or length of residence. *Autochthonous* is in many senses a better term in that its original Greek meaning is to come from the very earth in this place, but it is an uncommon term in American English.

The Model Dynamics

As indicated by the arrows, the dynamics of the model work both horizontally and vertically. A fundamental dynamic works vertically within each side, and then each side interacts horizontally at each level.

Sharing and Taking Without Giving (TWG) represent two different and opposed economic systems. On the one side are communally based societies extending back thousands of years, and, on the other, more than two thousand years of European societies dominated by forms of taking without giving, capitalism being the latest.

Connection and Disconnection represent the consequences, the necessary conditions for, and the goals of, the first pair. Connections make clear who is shared with. Establishing and maintaining connections puts the sharing into practice. Disconnection makes clear who or what is being taken from. Creating disconnections is the basis for putting TWG into practice, because if one were connected, then one would have to share. In both cases the goal is to maintain the connections or the disconnections.

Harmony and Disharmony represent goals and consequences of the operation of the first two pairs. Sharing and Connection work best when there is harmony. Harmony results from sharing and connection because the participants in the process are treated fairly. Falling out of harmony is a sign of becoming disconnected, and ceremonies are needed to restore the connections.

Conversely, Disharmony is the inevitable result of TWG and Disconnection, because those being taken from (whether human or nature) will resist. Those doing the taking must use force (mental or physical) to maintain the taking. In short, this is a society with much stress and conflict.

The processes described generally above need to be studied in the actual practices of European and Native societies to show how the model dynamics work out in detail and in reality. In this paper I focus on some important generalities applying to both sides, drawing examples mainly from Alaska and the North.

One fundamentally important observation arising directly from the model is the very deep practical and spiritual opposition between the two sides concerning all aspects of how life should be lived, which explains why Native peoples have almost universally resisted assimilation into European society.

Why would anyone coming from a sharing, connective, and harmonious society want, in their right minds, to exchange that for TWG, disconnection, and disharmony? In short, the model makes clear that Native resistance is not due to living in the past, being primitive or uncivilized or uneducated. On the contrary, it is a perfectly logical and rational reaction.

A way of life, not technology, is the fundamental issue. Native peoples have appreciated the technological from guns to ski-doos, but shopping at Wal-Mart or watching satellite TV in an Alaska Native village does not make a person less Native.

A second basic observation is that each side of the model represents at least one worldview/spiritual system/knowledge system that explains and justifies each side's way of life. People from both sides may be more or less aware of how they live out these systems. Spiritual systems are also knowledge systems, and the other way around. What we choose to know or not know, how we interpret our knowledge, is determined by the spiritual systems that influence us.

Native Worldview

Spirituality as a word and a practice came up repeatedly as I lived in and worked with Native communities. It became clear that something called *spirituality* and actual practical life are closely connected. Many examples of this can be found in Alaska.

The key for me personally regarding the connection of the spiritual and the practical came in the repeated comments by Native spiritual leaders that theirs is a way of life, not a religion. In short, Native peoples use spirituality to create a lived way of life in everyday practice by building the spiritual factor into the learning/experience process, by creating spiritual experiences—ceremonies, stories, songs, dances, vision quests—in forms that relate to all ages and experience levels.

Connection is critical. A connective spiritual worldview can become a lived daily practice precisely because it corresponds to the connective reality of the universe. Such a worldview can be lived by the great majority, not just a spiritual minority or only on certain days of the week or times of the year. Everyday life is a replication of the spiritual essence of that society. The living practice confirms and reaffirms the spiritual connections. The growing knowledge of connection confirms the correctness (workability) of the living practice.

The conscious and deliberate practices of Alaska Native peoples are deep examples of the above. Recent Native writers such as Shawn Wilson (2009), who presents the Native research process as a ceremony, and Oscar Kawagley (2006), who saw a Native connective spiritual worldview as essential to human learning, can be mentioned. The Navajo worldview summed up in the concept of *hozho*, which advocates for a state of moving in beauty and harmony, or, as I remember hearing many years ago, of walking in a ceremonial manner, assumes that a human being does not stand still—he/she moves through the world and best learns of it by moving in a ceremonial spiritual manner. This concept sums up the Native side of my model, and it implies its opposite, which is, for whatever reason, to fall out of balance and harmony or, still worse, to use one's life knowledge to benefit only oneself: taking without giving. The only cures for this are the proper ceremonies to restore the balance and harmony.

The great strength of Native societies lies, therefore, in the connective nature of Native spiritually. The more connections, the stronger one is. All humans are spiritual, but a connective spirituality has great strength as the glue keeping the society together. Because it is lived, it retains great strength and persistence even where "official" Native spiritual leadership and practices have been forcibly suppressed.

In sum, the recognition of the power of spirituality in determining what people actually do is an important contribution made by Native peoples.

European Worldviews

Three very important observations: First, TWG creates a divided society, which means its dynamics are more complicated because there is more than one spiritual/world view, and more than one social-economic and political group. In short, there is no "we," a term whose frequent use among Native people struck me from the beginning.

A critical question for those at the top of a divided society is how to put forward a spiritual system and worldview that can appeal to the majority and yet support the minority in their practice of TWG.

Second, TWG necessitates the assertion of superiority to justify the taking. The notion of European superiority became and remains a critical factor in the interaction of European and Native societies. More broadly, any form of TWG—interpersonal, within groups, organizations, religions or societies, etc.—always necessitates a notion of superiority.

On the society level, this need for superiority necessarily influences the two basic worldview/spiritual systems of Europe—Christianity and science. European superiority can be summarized as "blessed by God, proved by science." Either argument is quite persuasive; taken together, overwhelming. Christianity provides the spiritual proof, science the factual proof, and Native peoples appear as un-Christian heathens and unscientific superstitious primitives. Christianity and science have had their differences, but on this they could agree. The point here is that every society will use its available worldviews to explain and justify its own practices.

But the assertion of superiority is a lie that must be continually justified as being the truth. Maintaining that lie through both science and Christianity has had a deep influence on European views of Native peoples. Maintaining the lie becomes a critical ongoing source of conflict at all levels of the interaction of Native and European societies.

Third, disconnection itself causes lack of knowledge of the humans or nature being taken from. The disconnection blinds the person, the society, doing the taking from seeing or acknowledging certain facts. Additionally, there is a strong incentive not to understand, because understanding the true situation of connection would mean having to stop TWG. The result is a profound limiting affect on both European knowledge system/worldviews regarding what they are willing to see (more about this below).

A general conclusion is that no human knowledge system can be objective, i.e., able to directly know the objects, the facts, independently of a worldview and spiritual system, because all knowledge passes through our minds and our beliefs. We cannot escape being what we are, but we can become consciously aware of where we come from and act accordingly.

In other words, this is a physical process and is not the result of a social construction of knowledge, in that the social knowledge, while very influential, still must first pass through the physical process of how the human mind processes, understands, and acts on content.

Knowledge and the methods for obtaining it are never neutral: advocacy is built in. "The facts" are not neutral, because to tell the truth is to confront those who do not want the truth. This does not mean that truth cannot be determined. What it does mean is that different viewpoints are more or less connected to or disconnected from the truth.

Spirituality

Spirituality determines what we actually do. As noted, this observation made long ago by Native societies is a very important contribution to understanding how humans behave. As a community organizer, before working with Native communities, I learned one can offer many facts, but if people are not ready at what I then called the gut level, they won't change; thanks to work with Native peoples that opened my eyes to the existence and importance of spirituality, I now understand it at the spiritual level. Native peoples were generally quite consciously aware of this spiritual level of change and made use of it as a way to maintain behaviors that were and are the foundation of Native life.

But what is spirituality? Stressing its importance as a central factor in human behavior necessitates offering a definition of what it is. My own is biological.

All living organisms, even a single-celled amoeba, must be able to adapt to changing environments. I suggest that at a certain evolutionary point what we call spirituality is a very complex way by which living beings adapt and survive. This means it is built into our behavior—but not just human behavior; I think Native people are quite right in seeing spirituality at work in other living creatures.

In other words, humans by definition are spiritual, and spirituality is absolutely fundamental to the human condition. It is a matter of detail to examine how each group of humans has worked out spiritual systems to express that inborn spirituality.

Since spirituality is built in, no one group can claim to have a monopoly on being spiritual. This is why the practice of Christian missionaries toward Native people was too often so wrong and so hurtful.

A deeper and very important point is that the realness or factualness of spirituality lies in how it determines real human behavior toward other humans and nature. The human mind is free to imagine anything happening or existing spiritually, whether or not factual or provable. In fact, I suspect that the way humans think and feel about spirituality is in forms that are not necessarily factual as such, nor need they be. The point is how the beliefs and feelings affect actual behavior.

The scientist, focused on whether the spiritual can be factual, and the Christian (or member of any religion) who insists that one must believe certain spiritual events to be factual, both miss the point of the role that spirituality plays in connecting real factual human beings to real factual behavior in a real world. It is not whether an aerial photograph can be produced of Santa's North Pole workshop, but rather the spirit of gift giving that the story teaches that is important.

I am also aware that most Native peoples also see all processes in nature as living and having a spiritual character. Since it is a fact that everything in the universe is moving and changing, it is not extreme to interpret this as every process having a spirit that influences how humans should relate to all that is.

The Interaction of the Two Sides

There cannot be a better practical example than Alaska of the dynamics at work between Native and European-based societies.

On the European side, the development of capitalism beginning in the 13th century soon sent Europeans worldwide searching for three things—resources, labor, and markets—at the least cost and the greatest monetary profit possible. They sought labor to make commodities from resources, and markets to sell them in.

Alaska's main use to Europeans from the Russians onward has been resources. The history of non-Native Alaska is naming the resource, its discovery date, and its location. For the Russians it began with furs.

The main point here is that the taking without giving of resources results in resistance and disharmony. This is fundamental to understanding the interaction process in Alaska from the disharmony of the enslavement of the Aleuts by the Russians and the suicides of young Native people in the 21st century, to the resistance shown in the persistence of over 200 Native communities to the present day in the face of enormous pressures to change.

While Native labor was important for the Russians in Alaska and the Americans did hire some Native labor in connection with development of other resources, it was never as important as in Latin America or Africa, where the Indigenous populations were much larger. In Alaska there was a tendency to simply ignore the Native presence, push them aside if they were in the way of obtaining a specific resource, and to disregard the effects of resource exploitation on the Native population.

The tale of Native resistance ranges from the Aleut revolts against enslavement by the Russians to present-day lawsuits by Native organizations and tribes concerning resource development and the existence of Native sovereignty.

Assimilationist policies deserve special mention because they operate at the spiritual level. They thereby concern some of the deepest and most important interactions between Native and European societies. To control a people one must try to control their spiritual systems. In the case of Native peoples, this meant eliminating Native spiritual systems, taking away education of Native children, suppressing language—all of which are vehicles for the spiritual.

Sheldon Jackson's missionary efforts in Alaska and his federal appointment as general agent for education perfectly illustrate the understanding of spiritual control regarding beliefs and education. The content of and control over belief and education systems continue to be issues in Alaska.

Disconnective efforts to break up Native peoples as distinct peoples by assimilating them as individuals into the European system are reflected in the 1915 Alaska Territorial Law granting a Native citizenship on proof of "total abandonment of tribal customs, adoption of the culture of civilization," the repeated (and ongoing) attempts by the State of Alaska to eliminate tribal sovereignty and attach subsistence rights to rural individuals rather than Natives as a group, and the terminationist aspects of the original ANCSA.

The Native Side

Connective spirituality as a guiding force in determining Native reactions and the great strength of that connection are shown by the persistent survival in Alaska of so many small Native communities into the present day.

At the same time the strength of the system of connections is also measured by the depth and complexity of the problems resulting when the connections of people with each other and/or with nature are bent, strained, or broken. This is seen in the range of personal and community issues in present-day Alaska. The problems of Native individuals and families cannot be understood or addressed outside of the context of the connections to and within Native society.

It is seen in the fundamentally different definitions of what community development means for Native villages. One side measures development by monetary profitability for individual owners. The other side measures development in terms of how it strengthens the connections fundamental to the Native community. A practical example is how subsistence is understood and analyzed by the two sides. (1)

Where Do We Go from Here?

Beginning in the 1960s Native peoples in many parts of the world, including Alaska, began to reassert themselves. There is no question this was connected with the challenges to European domination physically, ideologically, and spiritually after WWII, although earlier 20th-century Native resistance certainly existed in Alaska and elsewhere.

What do Native peoples do once it is clear they have no intention of disappearing as they were supposed to? They focus on connections. My own observations since the 1960s are that Native communities have been concerned with maintaining the connections that still exist, repairing connections that have been strained or bent, and reestablishing connections that were broken.

Again, Alaska provides abundant examples of these efforts. They can be summed up as regaining the physical ground from the 1960s into the 1980s and then regaining the spiritual ground from the 1980s to the present.

This is a logical sequence: Native people need a place to live and are spiritually closely tied to those places. They need physical communities to live in. Thus the land claims of the 1960s that led to the passing of the ANCSA in 1971. It includes gaining control or influence over programs serving Native communities and using those programs to thoroughly rebuild the physical infrastructures of Native communities. This physical rebuilding is a clear statement of ongoing existence.

It follows that the next step is to regain the spiritual ground. If Native peoples are to continue to exist physically, it becomes necessary to construct, reconstruct, and restore a spiritual base for that continued existence in present times.

The list in Alaska is long, varied, and creative, and deserves much greater study and documentation. It includes the revival of ceremonies, celebrations, and dance, the creation of spirit camps, gatherings of elders and youth, charter schools, and efforts to promote and restore Native languages, etc.

There is a long and varied list of Native organizations that have arisen at the village, region, and state levels speaking to the needs of Native peoples in every area of concern, including politics, law, health, economic development, cultural institutions (including repatriation efforts), funding of studies and documentation, etc.

Alaska Natives reached out internationally to Indigenous peoples worldwide. The Iñupiat peoples on the North Slope were among the first anywhere in creating international ties, with the formation of the ICC in 1977.

Native involvement in Alaska state politics, going back to William Paul in the 1920s, has been more important because the Native relation with the federal Bureau of Indian Affairs has not been as direct and extensive as in the lower 48. However, the federal-level relationship of sovereign nations attained great importance from the 1970s onward with the steady and persistent assertion of Native sovereignty as a necessary tool for control over the rebuilding and survival process.

In response to these measures of connection, there have been consistent and ongoing attempts at disconnection, most notably by the State of Alaska but also by some private organizations, individuals, and legislators. With a couple of exceptions, such as the Millennium Agreement in 2001 between Governor Knowles and Alaska tribes, the State of Alaska has maintained a consistently aggressive resistance to tribal sovereignty and to the continued existence of Native peoples as distinct groups, spending well over a million dollars in legal costs. Very recently, the state succeeded in having tribal courts in Alaska excluded from jurisdiction over non-Natives in the Violence Against Women Act of 2013.

Native Worldviews Today

One of the most significant developments in the last ten to fifteen years is a rapidly growing literature expressing systematic Native worldviews for the 21st century coming from Native communities and Native academics. This work has both confirmed and informed my own thinking, although it is necessary to mention Vine Deloria's important and prolific contributions dating back to the 1960s when I first read his *Custer Died for Your Sins.* Native Studies programs play a significant role in this ongoing process.

This is part of the process of regaining the spiritual ground, reflecting the fact that by the 1990s the number of Native peoples achieving higher degrees in the European higher-education system had reached a critical mass where they were becoming active participants in the academic world.

All the restatements of Native worldviews include spirituality as a central operating factor. The connective nature of Native spirituality is a very practical asset as an analytical tool that helps cut through the disconnective influences of European Christianity and science. One sees more facts more deeply and more accurately through connection than through disconnection.

The assertion of a distinctly Native worldview and spiritual system necessarily means challenging the European worldviews/spiritual systems of science and Christianity—an ongoing and very productive process. Whatever European missionaries intended, it should be noted that Native peoples nativized Christianity to fit it to their own basic worldviews. This can be seen in Alaska, for example, in how the Russian Orthodox religion has become "nativized." The challenges include such steps as the restoration of public Native dancing in Noorvik as part of the official beginning of the 2010 U.S. Census process. Native academics are reevaluating and challenging the practices of science, both natural and social, as developed by Europeans (Cajete 1999; Wilson 2009).

European Societies Today

Being of European background, I am concerned with important changes happening in European-based societies. Certain of these changes have a profound impact on the conditions for survival of Indigenous peoples.

There are two major concerns for Native societies. First is how Native peoples are seen by the representatives of the two basic European worldviews, science and Christianity. Second is how Native peoples and issues are seen by groups and movements arising inside the European context who challenge TWG within their own European world. One would expect these forces to be sympathetic to Native issues.

In regard to the first concern, strong criticism from Native peoples since the 1960s has caused many practitioners of both science and Christianity to reevaluate their approaches to Native peoples in a positive manner, moving toward rejecting notions of inherent European superiority. This is to the good. At the same time, resistance continues on the part of some scientists and Christians. Even where the reaction is positive, the question remains of how deep the understanding is of Native peoples' perspectives.

Science, even when trying to be positive, has a special problem in that it cannot or will not deal with spirituality yet, I suggest, has become a spiritual system of its own (this is discussed further below). Here I refer to science as a worldview and spiritual system, in contrast to what is called the scientific method, which can be a very useful method of study of the real world.

Christianity obviously does see itself as a spiritual system, so could it relate better than science? It can to the extent that it does not play a role as spiritual spokesman for European societies, which necessarily introduced much disconnection, disharmony, and taking without giving.

The problem for both European worldviews is the limits imposed by disconnection. There are still great pressures on Christianity and science to remain limited. Not seeing can be deliberate and enforced but can also operate unseen, unquestioned, and unconsciously.

Regarding the second concern—attitudes toward Native peoples and Native issues on the part of Europeans who resist what is happening within their own societies—European societies are divided, and there always has been an active resistance to TWG going back to the slave revolts of ancient Rome.

Unfortunately, those who resist have not always understood Native peoples, and one must ask why. Some of this is due to simple ignorance: the focus was often on issues within the European framework, not on relations with others.

However, the major factor is the spread of the virus of European superiority, so that too often European critics have seen their own criticisms as the most superior criticisms—in particular, superior to anything Native societies have to offer (more below).

Role and Tasks of Native Studies

Native Studies goes back to the 1960s protests to establish new fields of study other than of dead white men and to have these studies taught and developed by other than just living white men as more and more minority and women students entered colleges.

An essential task for Native Studies has been to insist on and provide space for Native scholars and scholarship. Another challenge is to develop and express the essentials of a Native worldview and research methodology, in that each actual Native worldview is grounded in specific tribal worldviews worldwide, and to undertake studies in ways that support and maintain connections with and within the Native communities that are the living base of Native worldviews and practices.

More particularly Native Studies can be seen as studying the contrasts, the connections, and disconnections of the Native/non-Native interaction, what they are, how they work, and, very important, why they exist in real-life situations past, present, and future.

Native Studies is inevitably a confrontational field of study, insofar as it supports the sharing, connection, and harmony that constitute the Native side. To tell the truth about what has happened to Native peoples means confronting both those who cannot see the truth and, especially, those forces that do not want the truth told. These truths concern fundamentally important and current issues of concern to both Native and non-Native societies, resulting in the involvement of powerful interests on both sides.

Native Studies as part of the European higher-education academic framework necessarily concerns the Native/European interaction as expressed within that framework. A good deal of institutional disconnection is involved, which can put Native Studies practitioners in uncomfortable positions, individually and on behalf of their Native Studies programs.

The Necessity of a Model: Some Deeper Aspects of the Interaction

In 1974 Yupiktak Bista published an important booklet entitled *Does One Way of Life Have to Die So Another Can Live?* (2) In the longer and deeper run, my answer is yes. On the deepest levels, the long-term survival of the one side of this model is the death of the other. Given these high stakes and the breadth and depth of the Native/European interactions, some kind of model of the interaction process is necessary.

As noted above, from the times of first contacts to the present, Europeans and Native peoples have been remarking on the differences between their societies. The content of these comments are at three levels—*what* the differences are, *how* these differences work, and, most deeply, *why* these differences exist. The focus of the model in this paper is on the *why* level. The great majority of studies do not venture beyond the *what* and the *how* levels. This is true even of more recent writing.

There is a long history of explanations for why differences of civilization exist or what measures should be used to determine different levels.

Columbus himself in his journals (1492) remarked on differences. There are the debates between Bartolome de las Casas and Juan Gines de Sepulveda in 1550 concerning the humanity of Indians, and Montaigne's 1589 essay "Of Cannibals," Jean-Jacques Rousseau's "Discourse on the Origins and Basis of Inequality Among Men" (1755), Benjamin Franklin's "Remarks Concerning the Savages of North America" (1784), the multivolume, multi-year observations by Jesuit missionaries of the interaction of Native and European societies in the *Jesuit Relations*, and the annual reports of the commissioner of Indian affairs in the 1880s and 1890s.

In the United States there is James Fenimore Cooper's remarkably sensitive exploration of the relationship and differences of the two societies as he traces the adventures of the Deerslayer as he fights Indians across five novels of *The Leatherstocking Tales* (1823–1841) from New York westward to Illinois. On the other hand, there is also the outright undiluted racist explanation seen in popular novels such as Montgomery's *Nick of the Woods* (1857) and Bennett's *The Forest Rose* (1850). Herman Melville's 1857 essay "The Metaphysics of Indian Hating" explores the source of the violent attitudes of American frontiersmen toward Indians.

Why-level analysis—when it is attempted—can be summed up in several fundamental contrasting differences. These include differences of race and of civilization levels—sometimes connected where race is seen as determining civilization level.

Even though racial explanations began to be challenged in the later 1800s, the civilization explanation persists in different forms to this day; for example, in modernization theories with assumptions about who is modern and who is backward.

In regard to any of these differences, one can ask how fundamental the explanation is in regard to the basic cause at work. With race, the basic cause goes back to biology in some form, or in some older writing to God's creation.

Twentieth-century anthropologists have tended to move toward cultural-system differences as a supposedly more neutral explanation but still often question which cultures are more likely to survive. Well into the 1960s, most anthropologists simply accepted that European-based societies were the most modern and that Native peoples would gradually be absorbed, even if many anthropologists were critical of the behavior of Europeans and felt that Native cultures deserved respect. But cultural differences fall, actually, more in the what-is category, in that there rarely is any attempt to explain *why* these cultural differences exist and persist. There is very little attempt to explore why European societies have acted as they have. I have discussed this literature in some detail in an earlier paper (Kaliss 1997).

Recent years have seen many useful studies of what happened to Native peoples and how it happened, such as Harold Napoleon's *Yuuyaraq: The Way of the Human Being* (1996) in Alaska. But deeper dynamics of the interactions are not so clearly or easily seen.

What struck me in my own search for deeper answers was the lack of systematic models, or of any models at all. More often than not a single word or phrase is used to describe each side, and more often than not these words refer to symptoms rather than ultimate causes. This is true among both Native and non-Native writers.

This lack of clarity about the European side can be seen in the existence of more than 35 terms to describe what came from Europe. Of these, terms like *white*, *Western*, *culture*, and locational terms (*European*, *Euro-American*, etc) are the most frequent. I suggest that a color, direction, or location do not and cannot explain the fundamental *why*s of the two different social-economic systems. Anthropologists prefer the term *culture* as in "culture clash," but the factors at work here are far deeper than just a clash of cultures.

Two recent Euro-Canadian writers with much experience working with northern Native communities did attempt a deeper look but still focus more on the symptoms—even if somewhat deeper ones (Berger 1999; Brody, 2000).

The phrase "Native Science" such as used by Gregory Cajete (1999) to describe the Native approach to studying the world is another good example. I understand why some use it to argue that the Native view is just as "scientific" as the European science. However, until there is real clarity, especially on the European side, of how loaded the term *science* is with European beliefs and assumptions, and until science admits and deals with the great difficulty it has with spirituality, I hesitate to apply the term to Native ways of knowing for all the reasons so far discussed. Science as developed and practiced by Europeans has too many built-in limits compared to the Native worldview.

More recent explanations for European behavior, if given at all, tend to refer to Judeo-Christian values of humans dominating nature, enlightenment philosophies stressing individual rights, or the development of linear theories of social and physical evolution showing Europeans at the advancing tip of human progress. These viewpoints exist but are justifications for a certain behavior, not the explanation of that behavior.

In the last 30 years, some writers have tried to use advances in physics, particularly quantum physics, and chaos theory as a basis to challenge what is seen as European linear thought, to suggest that Native worldviews are close to those ways of thinking and that this may serve as an avenue for the Europeans to recognize Native understandings as a basis to work together. Good examples of these are David Peat's *Blackfoot Physics* (2005) and the use of chaos theory by Barnhardt and Kawagley (1998, reprinted 2011) to suggest that Native and non-Native education systems can work together. While they are interesting and thought provoking, can physics theories explain differences between human societies or, more specifically, why the Native and European education systems have been in conflict?

Economic factors are sometimes referenced, and I have indicated my own conclusion that fundamentally different social-economic systems are basic to the Native-European interaction. But here, also, too often, economic symptoms such as human greed, imperialism, and colonization are referenced without deeper examination of the economic framework they are symptoms of. Colonization as an analytic term appears fairly frequently in more recent discussions of the European-Native interaction, due in good part to Linda Tuhiwai Smith's

Decolonizing Methodologies: Research and Indigenous Peoples (1999, 2nd 2012). See also the essays collected by Marie Battiste in *Reclaiming Indigenous Voice and Vision* (2000), where *colonization* is the term most used to describe what came from Europe. I suggest that a difference needs to be made between using this term to accurately describe an important tactic and method used by Europeans and the more fundamental economic processes that led to its use.

In this regard it is impossible to avoid Karl Marx's profound analysis of the actual economic dynamics of taking without giving that underlie and are built into the very core processes of the capitalist social-economic system. It is these processes that drove this system from Europe around the world to a scale threatening the very survival of life. I say this not as a partisan of Marx but because no one else has penetrated as deeply into the actual dynamics of the system.

Sandy Grande in her *Red Pedagogy* (2004) is one of the very few Native writers who do see Marx's economic analysis as fundamentally useful. However, Grande remains wary of a common European linear type of reasoning about social progress that has been present among many Marxists (individuals, political parties, and the ruling governments in some would-be socialist countries) that sees the essentially "primitive" communism and advanced modern communism as being at the two ends of an onwards-and-upwards progression with proletarian revolutions in the lead. This led some Marxists to disregard Native wishes and to actually oppose Native desires to remain as distinct peoples on the basis that this isolated Native peoples from the progress of history. Strong Native criticisms of this can be found in the essays collected by Ward Churchill in his *Marxism and Native Americans* (1983). However, Grande stresses, and I agree, that Marx's original economic analysis of the dynamics of capitalism is essential and fundamental to understanding the source of TWG on the European side.

I deliberately chose the terms of my model to combine the practical and the spiritual, since I believe their interaction is key to deeper understanding. But it is necessary to first explore each separately and then to examine how the practical and spiritual interact with each other to create the dynamics of the interaction. The practical basis of TWG (in my model) lies in the capitalist economic system.

What happened to Native peoples is so deeply an example of taking without giving that any discussion of what happened, and how it happened, inevitably must confront the lies necessary to justify the taking.

In the United States, the economics profession is committed to defending the capitalist system on theoretical, allegedly scientific, grounds as a system that not only does not take without giving but is the most advanced social system most fitted to what they see as human nature.

The spiritual basis of TWG, however, extends beyond the immediate practical economic system that it supports. I have noted that TWG and the assertion of superiority that goes with it is found in any relationship where one side takes advantage of another.

For example, it is not just that resource developers in Alaska saw and see Native peoples as obstacles to resource development. It is that, on a deep spiritual level, they cannot comprehend why

Native peoples should wish to or be allowed to live a lifeway so deeply contrary to what seems natural and superior to them. Reactions like this are easily documented in Alaska history.

As noted, the virus of superiority is such that even those very critical of TWG in European society often believe that their criticisms are superior to anything that Native peoples have to offer. One sees this in the attitudes of some European environmentalists toward Native peoples.

It explains why the Soviet authorities worked so very hard to eliminate the only already-working examples in the intended socialist USSR of a communal sharing society as, for example, policies toward the Eskimo and Chukchi peoples in Chukotka.

Also, to the extent science, as a European worldview, plays a role in defending TWG, it also necessarily carries the virus of superiority, leading some scientists to claim an imperial right to pursue facts anywhere, anytime, and to use them as they please because the so-called scientific worldview is superior. So taking Native knowledge, even Native genes, without giving is acceptable because science just gathers facts for the good of the human race.

In essence the spiritual attitudes developed across several thousand years of European economic systems based on TWG have unavoidably influenced the outlooks of all Europeans, including those who were deeply opposed to the practices of those economic systems. The implication of all this is that it is not enough to just change the practical economic arrangement from an economy of taking to one of sharing. After all, in the Soviet Union the basic productive forces of the economy were legally declared to belong to all the working people, who would share in the benefits of their own labor. What is necessary is also a change at the spiritual level.

The year I spent on the Russian side was a turning point for me in that it forced me to seek the common elements in European behavior that leads to this. Why did European communists, capitalists, or Christians, who often disagreed about many things, basically hold the same view of Native peoples: Europeans are civilized, advanced, and modern; Native peoples are primitive, backward, and traditional? All three conclude that Europeans have a duty to lift up the Native peoples to a higher—of course, European—level.

Science as a European worldview also has a special problem of concern to Native peoples: its inability and/or unwillingness as a knowledge system to deal with spirituality. This inability is a deep example of the effect of disconnection that is, in turn, tied back to the TWG use of science to focus only on the facts needed by and useful to those who take: please keep the spiritual/moral out of the process.

This is a major obstacle in relation to Native societies. How can European-based "scientists" understand a society where spirituality is the key factor in the everyday existence and worldview? Science cannot get to the spiritual "facts" that are fundamental to understanding the Native-European interaction. This shows in the relationship toward Native peoples of both the so-called natural and social sciences.

Yet science as a worldview is by definition also a spiritual system, one that has, in fact, become a faith deeply believed in and deeply, emotionally defended when questioned. I have seen this in the intense emotional strength of scientists defending their belief, in connection with certain issues of concern to Native peoples, akin to that of a member of a religion defending a perceived attack on the faith.

The more faithfully they (scientists, including Marxists who believed in a science of history) believed in what allegedly did not include faith, the less they understood the basis for belief by peoples who held differing worldviews from their own.

As noted above, Native knowledge systems have no issue with integrating spirituality with their knowledge systems as a necessary factor in better understanding the connections in the world and how humans can and should relate to those connections. This is not because Native societies are somehow more spiritual, but because it is a spirituality that is not in contradiction to how the universe really works. This lays the basis for an everyday interaction of the spiritual and the practical, and a knowledge system that goes with it.

The connective nature of this spirituality is the key to understanding the recent legal defense by Yup'ik fishermen that their practical activity has a spiritual base. By the same token, the persistence of Alaska Native peoples to remain as distinct peoples in spite of what would seem like overwhelming pressures to disappear has its basis in deeply held lifeways that operate at the spiritual level and express themselves in the practical issues that today exist between Native and non-Native societies.

Relevance of Native Worldviews to Non-Natives Generally

Taking without giving, disconnection, and disharmony cannot be a recipe for long-term human survival. Humanity must learn to live with the world and not against it. This means that for the majority of humanity the most compelling reason to know facts is to better learn how to live with the world.

The connectiveness of Native worldviews has much to contribute to a worldwide discussion, and many Native spokespeople have made this point. The connectiveness of present-day communications technology makes possible worldwide discussions of critical issues. In particular, changes in European societies that recognize the importance of connections make room for Native views. For Europeans, there is the important question of what went wrong with attempts within the European world to return to some form of a sharing or communal society. In contrast, Native peoples have been able to construct and maintain communal societies for several thousand years.

However, it needs be noted that each society must develop its own answers from its own roots. While the Native worldviews have much to offer, others cannot just take those views and use them. That would be another case of TWG, and it would not work in any event. What is important about the Native worldview is not that it is Native but that it is based on a spiritual- level recognition of the connectiveness of the universe. One need not be Native to discover connection.

A Note on Good and Evil

Consistent with the model presented is the suggestion that the ultimate basis for good or evil becomes the practical way of life that either recognizes and lives with the connections of the universe or tries to ignore certain of those connections. The spiritual aspect concerns human beliefs about living in the one manner or the other. I suggest that that which promotes sharing, connection, and harmony is good; that which supports TWG, disconnection, and disharmony is bad.

When we understand both societies on the spiritual level, we can see that knowledge is both a practical and a spiritual issue that can act to support one side or the other. To live in a "good" way is more than a moral statement. It becomes the only practical way to live as a real human being. This is what walking in a ceremonial manner is all about.

Conclusion

The best advertisement for an accurate model is the degree to which it can be a guide to navigating this complicated process. My own model has evolved and changed as my understanding and experience has changed. Indeed, one more recent (2007) step in this process was coming across a striking comment by Vine Deloria Jr., a very well-known Standing Rock Sioux spiritual person and academic scholar in the European tradition. Regarding the expression of the connection between human actions and the universe, an expression that is the basis of Native ceremonials, he concludes that, "In the last analysis one might describe ceremonials as the cosmos becoming thankfully aware of itself."

This is a profoundly important factual and spiritual observation. The ceremonials are the recognition that human beings are completely connected to all that is, that humans are a product of all those connections and, as a living form of those connections, have both the moral duty and the intellectual possibility to be thankfully aware that these connections exist and therefore to live accordingly. In other words, living beings (not just humans) are the moral and spiritual expression of the reality of a connected universe.

In this spirit I very much welcome comments and further discussion. I can be reached by email at tkaliss@yahoo.com.

Endnotes

i. Territory of Alaska. Session Laws Resolutions and Memorials. 1915. Ch.24 S.B. 21 p.52

   The language about separation from the tribe and living in a civilized manner is taken directly from the General Allotment Act of 1887 (the Dawes Act) probably the most famous (or infamous) federal act aimed at the termination of tribes and the individual assimilation of Native peoples. Chapter 119 Sec 6 Feb. 8, 1887. 24 Stat., 388. (49th Cong. 2nd Session 1887).

ii. A nonprofit arm of Calista Regional Corporation that dealt with issues concerning the Yup'ik people in the Yukon-Kuskokwim Delta area.

References

Bibliography Note

In addition to works referred to in the text I have included some additional recent writings, mostly by Native authors, which provided useful and worthwhile analysis and perspectives.

Alfred, T. (2005) Wasase: *Indigenous pathways of action and freedom.* Peterborough, Ontario: Broadview Press Ltd.

Barnhardt, R. and A. O. Kawagley. (1998, reprinted 2011). *Culture, chaos, and complexity. Catalysis of change in Indigenous Education.* in Barnhardt, R. and A. O. Kawagley (Eds). (2011). *Alaska Native education: Views from within.* p.199.

Battiste, M. (Ed.). (2000). *Reclaiming Indigenous Voice and Vision.* Vancouver: Univ. of British Columbia Press.

Bennett, E. (1850). *The Forest Rose.*

Berger, T. *A long and terrible shadow: White values, and native rights in the Americas since 1492.* (1999). Seattle: Univ of Washington Press. 2nd edition.

Brody, Hugh. (2000). *The other side of Eden: Hunters, farmers, and the shaping of the world.* NYC: North Point Press.

Cajete, G. (1999). *Native science: Natural laws of interdependence.* Santa Fe, New Mexico: Clear Light Publishers.

Columbus, C.. (1991). *The Diario of Christopher Columbus's First Voyage to America, 1492-1493.* (O. Dunn & J. Kelley Jr., Trans.). University of Oklahoma Press.

Commissioner of Indian Affairs--annual reports. In the 1880s and 1890s these are issued separately or as part of the

Annual Report of the Secretary of the Interior and can be found in the Serial Set of Federal documents.

Cook-Lynn, E. (2007). *New Indians, old wars.* Urbana, IL: University of Illinois Press.

Cooper , J. F. (1823). *The Pioneers: The Sources of the Susquehanna; A Descriptive Tale.*

_____. (1826). *The Last of the Mohicans: A Narrative of 1757.*

_____. (1827). *The Prairie: A Tale.*

_____. (1840). *The Pathfinder: The Inland Sea.*

_____. (1841). *The Deerslayer: The First War Path.*

Deloria, B., & Kristen F., & Scinta, S. (Eds.). (1997). *Spirit & Reason: The Vine Deloria Jr., Reader.* Golden, Colorado: Fulcrum Publishing, 1999:332.

Deloria, V. (1969). *Custer Died For Your Sins.*

Fixico, D. (2003). *The American Indian mind in a linear world: American Indian studies and traditional knowledge.* New York: Rutledge.

Franklin, B. (1784). *Remarks Concerning the Savages of North America.*

Garroutte, E.M. (2003). *Real Indians.* Berkeley: University of California Press.

Grande, S. (2004). *Red pedagogy.* London: Rowman & Littlefield Publishers, Inc.

Irwin, L. (ed.). (2000). *Native American spirituality: A critical reader.* Lincoln: University of Nebraska Press.

James, K. (Ed.). (2001). *Science and Native American communities: legacies of pain, visions of promise.* Lincoln University of Nebraska Press.

Kaliss, T. (1997). *What was the 'other' that came on Columbus' ships?* The Journal of Indigenous Studies,3(2), 27-42.

Las Casas, B. De. (1992). In Defense of the Indians: The Defense of the Most Reverend Lord, Don Fray Bartolome De Las Casas, of the Order of Preachers, Late Bishop of Chiapa. Stafford Poole (Foreword). Northern Illinois University Press.

Marx, Karl. (1867). *Capital.*

Melville, H. (1857). *The Metaphysics of Indian Hating.* Chapter 26 of H. Melville. *The Confidence-Man.*

Mihesuah, D. A., Wilson, A.C. (Eds.). (2004). *Indigenizing the academy: transforming scholarship and empowering communities.* Lincoln: University of Nebraska Press.

Montaigne. (1589). *Of Cannibals.*

Montgomery, R. (1837). *Nick of the Woods, or the Jibbenainosay: A tale of Kentucky.*

Moore, K.D., Peters, K, Jojola, T., Lacy, A. (Eds.). (2007). *How it is: The Native American philosophy of V. F. Cordova.* Tucson: University of Arizona Press.

Nabokov, P. (2002). *A forest of time: American Indian ways of history.* http://www.amazon.com/Forest-Time-American-Indian-History/dp/0521568749/ref=sr_1_1?s=books&ie=UTF8&qid=1370565101&sr=1-1&keywords=a+forest+in+timeCambridge University Press.

Napoleon, H. (1996). *Yuuyaraq: The Way of the Human Being.*

Alaska Native Knowledge Network.

Peat, F. D. (2005). *Blackfoot physics.* York Beach, ME: Weiser Books.

Rice, B. & Oakes, J.E. & Riewe, R. (2005). *Seeing the World With Aboriginal Eyes.* Winnipeg: University of Manitoba Press.

Ross, R. (2009, reissue of 1992 with new Introduction). *Dancing with a ghost: exploring Indian reality.* Toronto: Penguin Global.

Rousseau, Jean-Jacques. (1755). *Discourse on the Origins and Basis of Inequality Among Men.*

Smith, L.T. (1999, 2012 2nd Rev.). *Decolonizing methodologies: research and indigenous Peoples.* London: Zed Books.

Society of Jesus. The & P. Le Jeune. R. G. Thwaites (Editor). (1610-1791). T*he Jesuit Relations and Allied Documents.* The Burrows Brothers Company, Cleveland. 71 volumes.

Tinker, G.E. (2004). *Spirit and resistance: political theology and American Indian liberation.* Minneapolis: Fortress Press.

Warrior, R.A. (1994). *Tribal secrets: recovering American Indian intellectual traditions.* Minneapolis: Univ Of Minnesota Press.

Waters, A. (2004). *American Indian thought.* Malden, MA: Blackwell Publishing.

Waziyatawin, A.W. & Yellow Bird, M. (Eds.). (2005). *For Indigenous eyes only: a decolonization handbook.* Santa Fe: School of American Research Press.

Wilson, S. (2009). *Research is ceremony: Indigenous research methods.* Black Point, Nova Scotia: Fernwood

Publishing Co., Ltd.

Yupiktak Bista. (1974) *Does one way of life have to die so another can live? A report on subsistence and the conservation of the Yupik life-style.* n.p.

PART IV
THE ALASKA NATIVE CLAIMS SETTLEMENT ACT (ANCSA)

The Alaska Native Claims Settlement Act Corporation: A Case Example for Indigenous Peoples' Business Development?

George A. Geistauts and Sharon Lind

Abstract:

Before the Russians came, Alaska already was home to Indigenous Aleut, Eskimo, and Indian peoples, and neither the Russian presence nor the US purchase negated their legal and moral claims to the land. In 1971 the US Congress passed the Alaska Native Claims Settlement Act (ANCSA). The Act created 13 Alaska Native regional corporations and over 200 Alaska Native village corporations, allowed Natives to select 44 million acres of land, and provided a cash payment of $962.5 million. Suddenly, a great many Alaska Natives, for whom culture and lifestyles had been tied to subsistence and the land, were thrust into a world of corporate structures and management. Today some of these corporations do business all over the US and internationally and have revenues in the billion-dollar range. This paper looks at the ANCSA experiment's unique aspects and implementation, focusing on the regional corporations, and examines the effectiveness of the ANCSA approach.

Alaska, now about 17 percent of the United States land area, was purchased from Russia in 1867. But before the Russians came, Alaska already was home to Indigenous Aleut, Eskimo, and Indian peoples, and neither the Russian presence nor the US purchase negated their legal and moral claims to the land. In 1971 the US Congress passed the Alaska Native Claims Settlement Act (ANCSA) The Act created 13 Alaska

Native regional corporations and over 200 Alaska Native village corporations, allowed Natives to select 44 million acres of land, and provided a cash payment of $962.5 million.

The act's corporate model, definition of shareholder eligibility, land-selection process, natural-resource ownership rights, requirements for resource revenue pooling and sharing, limitation on stock sales for the first 20 years, and other provisions made this approach dramatically different from the Indian tribal-reservation model commonplace in the rest of the US, and the dual ANCSA corporations' mission to achieve both financial performance and social performance distinguishes these corporations from mainstream US corporations. Suddenly, a great many Alaska Natives, for whom culture and lifestyles had been tied to subsistence and the land, were thrust into a world of corporate structures and management. Initially, most ANCSA corporations struggled to become profitable, and losses were common. Today, some of these corporations do business all over the US and internationally, and have revenues in the billion-dollar range. This paper looks at the ANCSA experiment's unique aspects and implementation, focusing primarily on the regional corporations, and examines the effectiveness of the ANCSA approach.

Introduction

The year 2011 was the 40th anniversary of the passage and implementation of the Alaska Native Claims Settlement Act (ANCSA). In 1971, through this act, the United States Congress addressed the land claims of the aboriginal peoples of Alaska. In a number of important ways ANCSA represents a significant departure from previous United States policies toward its Indigenous peoples, not the least of which is the establishment in Alaska of a Native corporate model as the socioeconomic settlement framework, rather than the Indian-reservation model commonplace in the 48 contiguous states.

This corporate framework created 13 regional Alaska Native corporations (R-ANCs) and over 200 village Alaska Native corporations (V-ANC). The corporations, and through them the Native shareholders, shared in a financial settlement of $962,500,000. The corporations were also entitled to select a total of 44 million acres of land from public lands in Alaska. The 12 R-ANCs were entitled to select land (the 13th R-ANC was not so entitled because it represented Natives living outside Alaska) and received full surface and subsurface rights to their land selections, as well as subsurface rights to the village land selections within their respective regions. This is significant because in Alaska subsurface rights generally are retained by the government regardless of surface ownership; thus R-ANCs became essentially the only significant private owners of subsurface rights in a resource-rich state. A provision of the act required that 70 percent of mineral revenues (after expenses) received by each R-ANC must be divided among all 12 regions proportionately, based on original enrollment numbers. These R-ANCs then shared the revenues with the V-ANCs in their respective regions.

Figure 1 shows the Alaska Native peoples' traditional geographic regions. Figure 2 shows the geographic areas represented by the 12 in-Alaska R-ANCs. It should be noted that shareholders enrolled in a specific region did not actually have to reside in that region, and in fact, many did not.

Figure 1: Traditional Alaska Native Regions

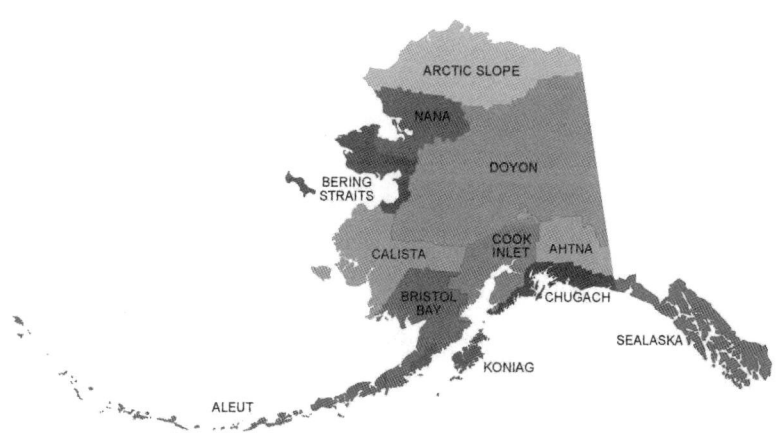

Figure 2: The 12 In-State Regional Corporation Areas

Approximately 80,000 Natives were initially enrolled as shareholders under ANCSA. Those living in villages received 100 shares in their V-ANC, and all enrollees received 100 shares in their R-ANC. In general, to be eligible for shareholder status you had to be at least one-fourth degree Native (i.e., Aleut, Eskimo, Indian, or some combination thereof). Eligibility to be enrolled as a shareholder under the act was limited to those born by its passage in December 1971. However, children of enrolled Natives could inherit shares. Initially, shares could only be sold 20 years after passage of the act, a provision that would later change.

In the years after the passage of the act, a number of flaws were recognized, and Congress amended the act on more than one occasion. However, its most basic structure remains in place. Over the 40 years since passage, Alaska Native corporations have undergone a steep learning curve. This included periods when many ANCSA corporations lost money. More recently, many corporations have had significant profits. During the eight-year period between 2004 and 2011, the 12 R-ANCs had $45.52 billion in gross revenues and $2.52 billion in net earnings.

However, financial performance is not the only measure of success for the ANCSA corporation. In a sense, ANCSA is a unique experiment in Indigenous peoples' socioeconomic development, and also a reaction to the perceived failures of the Indian reservation system. Thus performance must be measured both in economic and social terms. Additionally, in Alaska, as elsewhere, the aboriginal peoples are not just part of their own culture but also of the larger society. ANCSA corporations' success, then, is important for the state and the country. In fact, today ANCSA corporate investments and business activity extend far beyond the borders of Alaska. This paper looks at various factors shaping the ANCSA experience. Rather than attempting to reach an overall judgment about the viability of the ANCSA approach, it identifies some key issues and factors that have influenced ANCSA implementation and results. If these influences are replicated in other regions of the world where Indigenous peoples are seeking to achieve greater economic security through corporate business structures, ANCSA may serve as a model.

Literature Review

The basic intent and provisions of the claims settlement can be found in the *Alaska Native Claims Settlement Act of 1971* (Public Law 92-203). The history of Alaska Native claims goes back to the US purchase of Alaska from Russia in 1867, and detailed discussion of these claims and the ultimate settlement process is beyond the scope of this paper. In this paper we focus primarily on the ANCSA regional corporations, of which news stories about their activities are commonplace in the local media. Each year the *Alaska Business Monthly* publishes an annual issue focusing on the performance of the Native corporations. The regional corporations publish annual reports and have also published their mission statements. It should be noted, however, that they are not subject to SEC regulations and disclosure requirements. Because of provisions of ANCSA, no market exists for their stock, and there is no investment analyst following their performance. Over the years a number of reports have analyzed the history and effectiveness of ANCSA and/or performance of the Native corporations. Jones (1981) provides a history and analysis of ANCSA together with subsequent amendments. Colt (2001) focused on regional corporation performance over the period from 1973 to 1993, and found that "the 12 regional corporations lost 80 percent of their original cash endowment—about $380 million—in direct business operations." This was a period with a steep learning curve for these newly formed entities, and these losses are not representative of current performance.

Several books provide a broader context for thinking about Native cultural values, traditional lifestyles, economic conditions, land claims, and ANCSA. Berry (1975) describes the linkage between oil politics and land claims, Arnold (1978) provides a historical perspective, and Berger (1985) reports on a study revealing substantial discontent in Alaska Native villages. Hensley (2008), who was a major figure in the fight for Native land claims, describes in an autobiography what village life was like and his role in the land-claims effort.

Methodology

The passage of ANCSA represents a historic departure from traditional US policy toward its Indigenous peoples—i.e., the Indian tribal reservation system commonplace in the "Lower 48" states. In Alaska, a Native-owned corporate structure is the alternative to the reservations. (Before ANCSA there was one reservation in Alaska—Metlakatla in southeastern Alaska; it did not participate in ANCSA and remains a reservation.) But the ANCSA corporation is also, in many respects, not a traditional mainstream corporation like, say,

Ford or IBM. Thus the ANCSA approach may be a new and useful precedent. We focus on selected aspects of ANCSA and the regional corporations it formed. We deliberately ignore other aspects, such as the village corporation, because of space limitations and also because, in general, the regional corporations are economically the most significant.

In general, we make no attempt to specifically cite sources for every point being made, as we draw on what in Alaska is often general knowledge about ANCSA. We try not to draw many specific conclusions, preferring instead to enable the reader to draw his or her own conclusions—or perhaps better yet, raise further questions. We believe that this paper benefits greatly from the fact that one of the authors (Lind) is an Alaska Native and is also a board member of the Aleut Corporation, one of the 12 regional corporations. She also served as that corporation's board chair from 2006–2011.

Findings and Discussion

The Alaska Context

In order to understand the ANCSA experiment, we have to look at how it fits with some of the specific characteristics of Alaska. Alaska has about 17 percent of total US land area, and over 50 percent of its coastline. This almost guarantees that Alaska would be rich in natural resources—not because it necessarily would have more resources per acre, but because it has more acres. In 1867 Alaska was purchased from Russia for $7.2 million. For most of the next hundred years Alaska's economy was based on natural resources—gold and other minerals, fish, timber, etc.—and on its strategic location in

WWII and the subsequent Cold War period. Boom-and-bust economic cycles were common, as various resources were discovered and exploited.

At the time of ANCSA passage, the rural Alaska economy—essentially the whole state, other than a few larger cities—was sparsely populated (just over 300,000 people). The transportation infrastructure was (and remains) very limited; only a few major communities were connected by roads and railroads. For example, the state capital, Juneau, even today can only be reached by boat or air. Most Native villages had populations of less than 1,000, were off the road system and separated from major population centers by hundreds of miles. Food, fuel, and other necessities were supplied by air, and by barge in the summers; therefore, rural prices were very high. Few steady job opportunities were available in most villages. Consequently, many rural residents pursued a subsistence lifestyle focusing on hunting and fishing. Subsistence requires continued access to land and water; hence, land claims are a matter of both economic and cultural survival. But the cultural traditions and economic conditions in rural villages had done little to prepare rural Natives for the corporate model.

In 1959 Alaska achieved statehood. As part of the Alaska Statehood Act, the state had the right to select 103 million acres from federal lands, but Native lands were not open to selection. Despite this, the state attempted to select lands occupied or used by Natives. Natives organized in opposition, filed protests, and ultimately sued over land claims. In 1966 Secretary of the Interior Stewart Udall froze disposition of federal land in Alaska until Congress settled the Native land claims. The state lost a lawsuit to block the freeze.

However, what really changed Alaska was the 1968 discovery of a supergiant oil field at Prudhoe Bay on Alaska's North Slope on land leased by the state. Alaska was eager to become an oil state, and Prudhoe Bay oil would be very profitable for the industry and important in reducing US dependence on foreign oil. To get this oil to market, the industry proposed building an 800-mile-long 48-inch pipeline to the all-weather port of Valdez. But the pipeline would have to cross lands claimed by Natives, and the claims had not been resolved. In 1969 Secretary Udall issued Public Land Order 4582, which formalized the land freeze and blocked the construction of the pipeline. In addition to moral and legal claims, Natives now had powerful leverage to persuade Congress to pass ANCSA. They succeeded in 1971.

Congressional Findings and Intent

The act starts off with a statement of Congressional Findings and Declaration of Policy:

> (a) there is an immediate need for a fair and just settlement of all claims by Natives and Native groups of Alaska, based on aboriginal land claims;
>
> (b) the settlement should be accomplished rapidly, with certainty, in conformity with the real economic and social needs of Natives, without litigation, with maximum participation by Natives in decisions affecting their rights and property, without establishing any permanent racially defined institutions, rights,

privileges, or obligations, without creating a reservation system or lengthy wardship or trusteeship, and without adding to the categories of property and institutions enjoying special tax privileges or to the legislation establishing special relationships between the United States Government and the State of Alaska.

Notable here is the recognition of "conformity with real economic and social needs of Natives," which establishes a rationale for the R-ANCs to pursue both economic and social missions. Also notable is "maximum participation by Natives in decisions affecting their rights and property."

Some Key Elements of ANCSA

Like most federal legislation, ANCSA is a complex law with many provisions, some of which have significant long-term consequences and others that deal essentially with relatively minor problems and implementation issues. We briefly describe several of the more significant provisions below.

Who got to be a shareholder?

ANCSA defined eligible Natives as those of one-fourth or more of Native blood. Initially, ANCSA limited shareholder eligibility to "Natives who were born on or before, and who are living on, December 18, 1971." Figure 3 shows the initial regional enrollment percentage of shareholders per region, Table 1 shows the number of initial shareholders in each R-ANC; note that the regional corporations differ greatly in the number of enrolled shareholders today.

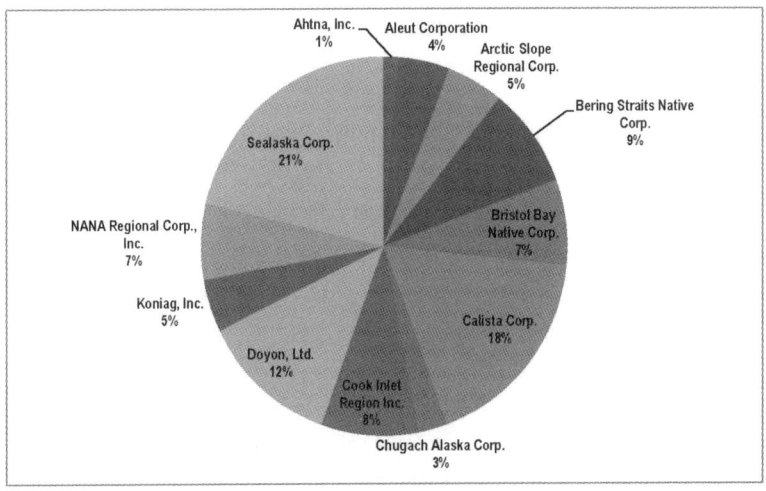

Figure 3: Initial Regional ANC Enrollment Percentage by Region

The 12 Regions	Original Number of Shareholders
Ahtna	1,074
Aleut	3,249
Arctic Slope	3,738
Bristol Bay	5,400
Bering Straits	6,333
Calista	13,308
Chugach	1,912
Cook Inlet	6,264
Doyon	9,061
Koniag	3,344
NANA	4,828
Sealaska	15,819

Table 1: Initial Regional ANC Enrollment

The December 18 cutoff point has two major implications. All shareholders enrolled by the deadline were protected from share dilution of their stock.

But this protection of their economic benefits came at a cultural price! If you were born on December 19, the next day, or thereafter, you were not going to be a shareholder except through inheritance. Thus the "afterborn" did not have an equal incentive to take interest in their Native corporations. Subsequent amendments corrected this apparent inequity by enabling each Native corporation to choose to issue additional stock, subject to a stringent decision process.

What protection will be provided the newly formed corporations during their learning process?

At the time of passage, it was obvious that many (but not all) Natives had limited experience with the corporate concept. They would not inherit established businesses, but rather would start from scratch. The corporations would have to establish governance and organizational structures. One of their key future assets, the lands they would select, would not be bought but conveyed to them by the federal government, with the true asset value of the land unknown. The land-selection process itself would be complicated and possibly contentious. These and other startup issues would be real challenges, even for those experienced in corporate management.

ANCSA provided a 20-year learning period, during which stock could not be sold by shareholders. Thus, an outside corporate takeover could not be possible for the first 20 years. Later, additional protection was provided by amendment. The boards of directors had to be shareholders. ANCSA corporations were subject to state and federal law but not regulated by the Securities and Exchange Commission.

The protection seems to have largely worked. As Colt has pointed out, initial losses from business operations were very high. However, R-ANCs have survived, and now all are generally profitable. What is not clear is what would have happened if, for example, corporate performance would have been subject to the influence of security markets.

How would perceived inequities from differences in resource distribution in the different regions be mitigated?

Although Alaska is resource-rich, the resources are not uniformly distributed throughout the state. While surface resources have long been visible, the presence and distribution of subsurface resources can only be fully known after a resource exploration process. To some extent, then, the land-selection process becomes a resource lottery.

ANCSA contains a provision commonly referred to as "7(i)." The provision states that " . . . 70 percent of all revenues received by each regional corporation from the timber resources and subsurface estate patented to it . . . shall be divided annually by the regional corporation among all twelve regional corporations . . . according to the number of Natives enrolled in each region . . . ." ANCSA goes on to provide a revenue stream to the V-ANCs by requiring the R-ANCs to then "share" half of their 7(i) revenue with the villages in their respective regions. This sharing also occurs on a pro rata basis once again, utilizing original enrollment numbers.

In the period closely following implementation of ANCSA, the 7(i) provision created numerous disputes among the R-ANCs, but in the early 1980s the R-ANCs reached a 7(i) settlement agreement. From a socioeconomic perspective, the 7(i) provision provided a more equal distribution of ANCSA-generated income. However, it also raises a question of fairness in the sense that shareholders of regions where, for example, there has been virtually no commercially valuable timber now benefit from this resource in another region. It can also influence R-ANC development decisions, essentially disincentivising future resource-development endeavors.

NANA's zinc mine is an example of the significant impact that 7(i) sharing has had on both R-ANCs and V-ANCs. NANA has estimated that the zinc mine alone has contributed over $341 million to the ANCs under this unique provision in ANCSA. NANA describes their role in this sharing to their shareholders in their 2009 annual report: "In December 2008, NANA paid $121.7 million in 7(i) royalties to the other corporations. This money helps other ANCs reach their goals, *uplifting all Alaska Native people.*"

Figure 4 below shows the significant impact 7(i) sharing can have on Alaska's ANCs. For the fiscal years 2005–2011, the Aleut Corporation reported $22,180,000 in 7(i) revenues. Using that number as a base, we have been able to estimate the overall impact for each R-ANC using the 7(i) sharing formula. Keep in mind the amounts shown here also represent the amounts that the R-ANCs in turn shared with their respective V-ANCs, when applicable. So once again using the Aleut Corporation as an example, that region also shared

$22,180,000 with their 13 V-ANCs, based proportionately on original enrollment numbers.

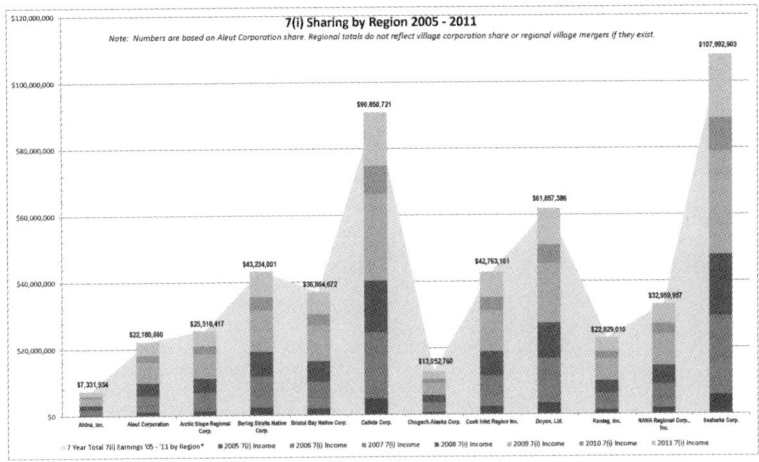

Note: the amounts here are calculated using the 7(i) sharing formula utilizing the Aleut Corporations reported 7(i) income as the base amount. Amounts reported by R-ANCs may differ due to varying fiscal year ends. This graph reflects the overall 7(i) effect by region. (Some mergers of R-ANC's and V-ANC's exist, however, are not reflected here.)

Figure 4: Regional Corporation 2005–2011 7(i) Revenue

The effect of 7(i) sharing on R-ANCs and V-ANCs has been significant since ANCSA was implemented. The seven years of sharing represented in Figure 4 totals over half a billion in 7(i) revenue among the 12 R-ANCs. This portion of the ANCSA model could be a case example for Indigenous peoples' business development.

How can the economically disadvantaged minority play on a level playing field with others?

In 1953 then–President Eisenhower signed into law the Small Business Act. This Act created the Small Business Administration in the US and was designed to aid, counsel, and assist the interests of small business. Section 8(a) of the act outlined the Business Development Program, a program designed to help small disadvantaged businesses. Over the years, the Small Business Act has been amended, and in 1982 American Indian tribes were allowed communal participation in this federal program, which allowed their involvement in federal contracting as a group, representing large numbers of economically disadvantaged tribal members. In 1988 ANCs were included in the program and allowed the ability to gain a foothold in government contracting.

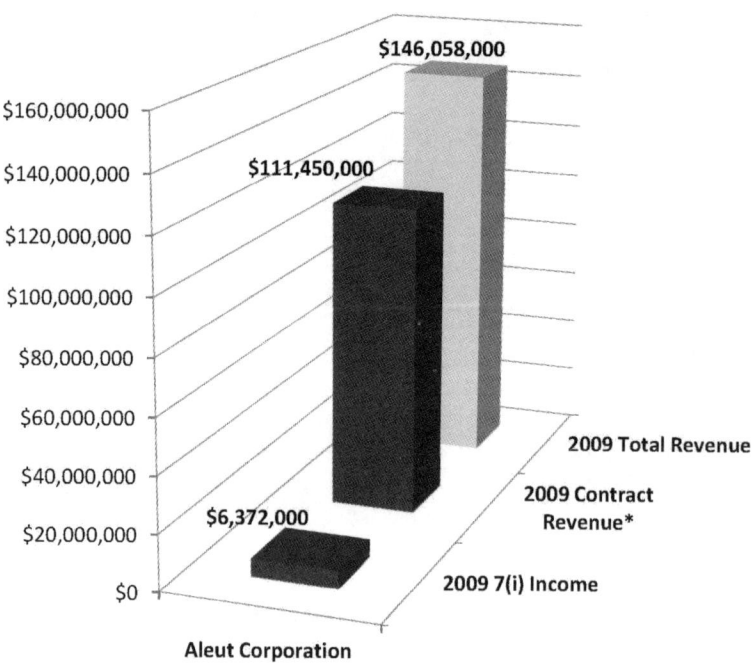

Figure 5: The Aleut Corporation—2009 Annual Report

Government contracting has become a mainstay among all 12 R-ANCs and many V-ANCs. The success of ANCs in this federal program has been significant but has not been without controversy. Early controversy centered on the ANCs' ability to acquire no-limit sole-source contracts. Early in this program, ANCs were realizing very large revenue streams partly due to sole-source awards. ANC participation in this special program has been scrutinized by various senators from other states. ANCs argue that the program, by its design, is working to accomplish what it intended. Sarah Lukin, advocate for the program and previous executive director of the Native American Contractors Association, stated, "Here's a federal program that the government actually got right for the Native people. The program is making a difference."

While ANCs lobby Congress to keep this program in place for ANCs, they also are making changes due to amended rules imposed predominately on ANCs.

Figure 5 shows what government contracting can do to the revenue of an ANC. While the margins on government contracts remain very thin, the end result usually nets big dividends to the ANCs who participate in this program. The bottom line can result in greater program benefits to ANC shareholders.

Government programs for minority Indigenous people could help level the playing field in local economies by providing a foothold to aspiring minority entrepreneurs.

How do ANCSA regional corporations perceive their mission?
Mission statements help corporations define their fundamental

sense of purpose, guide their actions, and inform customers and other stakeholders of the company's underlying reasons for existence.

Congress mandated that R-ANCs be profit seeking. However, these R-ANCs are in reality much more than just simply profit-seeking entities. It is more correct to think of them as socioeconomic development organizations, with both financial and social performance goals. This is reflected in the R-ANC mission statements below:

Arctic Slope Regional Corporation (ASRC)

- ASRC's mission is to actively manage our businesses, our lands and resources, our investments, and our relationships to enhance Iñupiaq cultural and economic freedom - with continuity, responsibility, and integrity.

Bristol Bay Native Corporation (BBNC)

- Enriching our Native way of life.

Koniag

- To sustain growth and provide increasing dividends while celebrating community and culture.

NANA

- We improve the quality of life for our people by maximizing economic growth, protecting and enhancing our lands, and promoting healthy communities with decisions, actions, and behaviors inspired by our Iñupiat Ilitqusiat values consistent with our core principles.

Aleut

- The Aleut Corporation is committed to promoting economic, cultural, and social growth for its shareholders through its subsidiaries, partnerships and foundation.

In practice, few corporations can successfully pursue social goals without being profitable. In the early stages of ANCSA implementation, profitability was not common. R-ANCs were in the business learning-curve stage, but pressure for social performance was significant—particularly for shareholder jobs—especially from rural shareholders. Colt tested "the hypothesis that the regional corporations traded off business profits for Native jobs. The data strongly rejects this hypothesis. Quasirents from Native shareholder employment were important to only three firms—the rest lost money without any countervailing employment."

The R-ANCs' mission statements clearly reflect a sense of social mission. Concrete corporation actions in this area include shareholder scholarships, protection of subsistence rights on corporate lands, general cultural-preservation efforts, supporting parallel Native nonprofits, and yes, jobs.

But the path to success, even for many of the best-run and most successful Alaska Native corporations, has not been smooth. There has been controversy about the directions individual corporations have taken, battles for board control, executives hired and fired, complaints about low dividends, complaints about the limited creation of Native jobs, and complaints about excessive executive compensation. Angry shareholder letters to the newspapers are not unusual. Some Natives have little confidence that they will receive significant benefits from their corporations and increasingly look instead to tribal identities and governance for a better future. An example of dissatisfaction is the following comment:

> *Native corporations and their management are easily CAJOLED by far, into believing that Native preference and shareholder hire will be implemented into the multi-million dollar contracts they give away to non Native contractors. I am a CIRI shareholder. I have completed my 4 year 8,000 hour carpenter apprenticeship and have years of journeyman experience excelling in all of the specialties of my trade, including certifying as a journeyman millwright working out of several locals in the state. Yet, when I apply for work as a shareholder, to superintendents and project managers at CIRI and South Central Foundation construction sites throughout Anchorage I am told the same thing over, and over again. That my foreman has ALL the help they need and we are JUST starting to cut down. Their prime non Native contractor even told me that they have their FULL QUOTA of Natives on the S.C. Dental Center, and I did not see any Natives on the entire job site. Native Corp. shareholder hire is a lie!* Entry by Dukdaneton2003. (2009, February 18). *Anchorage Daily News* Blog.

This was posted following the announcement of an educational partnership between the University of Alaska and the ANCSA regional corporations. It is notable that this is a shareholder in CIRI, the Native corporation that had the highest cumulative dividend payout of over $113,000 and the highest single-year dividend of $50,000!

What role has and does power and politics play in the ANCSA world?

The passage of ANCSA was a process where political power played a major role. From a moral perspective, American values had undergone a significant change, as exemplified by the civil rights movement in the '60s and the passage of the Environmental Protection Act in 1970. But how far the moral agreement would have gone to persuade Congress to settle the claims is unclear. What is clear is that the discovery of Prudhoe Bay oil, and the need for a pipeline, made the oil industry a powerful ally in the claims process. Alaska Natives gained political experience and a new generation of leaders.

In the period after ANCSA's passage, Alaska Natives have, for the most part, played their political cards very well. This was facilitated by Ted Stevens, Alaska's senior senator and the longest-serving Republican senator. Amendments to ANCSA, funding for infrastructure and for health services, legislation to enable R-ANCs to sell their tax losses as tax offsets to other profitable corporations, and preferential federal 8(a) contracting opportunities are some examples of benefits from the political process.

Of course, Senator Stevens is now gone, and federal earmarks are in disrepute. But Natives demonstrated political power in the last senatorial election when Republican incumbent Lisa Murkowski, who had lost the primary to Tea Party candidate Joe Miller, defeated Miller through a write-in campaign. She was only the third senate candidate to do so in US history. Murkowski owed much of her victory to organized support from Alaska Natives, who reacted to Miller's announced opposition to the 8(a) minority contracting preference.

Regional Corporation Economic Performance

As stated earlier, the ANCSA corporations experienced a serious and long learning curve during the first 20 years after the passage of the act. This should not be surprising, given that many Natives were masters of a subsistence economy but relative strangers to the corporate world. Therefore, recent economic performance is a better indicator of the ultimate success or failure of the ANCSA approach.

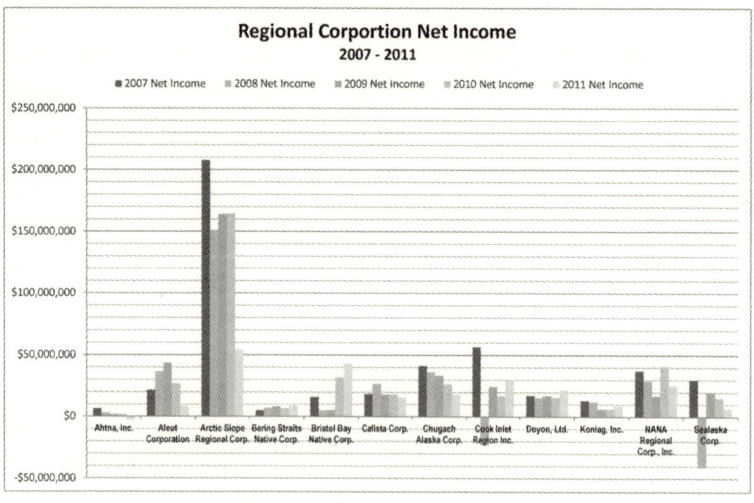

Figure 6: Regional Corporation 2007–2011 Net Income

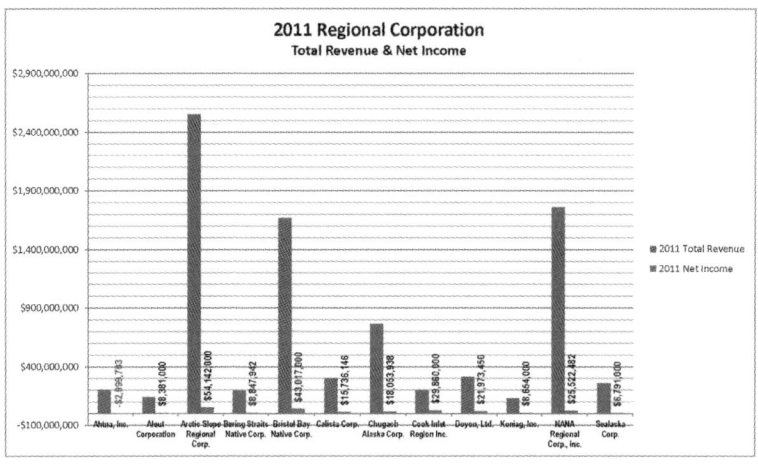

Figure 7: Regional Corporation 2011 Total Revenue and Net Income

Figure 6 shows that while the 12 R-ANCs are generally profitable, there is considerable variability in net income levels from year to year, and occasional losses do occur (Ahtna and ASRC in 2004—not shown here, CIRI and Sealaska in 2008). In this respect, the R-ANCs are not significantly different from mainstream corporations.

An examination of Figure 7 reveals that in 2011 11 of the 12 R-ANCs had positive net income. Arctic Slope Regional Corp, a giant among the corporations, had revenues exceeding $2 billion and net income of over $54 million (down from a net income of over $164 million in 2010). Koniag had the smallest revenues at $131 million, while Ahtna was the only R-ANC to report a loss at –$2.9 million.

R-ANCs have achieved profitability over the years in a variety of areas, including 8(a) federal government contracting, resource development (the NANA Red Dog mine is the largest zinc mine in the world), construction, energy services,

235

petroleum refining, tourism, hotel management, real estate, investment securities, and gaming, to name a few. CIRI's sale of its telecommunications investments in 2001 allowed distributions to shareholders of over $300 million.

Figure 8 below shows both year 2011 shareholder equity and the 2006–2010 average shareholder equity. Ten of the 12 R-ANCs improved in 2011 over their prior five-year shareholder equity average. Again, substantial differences exist between the 12 different R-ANCs' equity levels, Arctic Slope (ASRC) and Cook Inlet Region (CIRI) having the highest equity. It should be noted that CIRI is the corporation for the state's most urban area (Anchorage and vicinity) and ASRC is a corporation for a mostly rural area. In both cases, a significant amount of the business activities and investments are outside Alaska.

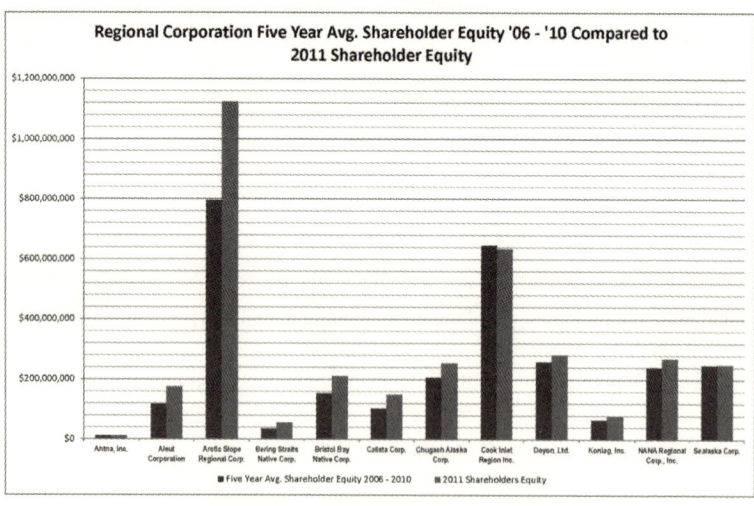

Figure 8: Regional Corporation Shareholder Equity

Conclusions

The question raised in this paper has been whether the Alaska Native Claims Settlement Act Corporation was a case example for Indigenous peoples' business development. The answer is *perhaps*, at least portions of it could be replicated and utilized by the Indigenous of other lands. ANCSA is not just a business model, it is a model of cultural preservation of various Indigenous peoples within Alaska. ANCSA was and is the US federal government's response to land claims by Alaska's Indigenous people. Parts have proven successful, and parts are in need of updating and amending.

Can the US federal government now be assured that the land-claims process is a success for the Alaska Native people? Do Alaska Natives feel fairly compensated through the land-claims process? There are many answers to these questions that may vary from village to village and region to region. In a recent survey conducted by the Aleut Corporation, in which 46 percent of shareholders responded, 90 percent stated they were *very* or *mostly* satisfied with the direction of the corporation. Those same respondents want to ensure that the ownership of the Aleut Corporation stays in Aleut hands, with 67 percent of the shareholders saying they would support the addition of "afterborns" into the corporation.

R-ANCs look to each other for support and sometimes guidance. An overriding effect of ANCSA cannot be ignored, and that is community. Native people want success for other Native people, and the cooperation amongst Native corporations has helped flatten the learning curve that took so long to climb during the first 20 years of these unique organizations. The second 20 years can be characterized as growth for the 12 R-ANCs. Yes, failures in the corporate world were still realized in the second 20 years, but for the most part, these R-ANCs have built strong, lasting foundations that will support future Alaska Natives for generations to come.

References

2008 NANA Annual Report.

Alaska Native Claims Settlement Act of 1971 (43 USC 1601-1642)—Public Law 92-203.

Arnold, Robert D. 1978, *Alaska Native Land Claims*, Anchorage, Alaska: The Alaska Native Foundation.

Berger, Thomas R. 1985, *Village Journey: The Report of the Alaska Native Review Commission*. New York: Hill and Wang.

Berry, Mary Clay. 1975, *The Alaska Pipeline: The Politics of Oil and Native Land Claims.* Bloomington: Indiana University Press.

Bohi, Heidi. 2010, *8(a) Advantages History in the Making.* Alaska Business Monthly September 2010.

Colt, Steve. 2001. *Two Views of the 'New Harpoon': Economic Performance of the ANCSA Regional Corporations.* Anchorage, Alaska. Institute of Social and Economic Research.

Hensley, William L. Iggiagruk. 2008, *Fifty Miles from Tomorrow: A Memoir of Alaska and the Real People.* Sarah Crichton Books/ Farrar, Straus & Giroux.

Jones, Richard S. 1981, *Alaska Native Claims Settlement Act of 1971 (Public Law 92–203): History and Analysis*

Together with Subsequent Amendments. American National Government Division. Report No. 81–127 GOV. Washington, DC: Library of Congress.

ANCSA as X-Mark: Surface and Subsurface Claims of the Alaska Native Claims Settlement Act
Eve Tuck

Abstract

This article analyzes settler colonialism in the context of Alaska and the Alaska Native Claims Settlement Act (ANCSA), the largest land-claim settlement in United States history. The article presents a critical overview of the settlement act and theorizes what is meant by surface and subsurface rights to land. It discusses the entrusting of land to Alaska Native corporations instead of tribal governments and the recasting of Alaska Native peoples into shareholders as ideological invasions, and theorizes Alaska Native resistance to settlement in the form of *x-marks*.

Keywords

Alaska Native Claims Settlement Act (ANCSA), Alaska Native corporations, ideological invasion, Indigenous futurity, x-marks

> *When Willie [Hensley] and I and a few of us young rebels got together 15 years ago we weren't trying to form a corporation. That never even occurred to us until later. It was the land we were after. We were pretty young back then but you supported us anyway, at least some people in most of the villages did, because we all knew land was important to us. We filed a claim for 25 million acres because we knew it was the right thing to do. We ended up with a little less than 2½ million acres, a*

*corporation, and some money. But it was the land
we were after because our people need that land to
live, to survive.*

—John Schaeffer, first executive
director of NANA Corporation
addressing NANA shareholders
at a village meeting, 1981

The 1971 Alaska Native Claims Settlement Act (ANCSA) comprises the largest land settlement in United States history. Made clear in John Schaeffer's comments, there were important political and philosophical differences between the claims sought by Alaska Native leaders and the settlement that resulted. As I will argue, Alaska Native leaders and Elders acted on behalf of Indigenous futurity, whereas representatives of the US government worked to ensure a settler futurity. The settlement, prompted by the discovery of oil fields in northern Alaska, ceded 44 million acres of land to Alaska Native peoples via regional and village corporations in exchange for desisting further land claims. Village corporations secured titles for the surface of their respective lands, while regional corporations secured subsurface rights—an arrangement informed by neoliberalism, not Alaska Native conceptualizations of land.

This article critically engages ANCSA in order to theorize what is meant by surface and subsurface rights to land and the impacts of entrusting land (only) to Alaska Native corporations. First I will provide an overview of the context that prompted the settlement act. Then I will discuss some of the core preoccupations of settler colonialism, including the corporate makeover of Indigenous land and life, which is uniquely enacted in Alaska. In the next section I will critically analyze several forms of ideological invasion represented in ANCSA. Finally, I will engage Scott Lyon's (2010) concept of the *x-mark* to render an alternative understanding of what ANCSA has yielded for future generations. Scott Lyon's conceptualization of the x-mark—the scrawls and signatures made by Indigenous peoples that resulted in uneven agreements with the US Government—provides a frame through which we can rethink treaties and other negotiations in which it seems that too much was given away. Though I use the space of this article to critique the settlement act, I acknowledge the work of Alaska Native leaders and elders to negotiate a settlement that would sustain Alaska Native life. Like the protectors of the seals on the Pribilof Islands, where my family is from, Alaska Native elders have a different narrative about the settlement, one concerned with protecting land and people—one that unsettles the finality of the settlement act and its desired settler future. (i) The last section of my article attends to that narrative and theorizes ANCSA within the context of Alaska Native futurity.

Wanting Alaska

Alaska Native peoples have oral histories of their lives in Alaska that stretch back more than 10,000 years, to time immemorial. Most communities disbelieve the land-bridge story that has been applied to them, and have their own origin stories of how they came to be in a particular place. The Aleutian Islands and Alaskan Peninsula were partially colonized by Russia just about 270 years ago, in the mid-1700s. Russia established its first permanent settlement in 1784, and several others scattered throughout the Aleutians and mainland Alaska (Chaffee 2008). In 1867 US Secretary of State William Seward convinced Congress to purchase the land from Russia, even though, as some legal experts have pointed out, Russia did not have "control" of the land to do so. Yet 586,400 square miles were sold to the United States for $7.2 million. In the negotiations of the Treaty of Cession, Russia and the United States characterized Alaska Native people as "uncivilized tribes," who under the treaty would be "subject to such laws and regulations as the United States may, from time to time, adopt in regard to the aboriginal tribes of that country" (Chaffee 2008). As many schoolchildren in the US have learned, the purchase of Alaska was ridiculed in the US press as "Seward's Icebox" or "Seward's Folly," until the discovery of gold in the 1890s, which redeemed William Seward in the public eye, and the purchase of Alaska as prudent and profitable. Ultimately, this purchase allowed for the extraction of wealth for the United States from Native land, via gold and oil, and from Native labor, via the harvest of the northern fur seals in the Pribilof Islands.

When Alaska was purchased by the United States, few in the contiguous US imagined that it would ever become a state. It was considered too far away, too foreign, and too remote. However, increasing tensions with the Soviet Union, the discovery of oil on the Kenai Peninsula in 1957, and the growing number of white settlers and prospectors in the region prompted the designation of Alaska as the 49th state in 1959. Congress permitted the new state of Alaska to identify and allocate 102.5 million acres of land as federal land, which Alaska state government would develop and oversee. Alaska

Native people opposed the designation of their land as federal land under the control of the state, and filed formal protests as early as 1961. At the same time, oil fields were discovered in other regions of the state, yet oil companies could not proceed without clear lines of land holdings and ownership. From the perspective of the US federal government, Alaska Native land claims needed to be resolved before they could get down to the business of profit extraction. A "land freeze" was enacted in 1967 so that no more land titles would change hands before a system was arranged (Chaffee 2008, p. 115).

That system was the Alaska Native Claims Settlement Act of 1971—ANCSA. The act represented a departure from prior ways of managing Indigenous peoples and their land claims by the US federal government. Understanding ANCSA is important not only in understanding the particular nature of settler colonialism in this instance, but for other Indigenous communities who have members who have spoken publicly about their desire to achieve a similar arrangement with the US federal government.

ANCSA and Settler Colonialism

As Patrick Wolfe emphasizes, "Settler colonies were not primarily established to extract surplus value from indigenous labor, but from land, which required/requires displacing Indigenous peoples from their homelands" (Wolfe 1999, p. 1). As I will discuss, within the framework of ANCSA, Alaska Native peoples are not displaced from lands outright, yet the titles are negotiated by corporations that serve as intermediaries and possibly soft-pedals on Alaska Native sovereignty. Settler colonialism is concerned with remaking land into property, remaking tribal membership into blood quantum, and—as demonstrated most powerfully in the case of ANCSA—the corporate makeover of tribal land and life. I discuss each of these in turn:

Remaking land into property

Settler colonialism can be differentiated from other forms of colonization because in this version the colonizers arrive at a place ("discovering" it) and attempt to make it a permanent home (claiming it). Settlers enforce their interpretations on everyone and everything in their new domain, and their new societies require corporeal and epistemic elimination of the Native (Wolfe 1999 & 2006; Veracini 2011). In settler colonial societies such as the United States,

> Exclusive rights of property in the land belonged to the nation who discovered the lands. Discovery was demonstrated by the appropriation of the lands for agriculture, which in turn secured the rights of the discovering nation to claim full sovereignty within the lands and against all other claims. (Barker 2005, p. 8)

Thus, in settler colonialism, a key preoccupation is the remaking of Indigenous land into settler property. When land is remade into property, human relationships to land—as life, as curriculum, as ancestor—are reduced to the relationship of owner to his property. When land is recast as property, place becomes exchangeable, saleable, stealable. The most important aim of recasting land as property is to make it ahistorical in order to refute prior claims, thus reaffirming the myth of *terra nullius*.

It is important to observe that settler colonialism also requires the forced labor of chattel slaves, often stolen from their homelands, whose *bodies* become settlers' property, and who are kept landless. In the Alaska context, where US settler colonialism occurs immediately after the legal abolition of plantation slavery, chattel slavery has to be fabricated from parts of the Indigenous world. The process of making property out of land *and people* is inherent and crucial to settler colonialism.

Remaking tribal membership into blood quantum

Another key preoccupation of settler colonialism is blood quantum. As J. Kehaulani Kauanui explains, blood-quantum logic erroneously "presumes that one's 'blood amount' correlates to one's cultural orientation and identity" (2008, p. 2). Kauanui's work examines the role of US colonial imposition on Kanaka Maoli genealogical practices and understandings of kinship, and how the imposition of blood racialization "constructs [Indigenous] identity as measurable and dilutable" (2008, p. 3, insertion mine). Blood-quantum laws are primarily geared to diminish claims to land and Indigenous sovereignty (Kauanui 2008; see also Wolfe 2006 and Tallbear in Latour 2012). Blood-quantum logics portray contemporary Indigenous generations to be less authentic, less Indigenous than every prior generation in order to ultimately phase out Indigenous claims to land and usher in settler claims to property (see also Tuck & Yang 2012).

Though they have no scientific basis, logics of blood quantum have been forced on tribes and Indigenous communities in ways that have attempted to undermine prior ways of determining tribal membership, an affront to tribal sovereignty. Blood-quantum laws (and one-drop rules that have been applied to black communities in the United States) have been imposed and required as part of the process of settler colonial making property, but also as part of another settler desire, which is to replace the Native. The aim of replacement is entwined in the acquisition of land, of course, but replacement taps a fantasy that plunges much deeper than land ownership. The settler fantasy of replacement is an attempt at resolution to a settler anxiety of unbelonging on Indigenous land—Indigenous peoples are not just in the way of settler expansion, but in the way of the settler desire to become/be Indigenous, a position of perceived moral right to the land (see also Tuck & Gaztambide-Fernández 2013).

Corporate makeover of tribal life and land

A third preoccupation of settler colonialism is epitomized by ANCSA. Under ANSCA, Alaska Native tribal communities were reimagined as corporations. It did not just remake land into property, it capitalized the land, forcing a corporate structure and profit-making mandate upon its people. ANCSA required Alaska Native communities to form regional and local corporations: 12 for-profit regional corporations were established based on geographical and tribal affiliations, and a 13th "region" corporation was established for Alaska Natives who did not reside in the state.

The settlement act also forced Alaska Native villages to become incorporated in order to secure funds, land, and other resources from the regional corporations. The settlement act requires that village corporations pass services and other benefits to village residents (ii). Thus, in most arrangements, village corporations maintain rights to the literal surface of the land (sometimes described as the top several inches of land) while regional corporations hold subsurface rights to the same land.

ANCSA prompted a corporate makeover of land into capital, that is, an abstraction of value that is based upon the market's perceptions of its worth (problematized later in this article). Such a makeover reflects the historical ascendancy of a neoliberal ideology, which would become more prominent in the following decade and those thereafter (Harvey 2005). As several Indigenous scholars have noted (Bargh 2007; Tuck 2012; Grande 2004), though neoliberalism is often positioned as a more recent or modern paradigm, neoliberalism as an expansionist imperative is only the latest configuration of settler colonialism.

In this context, the settler nation-state attempts to remake the Indigenous collective into bits of seizeable capital (shares). It also attempts to replace Indigeneity with incorporation that can then be disincorporated or taken over. In exchange for 44 million acres of land, Alaska Native people agreed not to make claims to additional land in the future. As declared by Congress, "[a]ll claims against the United States, the State, and all other persons . . . based on claims of aboriginal right, title, use, or occupancy of land or water areas in Alaska . . . [were] hereby extinguished" (43 U.S.C. §1601). Any reserves that were established prior to 1971, with the exception of Metlakatla Annette Island, were revoked.

Ideological Invasion

ANCSA represents several forms of ideological invasion on Alaska Native life and land. They are as follows:

1) The settler rationale for the settlement, which was to figure out how to allocate claims to land as natural resource from which capital would be extracted and distributed through shares.

2) The notion of surface and subsurface claims—tribal village corporations hold surface claims to land, and regional corporations hold subsurface claims, beginning literally a few inches below the surface of the earth.

3) The devolution of Alaska Native peoples as sovereign, original peoples of an occupied land into shareholders.

4) The requirement that Alaska Native peoples give up any future land claims, into eternity.

In this section, I will discuss each of these forms of ideological invasion in turn.

First form of ideological invasion: the rationale of the settlement

Alaska Natives' rights to use and occupy Alaska were recognized by the 1867 Treaty of Cession between the United States and Russia regarding the purchase of Alaska. Article III of that treaty recognized Alaska Native *tribes* as distinct peoples under principles of international and federal domestic law, while also describing Alaska Native tribes as subject to US Indian law and regulations (Case & Dorough 2006). The Bureau of Indian Affairs gained responsibility for programs for Alaska Natives in 1931, and in 1936 Congress expanded the Indian Reorganization Act to Alaska. As noted, the events that led to the Alaska Native Claims Settlement Act of 1971 included the discovery of oil in multiple locations throughout Alaska. Prior treaty language described Alaska Natives' rights of use, but did not make clear land ownership, and with oil producers wanting only to drill where clear title to the discovery lands could be established, the pressure was on Congress to settle land claims and settle them fast (Jones 2010).

Case and Dorough (2006) argue that Congress ignored international legal principles and the fuller recognition of Alaska Native peoples as distinct tribes in the design of ANCSA by transforming communal land claims into private corporate assets. They continue that, "The enactment of ANCSA did not allow for the collective right of Alaska Native peoples to consent to the terms of the act, an essential element of self-determination under international law" (2006 p. 13).

ANCSA opened Alaska Native land to corporate invasion by requiring Alaska Native people to reorganize their relationships to land—as property, as having monetary value, as investment. This is not to say that ANCSA introduced these dimensions to Alaska Native life but that learning the corporate structure was an urgent and consuming task, and people did not have time to collectively think together about how and if corporate conceptualizations could be integrated or reimagined in ways that were culturally appropriate. The introduction of legal fiduciary duties of corporate leaders in for-profit companies put immense pressure on Alaska Native peoples to learn corporate structures and adopt corporate conceptualizations of land and value (Chaffee, 2008).

At the outset of the settlement, the sale of Alaska Native Corporation stock was prohibited until 1991. Then, alienability restrictions would be lifted, and Alaska Native stockholders might have sold stock to non-Alaska Native persons. This provision, since modified, put the real intentions of the settler state on full display: to incorporate in order to disincorporate, to make claims in order to unmake claims. Apparent from the perspective of the settler nation-state is the hope that the land/ corporations might be unprofitable in the short term, or in the long term, and be privatized away from the tribal collective. Ultimately, the provision was modified before 1991, and alienability restrictions were not lifted. Under the Act as it is now written, a Native corporation can choose to suspend the sale of their stock indefinitely (Chaffee,2008, p. 188).

Second form of ideological invasion: claiming inches of earth

The land-selection provisions of ANCSA gave village corporations title to the surface estates of 22 million acres of land and gave regional corporations title to the surface estates of any of the 22 million acres left unselected by the villages and title to the subsurface estates of land selected by villages (iii) (Chaffee 2008, p. 122). Clearly, the need to differentiate between surface estates and subsurface estates draws from the potential for profits from oil drilling and mining, and the pressure from fossil fuel companies to gain access. Though the reasons for the differentiation are obvious, the fact remains that this distribution logic is absurd. In this particular feature of the settlement act, Alaska Native peoples are required to adhere to an understanding of land as vertical at the same time that other sections of the act extinguish hunting and fishing rights that traverse *across* land (iv):

> Section 1603 of the Act expressly extinguished Alaska Native hunting and fishing rights in exchange for money and definite tracts of land. Definite tracts of land, however, do not appeal to Alaska Natives leading a subsistence lifestyle because migratory animals do not choose their path based on land ownership. The Settlement Act, therefore, encases Alaska Natives within a system of governance and ownership that is in direct opposition to many of their traditional practices. (Chaffee 2008, p. 134).

I point to the arbitrary (except to fossil fuel companies) absurdity of surface and subsurface estates because it is one of the specific false logics of settler colonialism in Alaska, bending understandings of land to meet the needs of prospectors and settlers and refusing understandings that afford Alaska Native subsistence and land-based ways of life. The invention of subsurface estates is a remaking of *terra nullius*, as if somehow land a few inches below ground is uninhabited; it is a re-creation of the doctrine of discovery where there were/are already people.

In the daily lives of Alaska Native peoples, the designation of surface and subsurface estates has been a nuisance. Despite the requirement (v) that the 12 land-owning regional corporations share 70 percent of the revenues from subsurface estates and timber, disputes between corporations have resulted in substantial litigation, disputes entirely brought on by the settlement act (Chaffee 2008, p. 141). Alaska Native corporations already endure a heavy burden of complying with the legal requirements of ANCSA; indeed "lawyers and corporate consultants have been the major beneficiaries of an Act that was supposed to help Alaska Natives . . . Alaska Native corporations have paid nearly half a billion dollars to maintain and defend the corporations established by the Act," (p. 152).

Further, though the settlement act did not dissolve tribal governments or tribal governments' existing assets, ANCSA did turn over control of land and now resources to corporations, which can undermine the sovereignty of tribal governments. Corporations

> often frustrate and interfere with the role of Native governments . . .. For example, if one wanted to mine silver on Alaska Native corporate land, one would approach the corporation owning the land, rather than the Native government. Thus, the Settlement Act ultimately undercuts the role of Native governments in determining the use of land and resources because it vests power to make certain determinations in the boards of the corporations created as a result of the Act. (Chaffee 2008, p. 120)

Just after ANCSA was enacted, shareholders in Arctic Village and Venetie (village) Corporations voted to transfer all lands to the federated tribal government of the villages, prompting more than 25 years of litigation regarding the reach of tribal jurisdiction in the state of Alaska. When the tribal government taxed the state on a school construction project (citing Venetie as part of Indian Country as defined by federal law) the state sued to enjoin the tax, refusing both the recognition of Venetie as a tribe and its authority to impose taxes on lands that were part of the settlement act. Venetie was ultimately listed as a federally recognized tribe on a list ratified by Congress in 1994, but the Supreme Court ruled against Venetie as part of Indian Country (thus a dependent Indian community) because ANCSA lands had not been "set aside" for tribes but for corporations. Further, the lands were freely alienable as described in the design of the settlement act (see Case & Dorough 2006, p. 14).

Alaska Native tribes have persisted to gain recognition and sovereignty outside of the legal and discursive confines of ANCSA, especially in a government-to-government negotiation citing the UN Declaration on the Rights of Indigenous Peoples that resulted in the 2001 Administrative Order No. 186, which acknowledges tribes and their distinct legal and political authority in Alaska (Case & Dorough 2006). Also, several Alaska Native Corporation CEOs are both shareholders and tribal members, putting them in unique and possibly conflicting positions. Alaska Native communities are politically powerful in the state, both inside and outside the scope of the corporations, yet this power is staked upon the maintenance of alienability restrictions and other measures to keep subsurface and surface claims in right relationship.

Third form of ideological invasion: devolution of Alaska Native peoples into shareholders

The most immediate change introduced by ANCSA was the transformation of tribal members into shareholders. The settlement act employed a logic of blood quantum to describe and determine who could be a shareholder in Settlement Common Stock. Every Alaska Native person with the sufficient "degree" of Alaska Native blood alive on December 18, 1971, was entitled to 100 shares of the regional corporation where they resided. Those born after that date, called "after-borns" in common parlance, are eligible to be tribal members (rights to determine eligibility for tribal membership have been retained by tribal/village governments) but in most cases are not eligible to be shareholders unless by gift or inheritance. Because under ANCSA it is regional corporations and village corporations that own the land, the vast majority of those born after 1971 have no recognized or legal claims to the lands of their ancestors.

Opening shareholding registers/stock applications to include those born after 1971 is a subject of much debate, with those who want to ensure the active participation of younger generations (those now aged about 40 and younger) on one side, and those who do not want to "dilute" the value of the issued stock by creating more shares for younger generations on the other side. Most important for this discussion is how the question of stock applications pits shareholders and non-shareholding tribal members against each other (vi). Some shareholders depend on dividends to pay for basic needs, while others who do not hold stock could just as readily use dividend money (vii). The new tribal membership category of shareholder diminishes the significance and legal claim rights of tribal membership, as evidenced by the differences in the entitlements and decision-making opportunities between shareholders and non-shareholders. The result is that shareholder status overshadows tribal membership status.

Becoming a shareholder of one's land may also entice a person to push for short-term gains that cause long-term problems or environmental devastation. ANCSA, by design, may threaten subsistence living and other land-based life and cultural practices by titling land to corporations tasked by law to pursue profits. Indeed, "By focusing on financial performance, Alaska Native corporations act in direct opposition to the goals of many of the people that they are supposed to represent" (Chaffee 2008, p. 134). That is, being a shareholder of land puts tribal members into the precarious position of potentially financially benefiting from the extraction of the land-turned–natural resource even as it may devastate tribal homelands. By design, ANCSA inserts corporate measures of success that are contradictory to cultural aims of well-being, often characterized by attitudes of land stewardship (Chaffee 2008, p. 133). Corporate structures are inherently at odds with structures of Indigeneity. As for-profit entities, corporations are accountable to increasing the dividends of shareholders, not ensuring the vitality and viability of subsistence living and the thriving of land, flora, and fauna, even though those are the needs of the people that comprise the shareholders.

For Congress, a major impetus for managing land claims via the establishment of regional and local corporations was the desire to distribute the settlement, "without establishing any permanent racially defined institutions, rights, privileges, or obligations, [and] without creating a reservation system or lengthy wardship or trusteeship." At first this may read as a contradiction, because shares were in most cases distributed using criteria pertaining to blood quantum. It is important to see how this component of the settlement act—the deliberate deracination of Indigeneity—is a feature of settler colonial elimination of the Native through a policy of subtractive racination, or framing of Alaska Native peoples as an impermanent race.

As indicated, one of the core ways that ANCSA modified standard corporate law was by establishing alienability restrictions (prohibiting the sale of stock ownerships to others) until December 18, 1991. In accounts written by those who represented the interests of the United States, inserting alienability restrictions were important in order to prevent "establishing any permanent racially defined institutions, rights, privileges, or obligations" (43 U.S.C. §1601). Douglas Jones, former policy maker working on behalf of the federal government in Alaska, writing in 2010 in an essay called "What We Thought We Were Doing in Alaska, 1965–1972," writes that settlement "while inherently racially based," was designed to,

> point toward minimizing "racialness" over time. This is to say that features of normalization, such as establishing corporations requiring administrative and managerial skills in their running, making Natives financial shareholders with the ability (after twenty years) to alienate one's title (the opposite of traditional perpetual wardship status), and ending various protections, were a conscious part of the design of the settlement. (2010, p. 232, *quotation marks original*)

Indeed the act was designed to phase out a federally recognized status of Alaska Native that was based on tribal membership (designated as "race") in favor of a status based upon owning shares, potentially even if purchased on the open market (again this option has not been enacted, but it is built into the design of the act).

Alienability restrictions aside, the summative effect of bestowing rights or claims to land not to tribes or to tribal members but to those who have been recast as shareholders to their own land represents an important settler reconceptualization, one that displaces and re-stories land as capital and Indigeneity as a capitalist endeavor. It makes us all Alaska Native capitalists and reinterprets relationships to land as confined within the temporality of the rise (and falls) of capitalism, thereby diminishing prior and future stories of "how we/they came to be in a particular place—indeed we/they came to *be a place*" (Tuck & Yang 2012, p. 5).

The implied hope of the settler/speculators who negotiated ANCSA was that someday there would be Alaska corporations with no Alaska Natives in them. The evolution of [original inhabitant—savage—degree of Indian blood—shareholder] is an evolution that is accountable to settler futurity, or the "permanent virtuality" (Baldwin 2012, p. 173) of the settler on stolen land. It is a teleological assumption that the Native can be modernized away (2012, p. 174) and that the settler can finally, after all this time, replace the Native (viii).

Fourth ideological invasion: Relinquishing future claims

The most profound ideological invasion ushered in by ANCSA is the Alaska Native concession to give up all future claims. Extinguishment of future claims, and extinguishment of Alaska Native hunting and fishing rights to most of the land was a nonnegotiable set forth by the federal government, which wanted to settle the claims and settle them permanently. In recent decades, extinguishment has been explicitly denounced by United Nations human-rights review boards (Case & Dorough 2006, p. 14). This component of the settlement act undercuts tribal sovereignty by relinquishing the right to accumulate land and expand territory—a significant right of a sovereign state. It installed permanent borders on land and access for future generations who may have a different vision of how land should be appropriately shared and distributed. Most of all, this concession legitimized the occupation of Alaska by the US settler colonial nation-state and confirmed its permanence and the permanence of this particular configuration of relations between Alaska Native tribes and the federal government—except for, of course, that the "racialized" or tribal components of shareholding were designed to dissolve, so that Alaska Native corporations become simply corporations over time.

At least, this is what ANSCA and the relinquishing of future land claims has done if the only temporality we consider is one of settler futurity. ANSCA is invested in settler futurity. To say that something is invested in something else's futurity is not the same as saying it is invested in something's future; futurity also refers to the ways in which "the future is rendered knowable through specific [contemporary] practices," and specific anticipatory interventions, including precaution, preemption, and preparedness (Baldwin 2012, p. 173). ANCSA takes precautions against Alaska Native sovereignty by preempting the land and preempting future Native claims to the land, and prepares the way for settler takeover of Alaska Native corporations. ANCSA attempts to diminish Alaska Native sovereignty by preempting Alaska Native self-determinations of governance structures, land use, and abidance of corporate law.

ANCSA is invested in settler futurity, but we know from the written and oral accounts of those Alaska Natives who negotiated the settlement and its later amendments that they were and are invested in what we might call an Indigenous futurity, a tribal futurity, a land futurity. Indigenous futurity is a (for now) parallel temporality that is also concerned with (the repatriation of) land. As I will discuss in the final section of this article, these other futurities persist precisely because of Indigenous sovereignty and because of Indigenous cosmologies and epistemological relationships to land. The relinquishing of future land claims invokes a short vision of the future; by contrast, an Indigenous futurity disbelieves the permanence of the United States settler colonial nation-state as it now exists— parallel paths headed toward careening futures.

Alaska Native Resistance to Ideological Invasion of ANCSA

At this point, a reader might surmise that ANCSA has caused much damage to Alaska Native sovereignty and personhood, or that settlement was handled improperly so that too much was given away. This would indeed be the message if the conversation stopped here; but this is why it is so important to engage and theorize the settlement act from the perspectives of Alaska Native elders and leaders. In this final section of the article, I provide a different read of the settlement via Scott Lyons' conceptualization of the *x-mark*, a "sign of consent in a context of coercion" (2010, p. 1).

Alaska Native elders and leaders have had to resist ANSCA from its inception, even as they had to bring it into existence. For example, with regard to the alienability restrictions, in 1987, Alaska Native leaders were able to get Congress to agree to what are called the 1991 Amendments (H.R. 278) (ix), which allowed corporations to make the decision to lift restrictions; at this time, zero regional or village corporations have decided to make the stocks saleable. A related modification from standard corporate law is Alaska Native corporation exemption from various securities acts (1933, 1934, and 1940) at least until the unforeseen time in which stock can be owned by peoples or entities who are not Alaska Native and/or alienability restrictions are withdrawn (Chaffee 2008, p. 119). This is one place in which it is possible to see Alaska Native assent to ANCSA as a form of resistance, not acquiescence. By stopping the desired traffic in shares, Alaska Native corporations have resisted the wholesale capitalization of land into seizeable property and effectively the incorporation of settlers into the Indigenous collective via the buying/selling of shares.

Unsettling the rationale of ANCSA

It is imperative to highlight the contradictory desires that resulted in ANCSA, including the Alaska Native leaders'/elders' desires to preserve Alaska Native life as land, and the settler desire to remove Indigenous life on oil producing land. For the Alaska Natives that were part of the negotiations, ANCSA comprised what Scott Lyons calls an *x-mark*,

> a sign of consent in a context of coercion; it is the agreement that one makes when there seems to be little choice in the matter. To the extent that little choice isn't quite the same thing as no choice, it signifies Indian agency. To the extent that little choice isn't exactly what is meant by the word liberty, it signifies the political realities of the treaty era (and perhaps the realities of our own complicated age as well). (2010, p. 1, *parenthesis original*)

As x-mark, ANCSA represents both a) settler desires to alienate Native peoples from land, and b) Alaska Native desires for the proliferation of land and people. The settlement process required Alaska Native leaders to negotiate in terms of land as property and people as land owners. These represent significant departures from the ways in which Alaska Native peoples have described their relationships to land and place. Yup'ik elder Oscar Kawagley wrote,

> The cold defines my place. *Mamterilleq* (now known as Bethel, Alaska) made me who I am. The cold made my language, my worldview, my culture, and my technology . . . I grew up as an inseparable part of Nature. It was not my place to "own" land, nor to domesticate plants or animals that often have more power than I as a human being. (Kawagley 2010, p. xviii)

Iñupiaq scholar Edna Ahgeak MacLean speaks to how language reveals relationships to land and water: People use their language to organize their reality. (x) Iñupiaq and Yup'ik cultures are based on dependence on the land and sea. Hunting, and therefore a nomadic way of life has persisted. The sea and land that people depend on for their sustenance are almost totally devoid of landmarks. These languages have therefore developed an elaborate set of demonstrative pronouns and adverbs that are used to direct the listener's attention quickly to the nature and location of an object. In place of landmarks, words serve as indicators about proximity, visibility, or vertical position and implies whether the object is inside or outside, moving or not moving, long or short. For example, Inupiaq has at least 22 stems that are used to form demonstrative pronouns in eight different cases and demonstrative adverbs in four cases. American English has two demonstrative pronouns [this and that] (plural forms these and those), with their respective adverbs here and there. (MacLean 2010, p. 49)

These descriptions by Kawagley and MacLean illustrate exponentially more complex relationships to land and place—particularly land and place that outsiders would dismiss as barren except for oil—than corporate ownership. When Kawagley acknowledges a nature that is more powerful than him, it is not a romantic gesture, not a noble framing, but recognition of a cold that can kill, a landscape that can make itself unknown in a matter of moments. When MacLean writes about the need for 22 roots for demonstrative pronouns, she is referring to a profound nexus of nature and language and thought that yields deeply nuanced and coconstituted relationships with place. These ontological renderings of land and place show how incompatible settler colonial notions of place are for Alaska Native life, and it was these understandings that prompted the settlement on the Alaska Native side.

The region described by MacLean is owned by NANA Corporation. In a 1981 account of a series of village meetings held by NANA Corporation's first executive director, John Schaeffer (who held the position from 1971–1984), Schaeffer discussed the progress of the then-ten-year-old corporation:

> We've been doing pretty good . . . with the business anyway. So good in fact it was getting boring. I was thinking of leaving. Why not? NANA seemed to be doing okay and I was offered a lot more money to go and run a company for someone else . . .. But when I started to think some more about it, I decided it wasn't enough to take another job just to get rich. Why make more money? Compared with a lot of you I make pretty good money already. I can take care of my family, so what would I do with more money? (Schaeffer & Christensen 2010, p. 61)

Later in his presentation, he told shareholders, "We've got things too important to us to sell. In our corporation, land is not for sale." He continued,

> For a long time we resisted the white man's land ownership system but finally when it looked like we

264

were going to lose our land, we used the land ownership system because we had to . . . . [Our children] are being taught that land is worth money. . . . Our land is worth billions. The big corporations aren't going to mind paying a few million for it. . . . Some oil company or mining company will offer our kids $100,000, maybe more, for their shares . . .[If we let making money guide our decisions and we sell our stock and land] you won't have Iñupiaq anymore, just a bunch of poor, hungry people living in their shacks on somebody else's land. (Schaeffer & Christensen 2010, p. 65)

Conclusion: ANCSA as x-mark

Locating ANCSA within an Indigenous futurity and a settler futurity complicates what is meant by relinquishing all future claims. Scott Lyons, writing about the x-marks that indicate agreement on old treaties observes,

The x-mark is a contaminated and coerced sign of consent made under conditions that are not of one's making. It signifies power and a lack of power, agency and a lack of agency. It is a decision one makes when something has already been decided for you, but it is still a decision. Damned if you do, damned if you don't. And yet there is always the prospect of slippage, indeterminacy, unforeseen consequences, or unintended results; it is always possible, that is, that an x-mark could result in something good. Why else, we must ask, would someone bother to make it? (2010, p. 3)

Seen from this view, the ability to make an x-mark, like ANCSA itself, presumes Indigenous sovereignty and presumes that sovereignty supersedes the x-mark. ANCSA is constructed in a way that hopes to preempt any future x-marks; however, it cannot, and this is where settler logic unravels itself. The provisions of ANCSA are already undermined by settler impermanence, just like most corporations are undermined by their own ecological devastation and excess profiteering. ANCSA will no doubt be reorganized and legislated. This means there are future x-marks to be made, potential x-marks to defragmentize land, place corporations under tribal governance, allow for the expansion of Alaska Native corporations to acquire more land.

For example, an April 2013 DC district court decision made room for the US Secretary of the Interior to take additional land into trust for Alaska tribes. This was seen as a foreclosed possibility after ANCSA, but the case *Akiachak Native Community vs. Salazar* argued on behalf of Alaska Native tribes by Heather Kendall Miller of the Native American Rights Fund, reconfirmed the possibility of adding to the land bases of Alaska Native tribes.

Any treaty with a settler colonial state is impermanent—both because the colonizing state will violate or amend it at its pleasure and because the settler futurity is a myth that tries to make itself real. An Indigenous futurity acknowledges the strategic necessity of engaging a settler nation in its own terms but also in resisting its own terms. An Indigenous futurity also remembers the land/people/life inseparability that resists the logic of fragmentation. The literality of ANCSA need not supplant the Indigenous objectives of protecting land and life. If we consider ANCSA as an x-mark, then the literality of ANCSA is settler coercion, but the decision to sign, to petition, to negotiate—*that* is Indigenous.

Endnotes

i. I should note that even though I use the words *they, them,* and *their* to discuss Alaska Native people throughout this article, I am an Alaska Native person. In many cases it would also be appropriate for me to use the words *we, us,* and *our,* but I did not want for this differentiation to be distracting. Thus, I used the former for sake of consistency.

ii. There are important provisions of ANCSA that give Alaska Native corporations a different shape than other corporations, including provisions regarding profit sharing and selling of net operating losses.

iii. Regional corporations collectively hold title to another 16 million acres of land, and two million more acres were kept out of selections but kept under Alaska Native control as burial sites and other places of cultural significance (Chaffee 2008, p. 122).

iv. Case and Dorough (2006) observe that Section 1603 is in violation of International Covenant on Civil and Political Rights and the International Covenant on Economic, Social and Cultural Rights, both adopted by the United Nations (UN) in 1966 and both of which affirmatively state in Article 1(2), "In no case may a people be deprived of its own means of subsistence."

v. 43 U.S.C. § 1606(i)(1)(A)

vi. Various factors including natural "resources" and investment decisions have contributed to the value of each stock, and to the dividends paid to each stockholder—some regional corporations pay out dividends at more than $40.00 per share, while others pay out $0.00, with most regional corporations paying out between $3.00 to $5.00 a share (2005 payouts, as quoted in Edwards & Natarjan 2002, p. 85).

vii. Sometimes those unfamiliar with Alaska Native corporations are surprised to learn that jobs in the corporation are not usually held by shareholders. Some corporations are deliberate about hiring shareholders, other corporations are less intentional, which accounts for the wide disparities: 29.8 percent jobs held by shareholders, maximum; 1.6 percent jobs held by shareholders, minimum (2005 reports as quoted in Edwards & Natarjan 2008, p. 85).

viii. The teleos of [tribe—tribal individuals—shareholders—nothing] corresponds to [land/people—land/persons—shares /shareholders—settler property/settler replacements]. Ironically, just as the Alaskan Native is wished away by settler logic of a diminishing bloodline turned diluted shareholder, the Alaskan settler is positioned as increasingly Native. That is, settlers in Alaska engage a simultaneous undertaking to Indigenize themselves (at least on television) as "wild men" and homesteading women, gold diggers, and adventurists on the northern frontier, often in front of television cameras. This is possible only by imagining the settler's property as expansive (settlers can own more and more) and the Indigenous as subtractive (shares get diluted over time until they vanish in value—easily seized by the settler). The racialization of Alaska Natives as an impermanent race, to be washed away, follows the logic of other settler technologies, like blood quantum. However, the conversion of Indigeneity into shares, like blood, which can be eventually possessed by settler shareholders, is part of a different formulation of settler colonialism.

ix. The only way Alaska Congressperson Don Young was able to get the "1991 Amendments" bill passed was to assure Congress that it had nothing to do with tribal sovereignty. "The bill does not affect government powers, it does not grant new lands or funds and it does not have any significant fiscal impact on the federal government," Young told Congress (as quoted in the *Alaska Federation of Natives Newsletter*, 1987).

x. MacLean notes later in the manuscript that the Iñupiaq and Yup'ik word *kangut*, which meant "a herd of animals or large assemblage of people" was extended to include the concept of corporation—the suffix *uraq*, meaning "small," was added to the word, making *kannuuraq*, or subsidiary.

References

Alexie, S. (1996). *The Summer of Black Widows*. Brooklyn: Hanging Loose Press.

Baldwin, A. (2012). Whiteness and Futurity: Toward a Research Agenda. *Progress in Human Geography 36*, 172-187.

Bargh, M. (Ed.). (2007). *Resistance: An Indigenous Response to*

Neoliberalism. Wellington, NZ: Huia Press.

Barker, J. (2005). For Whom Sovereignty Matters. In J. Barker, (Ed.) *Sovereignty Matters: Locations of Contestation and Possibility in Indigenous Struggles for Self-determination,* pp. 1-37. Lincoln, NE: University of Nebraska Press.

Case, D. & Dorough, D. S. (2006). Tribes and Self-Determination in Alaska. *Human Rights Magazine 33,* 13-14.

Chaffee, E. (2008). Business Organizations and Tribal Self-determination: A Critical Reexamination of the Alaska Native Claims Settlement Act. *Alaska Law Review 25,* 107-149.

Deloria, P. (1998). *Playing Indian.* New Haven, CT: Yale University Press.

Grande, S. (2004). *Red Pedagogy: Native American Social and Political Thought.* Lanham, MD: Rowman and Littlefield.

Harvey, D. (2005). *A Brief History of Neoliberalism.* Oxford, UK: Oxford University Press.

Heynen, N. & Robbins, P. (2005). The Neoliberalization of Nature: Governance, Privatization, Enclosure, and Valuation. *Capitalism Nature Socialism 16,* 5-8.

Jones, D. (2010). What We Thought We Were Doing in Alaska, 1965–1972. *The Journal of Policy History 22,* 226-236.

Kauanui, J. K. (2008). *Hawaiian Blood: Colonialism and the Politics of Sovereignty and Indigeneity.* Durham, NC: Duke University Press.

Kawagley, A. O. (2010). Foreword. In R. Barnhardt & A.

O. Kawagley (Eds.) *Alaska Native Education: Views From Within*, xiii-xv. Fairbanks, AK: Alaska Native Knowledge Network Press, University of Alaska Fairbanks.

Latour, F. (2012, June 1) "The Myth of Native American Blood." *The Hyphenated Life Blog on Boston.com.* Accessed June 4, 2012, http://www.boston.com/community/blogs/hyphenated_life/2012/06/the_myth_of_native_american_bl.html

Lyons, S. (2010). *X-Marks: Native Signatures of Assent.* Minneapolis: University of Minnesota Press.

MacLean, E. A. (2010). Culture and Change for Inupiat and Yu'pik People of Alaska. In R. Barnhardt & A. O. Kawagley (Eds.) *Alaska Native Education: Views From Within*, 41-58. Fairbanks, AK: Alaska Native Knowledge Network Press, University of Alaska Fairbanks.

Schaeffer, J. & Christensen, J. D. (2010). Inupiat Ilitqusiat: To Save our Land and Our People. In R. Barnhardt & A. O. Kawagley (Eds.) *Alaska Native Education: Views From Within*, 59-72. Fairbanks, AK: Alaska Native Knowledge Network Press, University of Alaska Fairbanks.

Tuck, E. (2012). *Urban Youth and School Pushout: Gateways, Getaways and the GED.* New York: Routledge.

Tuck, E. & Yang, K.W. (2012). Decolonization is not a metaphor. *Decolonization: Indigeneity, Education, and Society* 1.

Veracini, L. (2011). Introducing Settler Colonial Studies.

Settler Colonial Studies 1, 1-12.

Wolfe, P. (1999). *Settler Colonialism and the Transformation of Anthropology: The Politics and Poetics of an Ethnographic Event.* New York: Cassell.

Wolfe, P. (2006). Settler Colonialism and the Elimination of the Native. *Journal of Genocide Research* 8, 387-409.

PART V

DECOLONIZING HISTORY: LEGAL AND INDIGENOUS VIEWS OF JUSTICE AND LEGISLATION

Alaskan Segregation and the Paradox of Exclusion, Separation, and Integration

Holly Miowak Guise

Abstract

Racial segregation in Alaska prior to the passage of the 1945 Alaska Equal Rights Act consisted of a hybrid between Jim Crow policies from the South and assimilation policies implemented by Bureau of Indian Affairs boarding schools. In the summer of 2008, 29 interviewed Elders reflected on memories of segregated spaces that enforced the color line between whites and Natives. Interviews with Elders indicate ubiquitous racial tensions and injustice in Alaskan cities, directed at the Native population. This study documents and analyzes Alaska Native Elders' testimonies, all of whom witnessed institutionalized racism firsthand, manifested in hiring and workplace discrimination, assimilation-focused boarding schools, and segregated spaces like restaurants and theaters. By centering key advice from Elders, this study moves toward dismantling the remnants of discrimination that developed since segregation.

Keywords: Alaskan segregation, Bureau of Indian Affairs assimilation, Elder interviews

The Alaska territory provides a unique example of Indigenous segregation, and pan-Alaska Native oral histories inform an understanding of US settler colonialism and the collective efforts of Indigenous resistance. Many Elders recount memories of pre-WWII Alaska when legalized segregation discriminated against Native people in Alaska's urban centers, including Anchorage, Fairbanks, and Juneau, among other locations. Elder interviews also reveal personal accounts of individual and familial identity formations that developed when they confronted stereotypes and overcame racial barriers.

Literature Review

Alaskan historian Terrence Cole's article entitled "Jim Crow in Alaska: The Passage of the Alaska Equal Rights Act of 1945" (1992) highlights prewar Alaskan segregation and parallels the experience of Alaska Natives to the plight of African Americans subject to Jim Crow segregationist regimes. In his comprehensive survey of Alaskan segregation, Cole (1992) also details the Alaska Native Civil Rights Movement led by activists like Alberta Schenck and Elizabeth and Roy Peratrovich. Branching from Cole's (1992) scholarship, this is research project expands the dialogue on Alaskan segregation, focusing primarily on separation, exclusion, and inclusion as well as the lived experiences and the uniqueness of Alaskan Indigenous segregation.

The fields of Alaskan segregation history, Alaska Native colonial resistance, and Indigenous empowerment are continuing to develop within academia and public history. *Aleut Story* (2005) and *For the Rights of All: Ending Jim Crow in Alaska* (2009) are important documentary film contributions jointly produced by Native communities. Other useful literature on Alaskan segregation derives from personal narratives transcribed by Native communities. *Haa Kusteeyí, Our Culture: Tlingit Life Stories*, edited by Nora Marks Dauenhauer and Richard Dauenhauer (1994), contains interviews that express stories about segregation. The Central Council of the Tlingit and Haida Indian Tribes of Alaska, Alaska Native Corporations, and other Native groups associated with the Alaska Native Brotherhood and Alaska Native Sisterhood have released publications on Alaska Native history, including abundant information on Native cultural adaptation and survival.

Waziyatawin Angela Wilson (2005) and Linda Tuhiwai Smith's (1999) scholarship both highlight the importance of recovering oral histories that incorporate Indigenous perspective within academia while simultaneously educating the community. Linda Tuhiwai Smith's *Decolonizing Methodologies* (1999) provides an excellent outline for facilitating a research project that empowers Indigenous voices and perspectives while reclaiming academia as an Indigenous space. Waziyatawin Angela Wilson's *Remember This!: Dakota Decolonization and the Eli Taylor Narratives* (2005) provides a useful framework for a research study that centers the Indigenous perspective and publishes a book in the Dakota and English languages so that community members may continue to study their Native language. The interviews in this study employ similar decolonizing methodologies that center around Alaska Native oral histories. In particular, Elder interviews uncover the everyday lived experiences of segregation. By recovering Alaska Native voices within Alaska history, we can assure that not only are we listening to, learning from, and empowering Indigenous perspectives, but helping to create an Indigenous archive of historical knowledge. Large block quotes from Elders is a purposeful methodology since it allows Native Elders' memories to flourish in this article.

Elders' stories reveal that Alaskan segregation in urban centers presented paradoxical elements of exclusion, separation, and integration (i). The Bureau of Indian Affairs (BIA) attempted to assimilate American Indian and Alaska Native students through boarding-school assimilationist policies, yet racial segregation and exclusion existed in Alaskan cities within churches, restaurants, public transportation, hiring practices, workplace conduct, health-care provisions, and other public spheres (ii). In this manner, Alaskan segregation paradoxically presented a hybrid between assimilationist and segregationist policies that attempted to confine Natives to lower rungs of the Alaskan racial hierarchy (iii). Alaska Natives resided in a liminal status in which the BIA expected Native assimilation, yet white settler colonial society would not fully integrate the Native population. Indigenous Alaskan racial segregation presented a new form of settler colonialism that inflicted cultural trauma that persisted over generations (iv). This article highlights excerpts from interviews that relate to segregationist signs, restaurants, theaters, hiring and workplace discrimination, BIA boarding-school experiences, and reflections on moving forward.

Collecting interviews in Anchorage, Juneau, Kodiak, Metlakatla, Nome, and Unalakleet provided for a wide sample pool as well as diverse experiences on segregation. From July through August 2008, 29 Elders composed of 25 Native Elders and four non-Native Elders shared their stories on Alaskan segregation (v). The interviewee population consisted of 15 male and 14 female Elders. A total of 11 interviews took place in Anchorage, from meetings at the First Alaskans Institute conference room, and at Elders' homes. In Nome, six Elders shared their stories at the Nome Eskimo Community Center, the senior recreational center, and inside their homes (vi). Three Elders in Juneau spoke about their experiences in a meeting room at the Central Council of the Tlingit and Haida Indian Tribes of Alaska and at their homes; and three Elders from Metlakatla were interviewed at their homes and at an inn. In Kodiak three Elders participated in interviews at the Alutiiq Museum. Three Elders participated in interviews in Unalakleet.

In the process of interviewing, Elders had the option to remain anonymous and to be audio or video recorded. Only three Elders selected to remain anonymous. Interview times ranged from ten minutes to over an hour. Two interview sessions consisted of married couples jointly interviewed, another interview consisted of two elderly friends, and another interview consisted of a mother and her son. These group interviews proved valuable in facilitating conversations on Alaskan segregation (vii). Interview questions asked for detailed experiences with Alaskan segregation prior to the 1945 Alaska Equal Rights Act, ways that individuals confronted or resisted segregation, beliefs on how Alaska society changed after the Alaska Equal Rights Act, and words of wisdom. Elders' words of wisdom ranged from the need to maintain cultural values, to the need to love oneself, to the need to tackle higher education.

During the post–Civil War Reconstruction Era, and after the *Plessy v. Ferguson* case of 1896, segregation known as Jim Crow spread throughout the American South and across the United States. Jim Crow also exhibited exclusionary practices, the denial of civil rights, the stigmatization of minorities as inferior to whites, and disenfranchisement. During the Jim

Crow segregationist regime, discriminatory signs in Alaska and the continental US excluded people of color from public venues (viii). In Alaska, such signs served as the visual boundary that excluded Natives from services reserved for whites only. Throughout the interviews, numerous Elders remarked that signs reading "No Natives and No Dogs" were particularly offensive because it paralleled Natives to animals. The word *Native* on discriminatory signs became synonymous with "inferior" to the white race and thus perpetuated exclusion and separation between the races.

Title: "A crew surveying the lot lines following the Louvre fire on Front Street, ca. 1908." A Juneau sign reads: "All White Help." Winter and Pond, Winter and Pond Photograph Collection; Alaska State Library, P87-1050

Lela Oman was born on the Kobuk River in 1915 before she moved to Nome as a young girl. She described the signs: "When I first came here to Nome, there were places where there were signs, 'Whites Only'" (Lela Oman, personal communication, July 19, 2008). Reverend Walter Soboleff, born in 1908, was originally from Killisnoo. He reflected, "We somewhat learned to live with signs on some stores and other places. 'No Natives Allowed,' so we didn't go into those places. And in some of the show houses our people [had to] sit in special places" (Reverend Walter Soboleff, personal communication, July 22, 2008). Kristian Didrickson, born in 1932 in Sitka, reflected, "'No Colored, No dogs, No Natives.' The hatred was always there" (Kristian Didrickson, personal communication, July 24, 2008). When asked about the segregationist signs and being treated unequally, he said, "I can name a few cusswords" (Kristian Didrickson, personal communication, July 24, 2008). Alice Jo Callahan, an Elder from Anchorage born in 1943, detailed the signs on 4th Avenue in Anchorage that existed after the passage of the 1945 Alaska Equal Rights Act: "I wasn't very old at that time [1945], but they still had signs up around town on 4th Avenue. 'No Dogs, No Indians Allowed.' I saw them when I was around ten years old in the 1950s" (Alice Jo Callahan, personal communication, August 4, 2008). These memories indicate that segregationist signs left lasting impressions, feelings of inferiorty, and the signs perpetuated racial animosity.

By excluding and separating Native patrons from restaurants, whites reaffirmed positions of superiority within the Alaskan racial hierarchy. Shirley Kendall was born in 1932 and

raised in Hoonah. She reflected on her childhood memory of
visiting the Juneau City Café with her family:

> Ah, I think my parents really protected us from the
> discrimination that was going on. But the things I do
> remember is that the only restaurant we ever went to
> was "City Café" in Juneau. And ah, it never occurred to
> me to question my parents as to why we always ate at ah
> City Café, but I liked it. It was really a fun place to go
> because there was lots of other Natives that were there.
> Um, it wasn't until I traveled by myself as a teenager
> that I discovered that there were signs on the restaurants
> doors that said, "No Natives Allowed." So ah, the signs
> that I saw, that were downtown in Juneau, were mostly
> on um cardboard, handwritten, or hand colored letters,
> you know, and they stuck it on their door. And, I was
> kinda surprised because I think up to then I wasn't really
> that aware of that fact that we weren't really allowed to
> go into the stores. Into the restaurants. (Shirley Kendall,
> personal communication, July 26, 2008)

For some Elders, the Jim Crow legacy perpetuates trauma
to the present day. Shirley described how trauma from racial
exclusion persists: "I'm still conscious of the fact that when I
go to a restaurant, I look around and see, you know, um, and
I'm kinda amazed that I'm in a restaurant with other people,
and I'm being allowed to be in there, because it still, apparently
it still affects me. My feelings about being in a place like that"
(Shirley Kendall, personal communication, July 26, 2008).

Title: "City Club and Café. 1938." Ray B. Dame, Ickes Collection; Anchorage Museum, B1975.175.516

More Elders reflected on how they could not understand the purpose of segregated restaurants. Arne Beltz, a non-Native Elder born in 1917, grew up in Reinbeck, New York. Arne came to Wrangell, Alaska, in 1948. She later went to Fairbanks, where she recollected, "They had signs around in the restaurants, 'No Natives Served.' And I hated that. That was in Fairbanks when I was up there" (Arne Beltz, personal communication, August 5, 2008). Alaska's Judge James A. von der Heydt, a non-Native Elder born in 1919 in Miles City, Montana, served as a US marshal in Nome from 1945–1948. He described, "Other times there were certain restaurants [where] the Native people had to sit at certain tables" (Judge James A. von der Heydt, personal communication, August 15, 2008). Rosa Miller, a tribal leader of the Klukwan Nation was born in 1926. She explained, "[W]e weren't allowed in restaurants. It was really hard back then, and treated like—we were just treated badly. We didn't understand. We were young. We didn't really understand why we were treated that way, and it stayed with us" (Rosa Miller, personal communication, July 22, 2008).

Even at entertainment venues, white Alaskan society segregated theaters to maintain strict racial boundaries and to restrict Natives to inferior spaces. In 1944, at the Nome Dream Theater, half-Iñupiaq and half-white Alberta Schenck refused to move from her seat to the Native side of the theater (ix). Schenck's activism combined with Native activism led by Elizabeth and Roy Peratrovich and the Alaska Native Brotherhood and Alaska Native Sisterhood facilitated the passage of the 1945 Alaska Equal Rights Act. Senator Frank Whaley opposed the passage of the 1945 act because he did not want to sit next to Natives at the theater (x). Segregated theaters confined and racialized Alaska Natives to separate seating areas. Cole (1992) writes, "Howard Handleman wrote in 1943: 'They have to sit on their own side of the theatre.' [. . .] nicknamed 'N----r Heaven,' [. . .] completely reserved for full-blood Eskimos" (xi). In this passage Handleman categorizes "Eskimos" with the extremely derogatory term "N----r." Racial slurs were yet another way to maintain the Alaskan racial hierarchy. Despite these segregationist measures, Alaska Native people created their own community spaces and, like Alberta Schenck, they protested theater segregation (xii).

Shirley Kendall shared distinct memories about sitting in the theater balcony as a small child:

> I was aware of the fact that we could buy tickets to the movies and I remember it was 20th Century Theater and Capitol Theater. And it seems to me that we always went to the Capitol Theater. And, they put all the Natives in a little balcony, and it's about as big as a third of [a conference room] and it curved around, and some people had chairs that were along the edge of the balcony and they were the ones that were serious about seeing the movies. I never really saw what the rest of the theater looked like. I think they just kinda shuffled us up the stairs and after we bought our tickets to go. And every now and then when something interesting happened on the screen people would kinda look to see what it is. Those are the things that I remember. (Shirley Kendall, personal communication, July 26, 2008)

Caroline Reader, born in 1928, remembered the Nome Dream Theater: "The theater was segregated. There was an aisle down the middle. The Eskimos sat on one side and the whites sat on the other side" (Caroline Reader, personal communication, July 18, 2008). Dan Karmun, born in 1927, from Deering, reflected on the segregation he experienced in Nome that did not exist in Deering:

> There was a theater here in Nome called "Dream Theater" and for the life of me, first time I've seen the move to separate the Eskimos and the white people in the theater at that time. That's one thing we've never

experienced in our little village of Deering, because we worked with gold companies, gold mines, and they respected us because we were the only work force for them, you know? And they treated us with respect on what our abilities were to do at the gold mine, which was done. And I'll never forget my first experience here in Nome of discrimination against the Eskimos at that time but that died out later in the life of our community here in Nome. (Dan Karmun, personal communication, July 17, 2008)

One of Judge von der Heydt's first recollections in Nome took place at the segregated theater:

The law at the time was segregationist. In the Nome theater, [there was a] center aisle. The Native people were required to sit on the left side of the aisle, white people on the right. The first time I got there, I sat on the wrong side. The usher came up to me and said, "You can't sit here." I moved. Such nonsense. (Judge James von der Heydt, personal communication, August 15, 2008)

The judge's example shows how theater staff enforced strict segregation standards that made whites adhere to their separate spaces.

Employment restrictions created economic differences between whites and Natives that few Natives could overcome. Native Elders from across Alaska spoke about their experiences with limited job opportunities, and some Elders commended others for breaking labor barriers. Reverend Walter Soboleff wisely stated, "The people did their best to survive. However, they weren't readily employed. In fact, very few had opportunities for employment. But when we had the fishing industry, our people went into the fishing industry. And it's a good thing fish didn't know racial problems. We did all right" (Reverend Walter Soboleff, personal communication, July 22, 2008). Jacob Ahwinona from White Mountain, born in 1923, expressed his pride in co-interviewee Lucie Trigg, born in 1930 on Little Diomede Island:

> I always admired [Lucie] because she went to school and become a nurse, that's the only Eskimo nurse we had up here [in Nome]. My mom always called up her, it's ah, she broke the ice. I'm real proud of her taking, you know, interest in nursing and stuff like that and working up at the hospital over the years that I knew her. And ah, that made me, that-that gives me a warm feeling inside, you know, when one of our people is a nurse see, registered nurse. I'm proud to say that. (Jacob Ahwinona, personal communication, July 18, 2008)

Lela Oman described the discriminatory nature of the Nome job market that only hired whites: "When I first came here to Nome there were places where there were signs, 'Whites Only'" (Lela Oman, personal communication, July 17, 2008).

According to Arne Beltz, the federal government practiced racial discrimination against Native employees:

> [T]hey had a place where the Federal government took care of the Eskimos who were working on the railroad. And I thought it was a dreadful thing they'd done to

the people. They gave them these little houses—you'd think it was a beautiful thing, but it wasn't. They had two rooms and they had to go [to the] bathroom outside their little house, and no facilities for washing that I remember. And, they had a lot of tuberculosis in that group, because they were so close together. They shared the water fountain, and they shared the toilets, and I thought that was discrimination. No white people would have accepted living like that [with] the railroad, under the federal government. (Arne Beltz, personal communication, August 5, 2008)

Nick Alokli, born in 1936 on Kodiak Island, shared his experience about working for the cannery that prohibited Natives from the mess hall:

We used to go down [to the] cannery, we had to take our own, everything back, we had to take our bedding, our dishes. Everything, cooking. So we could use it, 'cause we weren't allowed to eat in the mess hall. Natives weren't allowed to eat in the mess hall. We didn't really know the difference, I guess. We never really questioned why because, I guess, because we were just happy to have a job. They used to take leftovers and put them on the porch, and treat us like nothing. You know? If we wanna take it we take it, those leftovers. Now I start to think, why they treat us like animals? Giving us leftovers. But they wouldn't let us eat in the mess hall. Well, that's all changed now. (Nick Alokli, personal communication, August 9, 2008)

Nick's memories display the prevalence of Native exclusion that existed in the workplace and dehumanizing working conditions.

While public venues and jobs segregated and excluded Natives, the BIA and churches attempted to assimilate Natives into Western society. For many Elders, remembering boarding-school days brought anxiety and memories of physical and psychological abuse that prohibited Native languages in order to conform to the English language (xiii). Fortunately, language-revitalization programs from Alaska Native Corporations and Village Corporations have put forth efforts to preserve and revitalize Native languages.

Vince Pikonganna, an Elder from Nome born in 1948, spent the entire interview reflecting on harsh memories from the BIA school. He was originally from King Island but attended a BIA school in Nome. Vince reflected:

> When I went to school, the teacher there was very strict about languages, and every time I talked to the other students about what was going on the teacher would come over and hit us on the head with a yard stick. It has been on my mind ever since then because I thought you go to school to learn and not be hit . . . they hit you for talking your language. (Vince Pikonganna, personal communication, July 15, 2008)

Elder Dennis Knagin, born in 1930 in Afognak, recalled positive and negative childhood memories while attending the BIA school:

> I lived close by the school, a couple hundred yards from

the school. Back then I used to run home at recess time and grab my .22 and shoot a rabbit, and that would be our dinner (laughs). [We] weren't allowed to [speak Alutiiq]. They tape your mouth and they said you were mute. The teachers put tape on your mouth. That's all I can remember. There were quite a few guys with tape in their mouth. (Dennis Knagin, personal communication, August 9, 2008)

An Elder from Unalakleet also mentioned the abusive practices by the BIA teachers: "The school didn't want children to speak Native. They let them stand facing the wall so they won't speak" (Anonymous Elder, personal communication, July 30, 2008). Mary Ann Haugen, from Unalakleet, said, "Oh, in school, when I was going to school, you could not speak Iñupiaq in school or during recess. Even a word, a tattletale [would tell the teacher], the teacher then would have them hold the book with hands outstretched and if the elbow started to go down she would take a ruler and whack them in the elbow" (Mary Ann Haugen, personal communication, July 30, 2008).

Arnold Booth, an Elder born in 1919, from Metlakatla, reflected, "Education to the Natives was limited. I know my grandfather and his generation; they all came back as shoemakers or tailors" (Arnold Booth, personal communication, July 24, 2008). According to Hoxie (2001), BIA schools aimed to incorporate Alaska Natives into Western society as second-class citizens who served in uneducated craftsmanship roles to whites. Shirley shared how educators during his elementary school years would prohibit the use of Native language and say, "Your language is no good. Strictly English" (Shirley Kendall, personal communication, July 26, 2008). These messages from the BIA schools forced Native children to believe that their language and culture was inadequate compared to the Western culture. Arnold stated an unfortunate truth pertaining to language loss: "Now I doubt that 35 people can speak the language within our community" (Arnold Booth, personal communication, July 24, 2008).

Title: "Boys working in shoe shop, Sitka Industrial Training School." Elbridge W. Merrill, William A. Kelly Photograph Collection; Alaska State Library, P427-70

Reverend Walter Soboleff recalled biases from the Western schools:

> The public school system was very difficult. The Western culture race weren't so tolerant [. . .] It wasn't a happy experience for many of our Natives here. Not [a] very happy experience. Even the teachers came to be biased and that was the teachers; but also the administration tended to be biased. That certainly was not anything for Western culture to be proud of to say the least. (Reverend Walter Soboleff, personal communication, July 22, 2008)

William Johnson, or Bill as he liked to be called, was born in 1934 and raised in Angoon. He described discrimination that he faced as a student attending a Native school:

> I encountered more racial issues when I went to school in Juneau 'cause I went to Native school and we were treated like dumb Indians at the only school we could go to. The idea [was] that we had to go to our own schools, and we weren't allowed to go to other schools because of our color or race. (William "Bill" Johnson, personal communication, July 15, 2008)

Yet despite the biases and challenges of the Western education system, Alaska Natives continued to challenge the Alaskan racial hierarchy by desegregating schools and integrating the whit eterritorial schools. Kristian Didrickson shared his school-integration story: "My sister Arlene was one of the first to go to public school in Sitka" (Kristian Didrickson, personal communication, July 24, 2008). Alice Jo Callahan self-identified as a mixed-race Native, and she recalled attending school with white children: "One little girl said to me one time, 'I can't play with you anymore.' I says, 'How come?' She says, 'Because you're Native.' I says, 'What's that?' (Alice laughs)" (Alice Jo Callahan, personal communication, August 4, 2008). These stories display confrontations that Native children experienced with the integrated schools.

Bertrand Adams Sr. from Yakutat was born in 1937, and he grew up in Juneau. Elizabeth and Roy Peratrovich convinced Bert's father to enroll him in public school to commence school integration. As a second-grader, Bert recalled that on the first day of classes he was "one of the three [Native students] that showed up for school in the system that year." He described that the teacher encouraged his participation and integration in the classroom:

> So it was, ah, distressing at first because, you know, I was naturally just a shy kid, and most of time I would be, um, by myself sitting in the back of the room and, ah, the teacher, you know, was really nice; she tried to encourage me to participate more in classroom. She asked me if, um, you know, if I would sit toward the front so I could be closer to her. And I-I, you know, I just kept going back. And then, ah, during-during recess she tried to encourage me to, ah, to play with the other kids. (Bert Adams Sr., personal communication, July 11, 2008)

The encouragement that Bert received from the teacher and a schoolhouse friend exhibited a promising future for Alaskan race relations. Bert shared another story about his childhood friend. On the playground Bert became friends with a little girl named Amy who had freckles and blue eyes. Bert's friendship with Amy defied the racial boundaries that other children attempted to re-create on the playground. He reflected:

> And there was this girl who came up to me. And I was, you know, I was sitting there kinda sad. And she comes to me and she says, "Hi." And I looked up and there was this little girl, and she had red hair and pigtails, and wearing glasses and she had freckles and two missing teeth. And she said, "My name is Amy, would you like to play some jumping jacks?" And she was throwing a little ball and some jumping jacks around, and, ah, there was kinda a hesitation, and I says "Okay." So she knelt down beside me and we started playing jumping jacks. After that we became partners in jumping jacks, and then she finally got me involved playing with some of the other kids, you know. And when they saw her playing with me, they kinda got interested in me. I sort of got accepted by the group after that. There was one day, though, that I kinda, made me aware of, you know, the differences between Native and non-Native, because, as I said earlier, I didn't, because I had friends we played with on 9th street and, you know, Native and non-Native, we just became great playmates. Well, we were playing jumping jacks one day under this tree that we always played jumping jacks under, and there's

> this girl comes up to her and she says, "Amy, do you play with Indians?" And, ah, Amy jumped up and she said, "He's not an Indian! He's not an Indian! He's my friend!" And from that point on you know I-I-I kinda wondered, you know, what's goin' on here? (Bert Adams Sr., personal communication, July 11, 2008)

Bert's reflection on his friendship with Amy demonstrates identity growth and the self-realization of his own background as an Alaska Native who would confront racial issues in the future. Bert described the conversation he had with his mother on his Native identity:

> I went home, um, after school and I asked my mom. I says, "Mom, what's an Indian?" And, ah, she says, "Oh, who called you an Indian?" Then I told her the story, you know, and she sat me down and explained to me what my heritage was and who I really was and that, ah, sometimes, you know, during my lifetime I would have to deal with those issues. And she wanted us to—and she talked to my brother as well—she wanted us to deal with those. (Bert Adams Sr., personal communication, July 11, 2008)

Bert's story exhibits childhood memories of integrating the school, recognizing his own status as an Alaska Native, and remembering family conversations on racial identity. Many Elders like Bert expressed that their parents attempted to shield them from racial discrimination.

Conclusions

Widespread segregation spanning from the American South to Alaska displayed an institutionalized racism that formerly explicitly divided our country into racial hierarchies. Separate social spaces marginalized people of color. In Alaska, the opposing policies of assimilation, which attempted to absorb a culture, and segregation, which attempted to exclude a culture, created a pervasive climate of harsh intolerance and even dehumanization toward Alaska Native people. These forms of discrimination exhibited by racist hiring and workplace practices and segregation of public spaces, including theaters, restaurants, and assimilationist schools, collectively facilitated Alaskan social inequality.

Segregated spaces in Alaska generated racial boundaries between whites and Natives. Discriminatory signs represented a visual boundary and stigmatized Natives as socially inferior to whites. Bureau of Indian Affairs schools restricted upward class mobility by limiting Native students to become second-class citizens through vocational work (xiv). All of these forms of discrimination prevented social and economic upward mobility for Alaska Natives in the early 20th century. Former legislation like the 1925 Alaska Voters Literacy Act restricted the political and citizenship rights of many Natives who spoke English as a second language (xv).

In Alaska, racial boundaries proved to be complicated and at times malleable. Discrimination and racial boundaries varied from Alaskan city to city. Interviews expressed that feelings of racial inferiority last for decades and generations. Both segregation and assimilation policies created cultural trauma that caused individuals to feel ashamed of their family heritage.

Although many Elders confronted blatant discrimination, they are to be commended for resisting and terminating discrimination while encouraging the younger generations. Shirley Kendall from Hoonah detailed a story about how she educated Native students at East High School on the issue of racial segregation. She shared her personal experiences on segregation with Native youth, who then began to understand the historical complexities and underpinnings of cultural rifts today. She concluded her interview by saying, "All of this stuff is negative and we went through it for you. So now you need to make the best of what you have. So that's the only advice I have for the young people" (Shirley Kendall, personal communication, July 26, 2008). Civil rights leaders across the country, including Alaska Native civil rights leaders like Elizabeth and Roy Peratrovich and Alberta Schenck, combated discrimination with the power of words and civil disobedience to ensure that their children would not be treated as second-class citizens.

Many Elders remember the days of racial segregation in Alaska and recognize that their progeny continue to experience discrimination. While explicit segregation legally ended with the passage of the 1945 Alaska Equal Rights Act, implicit segregation and social inequalities linger. Many interviewed Elders claimed that segregation still exists through remaining forms of discriminatory attitudes.

It is possible to overcome racial discrimination, and it is also possible to forgive using methods by the truth and reconciliation commission. Therefore, racial hatred and discrimination from the past, however unpleasant, must be fully addressed in order to understand cultural trauma and present-day ramifications. Only once this has occurred will it be possible for all cultures to move forward toward the dismantling of racial boundaries. In Reverend Walter Soboleff's words of wisdom:

> I'm glad that segregation and discrimination is decreasing. It is so much better. It always, as I said I sound like an old record, it's always a problem of the people who feel they must be racially biased against *whatever race*: the Japanese, Chinese, or the person from Turkey or Egypt, or wherever. People just have to learn that the society of the world should be one big brotherhood and one big sisterhood. And that's so much better than trying to have a racial bias. What good does it do people? It's very harmful. Harmful to the person who opposes that way of life. And the people who are bias[ed] against whom they have a bias; [it] makes them unhappy. And after all, that's not how the world is created. We're all one big family. The less racial biases the better for civilization. (Reverend Walter Soboleff, personal communication, July 22, 2008)

Endnotes

i   During a discussion, Glenda Gilmore asked if Alaskan segregation exhibited elements of exclusion or separation. I have incorporated this language in my research.

ii For more information on BIA boarding-school assimilationist policies see Hoxie (2001), which contextualizes assimilationist policies within US politics and evolving efforts to confront the "Indian problem." Child and Lomawaima (2000) tell stories of Native survival and resistance from US assimilationist policies while contextualizing assimilationist policies that followed global patterns in Canada and Australia.

iii   For more information on racial hierarchies see Woodward (2001) and Fredrickson (2002).

iv   Napoleon (1996) provides important theoretical work to understand Alaskan colonialism and its impact on the Indigenous population. He also advocates for talking circles to bring community members together for healing.

v   I requested to interview Elders born before 1945, and all but a few met this qualification. I interviewed two individuals born after 1945 because they insisted that segregation did not end in 1945. Undergraduate funding and mentorship from the Alaska Native Policy Center made this Alaska Native oral history project research possible. In the summer of 2008, I received joint internships from Stanford University's Center for Comparative Studies in Race and Ethnicity Community Service Research Internship and the First Alaskans Institute that placed me with guidance from the Alaska Native Policy Center. This research resulted in my undergraduate honors thesis, titled *Rewriting the History of Racial Segregation in Alaska*. This paper derives from my research findings and feedback that I received from presenting at the Elders and Youth Conferences in 2008 and 2010.

vi   The Nome Eskimo Community Center was super helpful in connecting me with local Elders, as were Linda Scott and Karlin Itchoak.

vii   As part of his mission to collect oral interviews for his language-preservation project, Peter Boskofsky aided me with the three interviews at the Alutiiq Museum. In Unalakleet, I interviewed a family relative with my sister Jennine Elias's help.

viii For more information on the development of Jim Crow, see Woodward (2001), Kennedy (1990), and Gilmore (1996, 2008). Gilmore (1996) describes African American resistance and African American women's political activism that defied racial segregation. Gilmore (2008) analyzes world politics to detail continuous African American activism that defied and eventually terminated Jim Crow.

ix   See Marston (1972) for a chapter dedicated to Alberta Schenck, her activism, and Nome Iñupiaq activism. Marston also details how he encouraged Alberta to contact Alaska Governor Gruening. Cole (1992) also addresses Alberta Schenck's activism.

x   See Thomas (1991). Thomas recounts that Whaley did not want to sit next to Natives in the theater because "they smelled." Statements like this further perpetuated stereotypes of Alaska Natives as degenerate.

xi   Cole (1992), 441. I use dashes for the *N* word to indicate its racial violence and because common use of this as a vocabulary word has perpetuated social inequalities over the centuries.

xii For more information on Iñupiaq mobilization efforts against the Dream Theater see Marston (1972).

xiii For more information on Alaskan educational policies and historical trauma see La Belle et al. (2005). This article contains valuable oral interviews on boarding-school experiences, cases of molestation by BIA staff and other boarding-school students replicating behaviors, and the importance of spiritual healing.

xiv For more information on vocational school programs administered by the BIA see Hoxie (2001).

xv For more information on the Alaska Voters' Literacy Act, see Steven Haycox's (1986/7) "William Paul, Sr., and the Alaska Voters['] Literacy Act of 1925."

References

Alaskool. Institute of Social and Economic Research University of Alaska Anchorage. 10 February 2009. <http://www. alaskool.org/projects/JimCrow/Jimcrow.htm>

Alaskool. Institute of Social and Economic Research University of Alaska Anchorage. 10 February 2009. <http:// www.alaskool.org/projects/native_gov/recollections/ peratrovich/_Letter.htm>

Alexander, M. (2012). *The New Jim Crow.* New York: The New Press.

Blausten, A. P. & Ferguson Jr., C. C. (1962). *Desegregation and the law: the meaning and effects of the school segregation cases.* New York, NY: Vintage Books Inc.

Blueberry Productions, Dir. Jeffry Silverman. (2009). *For the Rights of All: Ending Jim Crow in Alaska.*, U.S.A.

Cole, T. (1992). Jim Crow in Alaska: The Passage of the Alaska Equal Rights Act of 1945. *Western Historical Quarterly.* 429-449.

Crockett, N. (1979). *The Black towns.* Lawrence: Regents Press of Kansas.

Dauenhauer, N. M. & Dauenhauer, R. (1994). *Kusteeyí, Our Culture: Tlingit Life Stories.* University of Washington Press.

Driscoll, J. (1943). *War discovers Alaska.* Philadelphia: The Cornwall Press.

Fredrickson, G. (2002). *Racism: a short history.* Princeton, New Jersey: Princeton University Press.

Gilmore, G. (2008). *Defying Dixie.* New York & London: W.W. Norton & Company.

Gilmore, G. (1996). *Gender and Jim Crow: women and the politics of white supremacy in North Carolina.* Chapel Hill: University of North Carolina Press.

Haycox, S. (2002). *Alaska: an American colony.* Seattle: University of Washington.

Haycox, S. W. 1986/87. William Paul, Sr., and the Alaska Voters Literacy Act of 1925. *Alaska History, 2,* 17-38.

Hoxie, F. (2001). *A final promise: the campaign to assimilate the Indians, 1880-1920.* University of Nebraska Press.

Hunter, T. W. (1997). *To 'joy my freedom: Southern Black women's lives and labors after the Civil War.* Cambridge, Massachusetts: Harvard University Press.

Johnson, R. D. (1998). *Ernest Gruening and the American dissenting tradition.* Cambridge, Massachusetts: Harvard University Press.

Joshi, S.T. (1990). *Documents of American prejudice.* USA: Basic Books.

Kennedy, S. (1990). *Jim Crow guide: the way it was.* University Press of Florida.

Kennedy, R. (2003). *Interracial intimacies: sex, marriage, identity, and adoption.* New York: Random House.

La Belle, J., Smith, S., Easley, C. & Kanaqlak (George P. Charles). (2005). *National Resource Center for American Indian, Alaska Native and Native Hawaiian Elders. Boarding school: historical trauma among Alaska's Native people.* Anchorage: UAA.

Lomen, C. J. (1954). *Fifty years in Alaska.* New York: David McKay Company, Inc. Van Rees Press.

Lomawaima, T. K., Child, B. & Archuleta, M. (2000). *Away*

*from home: American Indian boarding school experiences,
1879-2000.* Heard Museum.

Lowery, M. M. (2010). *Lumbee Indians in the Jim Crow South.*
Chapel Hill: University of North Carolina Press.

Marston, M. (1969). *Men of the tundra.* New York: October
House Inc.

McClanahan, A. J. (2002). *Our stories, our lives.* Anchorage,
AK: The CIRI Foundation.

Metcalfe, P. (1995). *Central Council historical profile:
Tlingit and Haida Indian tribes of Alaska.* Ed. Stark
Christianson, Susan. Juneau, Alaska: The Central
Council Tlingit and Haida Tribes of Alaska.

Morrison, W. R. & Coates, K. A. (1994). *Working in the north:
labor and the Northwest defense projects 1942-1946.*
Fairbanks: University of Alaska Press.

Napoleon, H. (Ed. Eric Madsen). (1996). *Yuuyaraq: the way
of the human being.* University of Alaska Fairbanks:
Alaska Native Knowledge Network.

Peratrovich, R. (1943). Letter to: Board of Director USO.
Juneau, AK. 16 Feb 1943.

Robinson, Carolyn K. Dir. Marla Williams. (2005). *Aleut
Story.* Anchorage: Sprocket heads Production.

Saks, E. (2003). Representing Miscegenation Law. Ed. Kevin
R. Johnson. *Mixed race America and the law.* NYU
Press.

Schenck, A. (1944). Letter. *The Nome Nugget.* 3 March 1944.

Senungetuk, V. & Tiulana, P. (1987). *A place for winter: Paul
Tiulana's story.* CIRI Foundation.

Smith, L. T. (1999). *Decolonizing Methodologies.* Zed book.

Stoler, A. (2002). *Carnal knowledge and imperial power: race and the intimate in colonial rule.* Los Angeles: University of California Press.

Thomas, E. K. (1991). *A recollection of Civil Rights leader Elizabeth Peratrovich 1911-1958.* Central Council of Tlingit and Haida Indian Tribes of Alaska.

Wardman, G. (1884). *A trip to Alaska.* San Francisco: Samuel Carson & Company.

Wilkins, D. E. (2002). *American Indian politics and the American political system.* Oxford: Rowman & Littlefield Publishers Inc.

Wilson, A. W. (2005). *Remember this!: Dakota decolonization and the Eli Taylor narratives.* USA: University of Nebraska Press.

Woodward, C V. (2001). *The strange career of Jim Crow.* Oxford: Oxford University Press.

Native by Policy: How Legislation Contributes to Dialogues about Indigenous Identity

Liza Mack

Abstract

Precedent-setting legislation in the United States and around the world has effectively changed the way that we as Native people define ourselves. This paper takes an in-depth look at the ways in which these biological, cultural, and personal definitions of *Native* have changed over time and how they play into our everyday lives. Using the knowledge, experience, and information learned from family and elders about histories that stretch from the Aleutians to Germany, I present my own examination of cultural identity.

Indigenous identity is an interesting concept. Until recently, I believed I was one-half Aleut, German, and Russian. Besides the obvious fact that this would actually be thirds, there is much more to it. I now understand that some of these ideas about identity are in fact legally binding colonial definitions that we have as Native people. What is an Indigenous way to define ourselves? What does it mean to be half Aleut or Unangax— which is how we refer to ourselves in Unangam Tunuu, the Aleut Language (i). Which half is it? Is it tangible or not? Can it really be quantified? Is Aleut the same as Unangax? (ii) These were some of the questions I began to ask myself as I undertook the task of defining my own Indigenous identity and outlining a family tree for my newborn son, Cohen.

One of the reasons I decided to go back to school in the first place was to answer one specific question. I used to have a problem with the difference between what is Native Alaskan versus Alaska Native. For me, I wondered and struggled with why a person who was raised in Alaska and whose families had been in Alaska for generations would not get the same treatment as Alaska Natives. Of course, as time has passed and I have become familiar with histories and legislations that define us as Alaska Native people I have a clearer understanding of why there is a difference. Now, having a child of my own, I understand better the importance of being able to define our legal and binding Indigenous relationships with our nation-state.

In 2012 I was introduced to a text by Eva Garroutte (2009) titled *Real Indians Identity and the Survival of Native America*. In it she writes, "The significance between Indians and other racial minorities, of course, is that legally defined Indian people enjoy rights and privileges, which other racial groups do not" (pg. 29). With a better understanding of treaty rights and what was given up in return for these rights and privileges, I began to think about these definitions. The United States government has a "trust responsibility" to tribes and individuals within federally recognized groups. These tribes have special rights to the land as well as eligibility for services such as health care, while also being exempt from taxation and some legislation on reservation lands (Garroute 2003). In Alaska, one such legislation was the Alaska Native Claims Settlement Act (ANCSA). ANCSA was a short, dense, comprehensive legislation that ultimately exchanged aboriginal title in Alaska for land and money. This act further confuses the situation and adds a whole new layer of disenfranchisement by creating a legal definition of who would and could participate in the capacities allowed, namely joining and participating in the newly created corporations. These changes and rules are now a reality faced by all generations of Alaska Native people.

David Case & David Voluck (2002) summarize aboriginal title in their text *Alaska Natives and American Laws 2nd edition*. Here they discuss much of the work by Felix Cohen (1972), who authored the *Handbook of Federal Indian Law*, and they further discuss some precedent-setting lawsuits that followed, including *Johnson v. M'Intosh*. Aboriginal title, they say, "is the first of all group or tribal title" and that it is "only the right of exclusive occupancy," and it does not allow occupied land to be convey freely (Case & Voluck 2002). It stems from the aboriginal title doctrine and the fact that people already inhabited places that were being "discovered" by other nations, thus the discovering powers only had title among other European powers. This title was then subject to the interests of aboriginal inhabitants. With this in mind, I will return to the discussion brought up by Garroutte (2003) about who these aboriginal people are, and why.

In her text, Garroutte (2003) takes a proactive approach to many of the concepts by simply addressing what many people may have a hard time even considering. It has been my experience that you often do not consider other ways of thinking about being Native besides the number on your Certificate of Degree of Indian Blood (CDIB). Garroutte states that there is a difference between the legal, biological, cultural and personal definitions of *Native*. It is a bit confusing but makes sense after you think about it. The legal definitions being the ones that are delegated by government and legislation, biological explaining the "blood" makeup of a person, and the cultural describing the ways that people live as Indian people.

Mandating legal definitions of Indian and Native was precedent-setting, and I believe the repercussions of this have been felt within all Native communities. Tribal governments in the United States of America have a unique privilege in that they have the ability to set the rules as to who is recognized as a member, therefore defining who has the ability to participate in the tribes and the programs that are available to them. Other Native entities also do this. For example, the World Eskimo Indian Olympics (WEIO) will not allow you to participate in their events if you are not ¼ Native of some kind, on your Certificate of Degree of Indian Blood (CDIB). Further, you must provide proof of this with your CDIB or an official tribal enrollment card prior to participation in their events. WEIO is just one example; there are many more that span health-care systems, family programs, culture camps, sacred rituals, ceremonies, and even employment opportunities. This degree of blood is also known as "blood quantum," and the way in which many tribes define who is eligible for their services is by blood quantum.

The blood quantum notion is that when two people have a child, that child's blood is made up of their cultural background, based on the ideas that state that biology defines race and culture. For example, if your father is Native and your mother is Native, then you would also be 4/4 Native. However, if your father was Swedish and your mother was Native, you would then be ½ Native. Note that not very often are you defined as half-Swedish. This idea is that the blood mixes to this exact equation and therefore defines you as a Native person. When looked at more closely, it is really kind of absurd. Who says that a person is mixed exactly as in the illustrations in the Bureau of Indian Affairs handbook? Further, what really defines a person as Native? Is it really the legal definition that matters, or is the biological or cultural? And does it vary by situation?

The legal and biological differences are addressed differently in different places throughout the United States. For example, the Santa Clara Pueblo in New Mexico recognizes people of paternal descent; the Seneca people recognize the maternal descent. The Tohono O'Odham give citizenship to any child whose parents both live on the reservation (Garroutte, 2003). This is interesting when you take into consideration things like adoption and how that plays a role in who is accepted into a tribe and allowed to participate within the culture. Garroutte (2003) uses Shania Twain as an example. Twain is recognized as an Anishnabe Indian because her adoptive father was Indian, while her biological parents were not. She became legally recognized as 50 percent Indian after the adoption. Throughout time, being recognized as 50 percent Native has allowed persons of Native descent to be included in certain programs. For instance, in the 1950s only people who were considered "native Hawaiian" by at least 50 percent could participate in the Hawaii Homes Commissions Act (Kauanui 2008).

Today, in 2013, the blood quantum issue is still present. An article published by the Associated Press and reprinted by the *Fairbanks News Miner* (2013) discusses the new health-care plan that will require that all persons who are receiving aide at Indian

Health Care clinics will also need to provide documentation that they are enrolled in one of the 560 tribes recognized by the US Bureau of Indian Affairs (AP 2013). This could be problematic because as mentioned above, there are different stipulations involved in different tribes about who qualifies and who is recognized under their own tribal jurisdiction. Erin Shields, a spokesperson for the U.S. Department of Health and Human Services says that there are almost a half a million Native American people who may be affected by the passing of the Affordable Care Act stipulation that they must be federally recognized. The problem is that some tribes are not recognized by the federal government, only state governments. Also, some tribes do not even enroll people until they are 18 years old and considered an adult. Therefore the language in the bill restricts the participation by people who may be Native, makes them ineligible, and potentially penalizes them for trying to utilize their treaty right to health care under the Indian Health Service. Further, the article lists that about 1/3 of the people who self-identify as American Indian or Alaska Native do not have health insurance. Although some people are voicing support stating people need to show proof, the article leads the reader to believe that more people are upset by the fact that they have to "prove [their] indianness" (Burke 2013).

In my own experience, I have also had to deal with the rules and regulations of being accepted into a tribe. Growing up, my sisters and I were enrolled in the Agdaagux Tribe of King Cove. I am not certain how we ended up being enrolled in that tribe. What I do know is that a year or so before my mom passed away, she was adamant that we needed to be enrolled in the

Belkofski Village Tribe, the tribe that represents the village where she grew up. After she passed, I took it upon myself to enroll us into the Belkofski Tribe. It was a time-consuming process. My sisters and I had to write letters to the Agdaagux Tribal Council asking that we be removed from their rolls. They then contacted us to be sure we wanted to be removed; they had to pass resolutions removing us from their rolls. Next we had to apply to the Belkofski Tribal Council, provide them with our Certificates of Indian Blood and the letters showing we were no longer on the Agdaagux rolls and fill out the applications that stated how we were descendants of the Village of Belkofski. This was done because of the stipulations that you cannot be dual-enrolled. Meaning that in both the Belkofski Tribe and the Agdaagux Tribe there are rules against dual enrollment or being enrolled in more than one tribe.

The legal and cultural precedents are very scary. For example, my son Cohen was born on January 1, 2012. He is 9/32 Native, based on the Bureau of Indian Affairs Calculation table; myself being 9/16 and his father being non-Native. Taking this into consideration, my grandchildren could be anywhere from 9/64 (basically that equates to 1/8), if he has a child with a non-Native, or 41/64 (or 5/8) if he has a child with someone who is 4/4 Native. Therefore, my great-grandchildren could potentially *not* be allowed to join a tribe based on the 1/8 rule depending on Cohen's choice of mate. And if WEIO is still hosting yearly events, they would also not be allowed to participate. On the other hand, my great-great-grandchildren will have no problem being recognized if Cohen 1) has kids with a fully recognized Native woman and 2) his kids also have kids with someone who is at least partially Native, as defined and recognized by the federal government and further by the tribe they are wanting to join. But as I have illustrated above, these rules about becoming recognized are not uniform and not always recognized at multiple levels of government. Also the requirements for participation in services, as well as in activities, are also not always the same.

With this in mind, I have begun to think through the ideas of Indigenous identity and the way I will define myself for my child. In essence, I have always learned about my cultural practices and from that constructed my own personal ideas about being Indigenous. I believe it begins with not only knowing where we come from, but understanding the landscape, the people, and the culture that is attributed to that place. Therefore, I will spend some time discussing exactly this, where we come from, who we are related to, and why this is important.

Cohen and I come from several very large mixed Aleut families who trace their origins to the villages of Pauloff Harbor on Sanak Island, Belkofski on the Alaska Peninsula, and King Cove, which is also located on the Alaska Peninsula. My dad is one of 19 children born to the Paul and Fannie Mack family. My mother was one of ten children, and her mother had 12 or more siblings as well. Since my dad was one of the children born later in the bunch of Macks, when he was born many of his siblings had already moved out and begun families of their own. Because of this, I have first cousins who are much older than me, one of them with great-grandchildren already. Of my dad's siblings, nine of them, including him, are still with us today. On my mother's side, I am the oldest of 27 grandchildren. I grew up babysitting all of the kids younger than myself and really felt as though they were more like siblings than cousins. Sadly, besides an infant that would've been the youngest sibling of my mother, my mother is the only one out of her family that has passed on. Thus, Cohen joins a very large, complicated, loving, and close-knit network of family in the eastern Aleutians.

My son, Cohen Kasux, is named after his maternal great-grandfather on my side, Alex Phillip Kenezuroff. He was one of four children born to Phillip and Annie Kenezuroff. My grandfather or "Ba," as I called him, was born in 1930 in Belkofski, Alaska, and many people called him by his nickname, Kasux. The Unangam Tunuu name Kasux is from the root word *kasulix*—which means to find something, as in, being able to find your seal on the beach when you are hunting. Cohen's great-great-aunt Margaret, Kasux's sister said it meant, "they found him." Besides Margaret and my Ba, there was also a boy name Robert and a girl named Galena, both of whom were older and both of whom died from tuberculosis.

In the old days in Belkofski and in other villages, there were always people who were raised by other families and with other family members. For instance, there is a woman named Irene Christiansen in King Cove who grew up in Belkofski. She has told me many stories about my Ba. However, when she talks about him, she calls him my dad. She talked about going out on the trap line with him and also helping with chores. It seems he was somewhat of a jokester. One time they were supposed to go out and collect alders for firewood, and he was too cold So, he took all of the feathers out of the pillows and stuffed them in his jacket, essentially making himself a nice warm parka. She also tells a story about traveling into the village of Belkofski from the west, which would be coming from King Cove and Cold Bay, where many people hunted for birds and had trap lines. They would travel by power dory and it would take several hours. But when they would get to the one point right outside of the village, my Ba would splash her in the face with saltwater; he had told her that this was good luck.

My Ba was also one of the last speakers of the Aleut language in the Belkofski dialect. He is acknowledged in the Aleut dictionary by Knut Bergsland as a contributor, as are his uncles and cousins. Millie McKeown, the director of the Cultural Heritage Department at the Aleutian Pribilof Islands Association, and a novice speaker of Unangam Tunuu, believes that the Belkofski dialect was one of the older dialects, since some of the words that are documented from there are not found in other dialects.

The village of Belkofski where my grandfather, Cohen's maternal great-grandfather, grew up is now a ghost town. It was established in the 1820s when Aleuts were moved by the Russians from Sanak Island to hunt sea otters. Belkofski became an economic and religious hub for the region. The Russian Orthodox church that was erected there was talked about extensively in travel journals and historic records. It is even included in the 1886 Elliot book.

The church was paid for entirely by sea otter pelts that were hunted by Aleut people. This was above and beyond the pelts that were required as taxes by the Russians. The population of Belkofski declined over time based on economics and also on the opening and closing of the Bureau of Indian Affairs School in the 1970's. Today there are only a handful of houses standing. The church, which was valued at approximately $13,000 in the 1890s, blew down approximately ten years ago. Luckily all of the icons and the embellishments were taken to King Cove, where they are today. As the economy of Belkofski changed from being focused on trapping to fishing, the people of Belkofski moved, many of them following the industry to King Cove, where the cannery was built in 1911. Sadly, in April 2012, some fishermen passing by decided to stop in and burn down every building standing except the Bureau of Indian Affairs school. Charges and investigations are still ongoing.

The people who lived in Belkofski have talked about the ways that they used to live in the village. They talked about the camaraderie that they had within the village. My grandfather and the others would travel by foot or by small skiffs with hand motors they called "power dories" to the trap lines or hunting grounds. They would also go out to what they called the "Sea Lion Rocks." They would go out in groups and would stop at on the island called Outer Iliasiks. There they would hunt for birds called chikanees or *qidungas* in Unangam Tunuu, small birds that nest in the ground that come out at sunset, and they would capture them as they were flying out of the nests. The next morning they would go out to the Sea Lion Rocks or Pinnacle Rocks. There they would get five to seven sea lions per dory that they would then take back to the village to share with everyone. It was common practice for the entire village to participate in butchering and sharing the harvest. The elders said that there was a distinct order for the meat to be handed out. Widows, then elders, hunters, then the rest of the community got their share of the sea lions. It was unspoken but understood by all of those within the community of families, fishers, hunters, and trappers.

Within the community of King Cove where my grandma and Ba moved to in the 1970s, my Ba was a well-respected elder. He was a successful fisherman and then began a career with the City of King Cove running the water-treatment plant. He would go up to the chlorine house daily and make sure that the fluoride and chlorine levels in the water were correct. He did this until he was diagnosed with cancer in 1994 and succumbed to the disease six months later in 1995.

Cohen's paternal great-grandmother on my side was Fannie Mack. She grew up in Pauloff Harbor, a cod-fishing station on Sanak Island located southeast of the Alaska Peninsula. Her father was George Ferguson and her mother was Matrona Ferguson. Her dad emigrated from Nova Scotia in 1886 when he was about 20 years old. The 1910 census says his father was from Scotland and his mother was from Ireland. However, in the 1930 census it has Fannie listed as ½ Norwegian. She was one of five children born to Matrona and George. This is a key point that brings the dialogue of biological versus cultural background, based on what was being reported on the census, the bloodline from my Grandpa George could've been from several places, and now the final say is based on documentation from one person, whose familiarity with the people he was surveying is questionable.

The Union Fish Company, whose headquarters was in San Francisco, built the cod-fishing station in Pauloff Harbor in 1886. Cod-fishing stations in the area began to close around 1930 (Maschner 2010), but the settlement of Pauloff Harbor was inhabited until the 1970s. After the cod industry dissipated, there were some people who actually started a cattle ranch on Sanak Island. The cattle were eventually set free when people moved permanently, and they are now owned by the Sanak Corporation and people go out and hunt them. The cattle survive the winter by going to the beach at low tide and eating the kelp.

Many of the people who came up to fish in the industry came through San Francisco. One of these people was my paternal grandfather, Paul Mack. He was born in Stolp, Germany, in 1883. My dad says that he was a stowaway when he was 11; my uncle recalled that he was 14. He arrived in Pauloff Harbor, married my grandmother, and had 19 children. My grandfather, who was a marine engineer, moved the family from Pauloff Harbor to King Cove in the 1920s, which is where my dad, all his siblings, and many of their kids grew up. The Mack family was one of the largest in King Cove. My dad talks about the way that the house worked. With so many people in the house, they took turns eating. First the men and older boys would eat. Then the kids would eat, and then the women and older girls who had cooked would eat. The Mack house was known for having great hospitality. My dad says that anytime people from neighboring communities would visit King Cove on their boats, they would come to their house for dinner. My Grandma would say, "Add more water to the pot, so-and-so is coming up the boardwalk." Along with there being lots of children in the house, my dad says their house was a big social gathering place. He says that my grandfather used to have a radio and would tune into the baseball games, and he especially liked to listen to the Yankees play. During the World Series, my dad says the house would be full of people there to listen to the games.

In 2011 the community of King Cove held their centennial celebration. I had the honor of going home to King Cove and gathering stories and photographs from the elders in the village to be used as displays for the event. This was a great opportunity for me to learn about the history of the people and the place that I use as one of the defining characteristics of my being. The people of King Cove had some great stories. One person talked about their dad, who was one of my late uncles on the Mack side, always hosting *Kaadax* which is a gambling game, at their house. People would bet money, clothes, boats, guns, fishing settlements, lots of things. It was a huge event. Another elder talked about the windmills that they used to have in King Cove and how their family had purchased glass batteries to store the energy, so even in the early 1920s and 1930s, the people of King Cove had electricity. They also had running water that they had piped to houses from streams on the mountain and wells outside of their homes. It may seem modest but was impressive to me nonetheless. It showed me that people in King Cove have always been forward-thinking and innovative; they were using the resources in the area to build a community that after 100 years is still flourishing. King Cove was settled by people who came to work, fish, and live off the land. For most people commercial fishing and living from the ocean is still providing people the opportunity to live where our ancestors lived. We have access to the same hunting and gathering places used for millennia and we have used them in such a way that our resources are still abundant. We have fish, we have berries, and we have plants and wild game that often appear on the dinner table. Hearing stories about survival and everyday life over the course of peoples' history gave me an understanding of what life was like and has made me appreciate the life lessons that are still taught and important today.

Between these memories and the information that I have collected about Pauloff Harbor, Belkofski, King Cove, and my family tree, I feel like I have been able to get a more holistic understanding of where my roots are. They are more than just the names on paper, they are the memories and the experiences that have been held by my family and been passed down. They have given me a great foundation to build into my personal cultural identity.

Luckily, several generations have been documented on paper, but we are even luckier still to have had people who were willing to share the histories that are not documented on paper and pass down information and lifeways that are understood from the landscape perspective. We have been present on the landscape for thousands of years, and the historical connection is engrained into me. From the smell and sound of the ocean to the knowledge about the plants, animals, and weather patterns, the contributions to what I would define as my Indigenous identity start at home, built by the people who raised me and the environment I was in. Weaver (2001) would call this a type of community identification, where "Indigenous identity is connected to a sense of peoplehood inseparably linked to sacred traditions, traditional homelands, and a shared history as Indigenous people."

It is a combination of knowledge of people, place, and culture, and I am thankful for having had role models that stressed the importance of family and took time to actively teach me about the surrounding environment. Only on paper and in the day-to-day rat race is it defined by a blood quantum. First and foremost, I am a mother, and an Aleut followed by a Belkofski Tribal member, an Aleut Corporation shareholder, a King Cove Corporation shareholder, and then finally, 9/16 ALT, which is what it says on my BIA Certificate of Indian Blood, however, I simply say half.

I know it should go without saying, but I have learned a lot by creating a family tree and taking a more in-depth look at the records. I have had to choose which spellings of names to include and whether or not to include some of the family siblings. As mentioned, the family dynamics present in the Aleutians have not always been the nuclear family structure that is dictated by the census itself. Thus the dynamics and the way that families were defined also had to fit a framework that was introduced. With this in mind, the amount of power that was bestowed upon the census workers is incredible. It was up to them to record and or document the family histories of each and every person. They decided how names were spelled and how they characterized nationalities and occupations. Which brings me back to where we began, with an outside entity defining who and what we are, and which of us could even be considered "Native."

Hilary Weaver (2001) discusses these issues of identity, the labels people use, and how Indigenous identity can be misrepresentative. She notes that often people have been defined from a non-Native perspective. It is actually taking the dominant way of thinking and applying it systematically across the board. However, it takes a much closer look to realize that not only are cultures different, there are different practices within families and other groups that may also contribute to a person's own Indigenous identity. These are often not considered in the greater scheme of things.

The ways in which those of the greater public define us is not always the way we have been defined. Thinking through what Indigenous identity means and how it affects us as Native people is important and imperative for the future. We need to address questions about how race and ethnicity must be considered when discussing sovereignty or Indigenous rights. It has been taken for granted, even by myself, that blood quantum is a part of who I am. But why? At the end of the day it is simply is dominant way of thinking. A precedent was set, and so it has become acceptable to be used as a defining characteristic. Scholars like Weaver have asked who does get to define what Native is? And even though we do have personal ties to our Indigenous identity, may times, as you see, we default to that dominant discourse. We need to have discussions about our histories and future simultaneously.

Like culture, identity itself is not static, and changes as a person's own perception of themselves changes (Weaver 2001). In exploring who my family is, I have discovered that blood quantum is a flawed classification system. I do not have an answer as to what is the best way to define a Native person, but I do know that the blood quantum classification system is outdated and inaccurate—with no biological basis, biased and misrepresentative of many of the qualities that I think make you Native. Hopefully, as we continue these discussions, we can get to a place where we can find a suitable alternative. Until then, I will take Cohen home to King Cove as often as I can, where his Papa Barney can teach him how to fillet, cut, dry, jar, and smoke salmon; his aunties can teach him which plants are edible and how to tell when berries are ripe, teaching him the phrases in Aleut they grew up hearing. His Krusnax or godmother will take him to church in a building that houses icons that are over 100 years old (that were purchased with sea otter pelts by his ancestors) where they sing in Slavic and Aleut. Kasux (as my son calls himself) can watch the tides and know when it is safe to dig clams. He will learn how to catch and clean an octopus and probably watch the tentacles as it tries to climb out of the sink. Most likely while he is visiting at his Papa Barney's he will be listening to the traditional Scandinavian music of his great-grandfather and also to the fishermen at the table talk about the weather as they play cribbage. All of this considered, at the end of the day, being present on the landscape and understanding how to survive on it far outweigh any notion of blood quantum.

Endnotes

i   William Laughlin (1980) explains that the term *Aleut* is of uncertain origin. The Aleut people refer to themselves as Unangan, in Unangam Tunuu (Aleut Language), which means "seasider" or "people who live by the sea" (Bergsland

1994). Recently there has been discussion among some politically active groups to change the name of the group from Aleut to Unangax̂ or Unangan depending on whether or not the word is being used to define one or many. The origin of the word *Aleut* is not known specifically, but is and has been used widely since the arrival of Russians in the 18th century. One of the issues people have with using the term is that it was so widely used, the peoples who were not of Unangax̂ descent were also fit under the Aleut umbrella term. In many cases the terms can be and are used interchangeably, but in this paper, I will mostly use Aleut, since it is what I identify with and what I was raised to understand. This is a personal preference, not representative of anyone else's views. However, when speaking about the language, I do refer to it as Unangam Tunuu.

ii This *x* in Unangam Tunuu has a ^ over the top of it, which is referred to as a circumflex. This symbol indicates the harder guttural sound that should be made when speaking many words in Unangam Tunuu.

References

Bergsland, K. (1994). *Aleut Dictionary: Unangam Tunudgusii.* Fairbanks: Alaska Native Language Center, University of Alaska Fairbanks

Black, L. T. (1995). *History and Ethnohistory of the Aleutians East Borough.* Kingston, OT: Limestone Press. p. 95.

Burke, G. (2013, May 13). Health reforms penalize some Indians, Native Alaskans. *Fairbanks Daily News Miner. Associated Press.* Retrieved from: <http://www.newsminer.com/news/alaska_news/health-reforms-penalize-some-indians-native-alaskans/article_d805cc98-bc08-11e2-a857-0019bb30f31a.html>

Case, D. & Voluck, D. (2002). *Alaska Natives and American Laws.* Fairbanks, AK : University of Alaska Press.

Elliott, H. W. (1886) *Our Arctic Province.* New York: Charles Scribner's Sons. pg. 121; Google eBook.

Garroutte, E. M. (2003). *Real Indians: Identity and the Survival of Native America.* Berkeley: University of California Press.

Kauanui, J. K. (2008). *Hawaiian Blood: Colonialism and the Politics of Sovereignty and Indigeneity.* Durham: Duke University Press.

Reedy-Maschner, K. & Maschner, H. (Eds.). (2012). *Sanak Island, Alaska: A Natural and Cultural History.* Pocatello, ID: Idaho Museum of Natural History.

Laughlin, W. S. (1980). *Aleuts: Survivors of the Bering Land Bridge.* New York: Holt, Rinehart and Winston.

Weaver, H. N. (2001). *Indigenous Identity: What is it and who really has it.* American Indian Quarterly. 0095182X, Vol. 25, Issue 2, Spring.

Bush Justice Unplugged: The Road Taken and the Research Trail Left Behind

Stephen Conn

Bush justice is the historical interplay between state and village law; both are critical to defining behavior and resolving problems in rural Alaskan villages. This was the focus of my teaching and research from 1968 until 2009.[1] For the discipline of Alaska Native Studies, the subject of bush justice serves as an interdisciplinary lodestone, drawing upon Alaska Native experiences with the territorial and state legal systems, especially with regard to alcohol problems.

I brought important lessons to Alaska, gleaned from time spent with the Navajo tribe and in Brazilian squatter colonies, there studying their internal real property laws (Conn 1969). These were, briefly, that more than one law can influence behavior and problem solving at the same place and at the same time, that the relationship between these laws and its history is best understood by local residents who receive and adapt to ever-changing postures by outside law imposed on them, and, finally, that for both legal processes to work together, links between each can and are best forged by people and institutions on the ground, often what the official system would term "paraprofessionals," literate in each law. I will examine these premises and show how I attempted to put them into play in Alaska.

Drawing on what might be termed "legal pluralism," I conducted field experiments with bicultural legal education, created with bush teachers, village problem (or conciliation)

boards that replicated village council legal process, and
Alaska Native paralegals, trained and placed with state justice
agencies and Alaska Legal Services (Vicenti, Jimson, Conn, &
Kellogg 1972; Barthel, McDearman, & Conn 1977; Conn &
Hippler 1973a, 1974a, 1974b, 1974c; Conn 1980). None of
these induced permanent and positive state change, nor did
comparative studies I did and reported on in Alaska about rural
justice experiences in Canada, Greenland, Australia, and Brazil.
During my tenure, Alaska justice agencies resisted formal power
sharing with villages, however useful. But new generations of
scholars can take up the challenges. And Alaska Native Studies
is an appropriate haven for such research, better because its
constituents are Alaska Natives and not justice agencies. In a
project to place both published and unpublished works online,
I have learned many new things by reviewing my own materials
in the University of Alaska Anchorage (UAA) archives and
watching my own thinking and efforts evolve. Perhaps future
students of bush justice will learn from my efforts at reform.

First, more than one law can exist at the same place and
at the same time. One law may have official dominance, but
the other may draw informal authority from official law as well,
because it can get the job done and because it is closer to and
followed by the local people. That second law may be called
"traditional," "village," or even, "squatters' law" (as in Brazil,
where it guides all matters pertaining to real estate in squatter
colonies not considered legal by the state) (Conn 1969). Both
laws are important. When a person schooled (or "literate") in
one system of law confronts a problem defined by a second legal
system, someone must help that person understand his or her

rights in the second law, using the law he or she knows as a comparative guide. From that discovery came, first, an effort both in Ramah, New Mexico, and again in Alaska, to develop bicultural legal education instruction (Vicenti et al. 1972; Barthel et al. 1977). The Navajo (and, later, the Alaskan) project was made of students, their parents' educators, teaching them to deal with relevant consumer, family, and community problems as defined by formal law through the prism of traditional law, tracing the history of that second form of law. Students also learned about official law; they also developed an appreciation for traditional law, which they may have perceived as "old-fashioned" or no longer relevant. They learned about the history of traditional law and its roots in the historical experiences of their people with both legal systems. So *Law of the People* (Vicenti et al. 1972) was directed at problems confronted by Navajo people and directed to young people who often helped adults literate in Navajo legal culture when their new problems arose. The second purpose of bicultural legal education was to teach young people the contemporary relevance of both legal cultures and how to use comparative law instrumentally to make wise choices for themselves (Conn 1982). *Alaska Natives and the Law* (Barthel et al. 1977) served the same purposes.

Second, local people who recognize that more than one law may be "happening" at the same time in the same place can do more to help people deal with their problems than those who are expert in one law only and blind (or indifferent) to a second legal culture. Navajo men and women hired to work with we poverty law attorneys as interpreter-investigators were taught relevant American and formal tribal law but were already expert in traditional law or had ready access to it from their elders. These, perhaps America's first paralegals, could better communicate with all clients who came in the office of legal services, be they desirous of a Western approach or solution to their problem or a traditional one (Conn & Hippler 1973a). I came to Alaska with the proven idea that Indigenous non-lawyers could do a better job than lawyers in welding both systems together just as then–Alaskan Chief Justice George Boney seemed to desire (Alaska Judicial Council 1970). And, of course, no better examples of these legal-culture brokers existed in the Alaska judicial system than District Court Judge Nora Guinn of Bethel and Barrow magistrate Sadie Neakok. I worked and learned from both and watched each in action. What I did not understand was that these women were used for the convenience of the state judicial system until it could implant legal professionals in both Bethel and Barrow.

Third, law, whether modern or traditional, is more than rules; it is a process or approach to a problem and its resolution. On the Navajo reservation many problems were solved at the hogan level; tribal courts were usually reserved for cases brought by the police or social service workers. The traditional approach was called by many names—mediation, conciliation, peace making, etc. It was well described in anthropological literature about Navajo people and was often used even by Navajo judges when an appropriate case came before them. My early Alaskan research showed traditional law's continuing role and relevance among small Athabascan and northern Eskimo villages (Hippler & Conn 1972, 1973a). In fact, it had been institutionalized by teachers, missionaries, and even the Indian Bureau in Indian

Reorganization Act councils (Peratrovich 1973). Extralegal village councils worked in tandem with commissioners, marshals and, later, with the early troopers assigned to the bush (Nix 1973; Hippler & Conn 1975). I learned about the Alaskan village council process by reading decades of council records, sitting in on council sessions, and interviewing council members, past and present.

Fourth, both laws have a history of working together, and the ones who best remember how both worked together (or failed to do so) were usually the consumers of law, not the ever-changing crop of professional legal representatives. This legal history—as a history of interaction between modern and traditional community law—was important, but history was and is a moving train. It does not start when one gets on (is hired) or stop when one gets off (retires). It was incumbent for representatives of the state system to learn about the past and its impact on current perceptions of the appropriate roles for state and village law. This history was grounded in hard facts and not in ideology, but was not taught in law schools or in police academies.

Local law is affected by the historical role of the state or federal law and the messages received from representatives of this powerful force. Bearers of traditional law learn to bend this outside power to their own needs or to deflect it—as when a traditional Navajo chief, Chee Dodge, became an Indian policeman and told the community after the return to the reservation under military occupation that the white man had given them "a long rope" (Williams 1970, p. 14).

A working relationship between traditional justice—whatever it is called or in whatever package it is wrapped—and powerful resources of state, federal, or official tribal law can make the entire legal process work for everyone's benefit. I have called this continuum different things at different times. For example, in a 1985 paper (Conn), I described it as consisting of three components—nonlegal social control, extralegal authority, and Western police, judicial, and correctional services. The pragmatic, working links are the most important thing—between towns and villages, between villages, between the state system and local system, between the past and the present, between professionals and locals, and between urban and rural legal processes. The lesser-empowered have a better sense of legal history than the newcomers who represent the more powerful law and use that knowledge to manipulate the system's impact on them whenever they can—for example, when Navajo chiefs become police or when Alaska Natives use the cover afforded councils or magistrates by state authority to reinforce a traditional legal approach or result. The local people have a better sense of the limits of that system than do the state representatives, especially the credibility of what they can do in the eyes of their own community and the limits of their authority based on their ability to access resources—for example, to successfully obtain a rapid response from the troopers when alcohol-related violence occurs.

Along with village council records from territorial days, I studied the records of official law in the bush (Conn 1977). Few, if any, modern agents of law are required to dig into these same archives to understand their historical roles as police or judges. They fly to a village with a message framed by their higher-ups or taught to them in academies or in law schools. On the other hand, villagers have seen agents of law come and go for generations. They have taken their promises, their threats, and their recommendations and, sometimes, written them down. They have adapted their traditional approaches to the ebb and flow of modern law and what it was realistically prepared to do at the local level, as best they could. By exploiting states' grants or authority, whether formal or informal, they have strengthened their own local authority (Conn 1976a). They also watched the relationship fail them in modern times as their ties to the larger world and its problems became more ubiquitous and their ties to the modern legal system became less predictable or reliable.

State and territorial law had been impacted by the local law tradition because overwhelmed professionals had often put it to use as a local problem solver, usually informally, not out of respect but out of convenience (Nix 1973). Early officials invented legal agents like "Native Police" or "Agents for Suppression of Alcohol among the Natives" that modern legal professionals would not recognize. So legal history of both systems matters—but the rural consumers of law are most aware of the relationships over time, their strengths and deficiencies. A flow of conferences on bush justice in Alaska and their recommendations documents this special knowledge (Alaska Judicial Council 1970; Alaska Legal Services Corporation 1974; McKenzie 1976; Alaska Federation of Natives 1985). All professionals in charge of each legal bureaucracy had to do was to listen and read these recommendations.

What I learned, first, from records of the Association of Village Council Presidents from the late 1960s was that members had told every agent of state and federal law they encountered that the councils needed more reliable police intervention when people did not listen to the councils. The councils did not ask for the state to provide all of the law, but to live up to its promises when the councils could not handle a problem, especially a problem that could become violent. From those records (republished in *No Need of Gold*, Conn & Moras 1986), I learned the Fairbanks district attorney helped draft village rules, each backed by a state law violation. If the person did not listen and abide by the council's advice, he promised, the Bethel trooper would intervene at the council's request. Of course there was only a single trooper in the Bethel region, and the letters he received (which I read in his office) told the same story as did the recommendations of statewide bush justice conferences over many years: the state could not and did not hold up its end of the deal. Again and again, consumers told a parade of agency representatives (and scholars) what the failings of village justice were. They tried to make up for deficiencies in state service by becoming more court-like but were boxed in by an absence of resources and the state's resistance to either shared jurisdiction, whether or not villages were cast as Alaskan second-class cities or as Alaskan tribes.

What I created for Alaska and the Alaska State Supreme Court in the early 1970s were "action plans" that connected each agency in the justice system to the village council (or another body capable of conciliation or mediation; see below) through paralegals in the villages capable of working both as locally supported authorities and as agents of state authority, be it judicial, in corrections and probation, in defense or in prosecution or in law enforcement (Conn & Hippler 1973b; Conn 1976b). Judicially and locally approved magistrates were to be used to keep a level of state judicial authority in the village. I knew it could be done because I had seen it work in Navajo country. Also, earlier relationships between troopers and councils had worked—until they were overwhelmed by alcohol importation and return of juveniles to villages for year-round residence, paracorrectional aides could supervise juveniles and probationers, for example, with the backing of the magistrate and councils. Lay advocates could argue for the prosecution and defense. My focus was on a working state system that would extend its authority to villages and limit its intervention to requests necessary to sustain village authority (Conn 1974). Village authority could anticipate violent crimes often associated with alcohol, save the state money, and make justice a daily, living reality in small villages. Many elements of this plan were field-tested. By the time that national experts on criminal justice were called upon to write the guiding document for the Criminal Justice Center at the University of Alaska (Strecher, Hoover, George, & Fox 1974), my plan for a complete, decentralized justice system at the village level, linked both to agents of state and village authority, became the guiding rationale for a bush justice component with the center (and the probable reason I was hired). (See appendix).

Professor Art Hippler and I experimented in Emmonak with what we had called a conciliation board to retain, officially, within the state system the historical approach to disputes used by the village councils (but not by the actual village council, which by then was focused on land-claims issues). We had several advantages. First, Bethel District Court Judge Nora Guinn understood the underlying process, embraced it, and even renamed conciliation boards in Yup'ik as "problem boards." Second, former council members who had worked on local problems wanted to be members of the problem board. Third, it was connected to a Yupik village magistrate and an educated, locally raised trooper constable who was both Yupik and a former Seabee held in great esteem. Each was prepared to refer appropriate matters to the problem board. Fourth, along with an *UCLA-Alaska Law Review* article (Conn & Hippler 1975), we publicized accounts of the experiment in two national legal magazines, *Judicature* and *Juris Doctor* (Conn & Hippler 1974a, 1974b) and compared and contrasted it to the then-fashionable and federally funded urban Neighborhood Justice Centers and their work. This made it hard for the state court system to ignore. We reported the results to the state Supreme Court (Conn & Hippler 1974c). The problems heard by problem boards were prelegal and anticipated violent behavior. How did the court react? It tried the experiment but initially cut out Emmonak (until we complained). It cut out local researchers entirely, hiring a national arbitration center to retrain Natives on how to solve their own problems! The court placed its own experiment into six villages (Alaska Court System 1975). Important links to local police and magistrates were not developed. The critical local context of each board within a larger village-state system was ignored.

As might be expected, the court's own experiment attracted few problems and failed except in Emmonak, which handled half of the reported matters. An official evaluation by a prominent lawyer and legal anthropologist said the process failed to replace courts (!) and had privacy and due-process issues (Marquez & Sedately 1977). In other words, the evaluators measured it against the wrong standards—its own, and not those of the traditional process. Thirty-three years late, early intervention to head off violence is again in vogue in the American legal culture as an alternative to court appearances. Once again, some form of mediation of embryonic problems before each turns violent, one that uses peer pressure and gossip as well as formal legal support to give it credibility, could be set in place within a state court system. Whether it is called a Peacemaker Court, a Healing Circle, or was an approach used by the handful of Alaska Native magistrates left in the state judicial system, it could still help both the village and the state.

In a second experiment in the 1970s, the Department of Law and Public Defender Agency in Bethel and Nome used to good effect—according to reports of their trainers—paralegal investigators, as did Alaska Legal Services in Barrow (Conn 1980). These positions disappeared when federal job-training funding disappeared. Permanent funding decisions were made in Anchorage and Juneau, not in the bush. Each bush office always needed more lawyers, even though the paralegals created new and reliable links to the villages. In the meantime, I helped the Criminal Justice Center to educate paralegals for private practitioners who came to value paralegals for monetary reasons. I developed courses and taught on live television to rural towns like Kodiak and Nome in that pre-Internet age. These paralegals took career positions in urban law firms.

The Navajo had taught me that non-lawyers with knowledge of local law can navigate the dual processes better than professionals to meet consumers' needs. I and my legal-services peers transformed Navajos hired as interpreter-investigators into tribal court advocates who could determine whether clients wanted Western or Navajo-grounded remedies. As stated, I took this enthusiasm for paralegals to Alaska. But, as I now realize, I overplayed a valid historical argument by telling Alaska legal professionals that nonprofessionals in Alaska had taken up the lion's share of legal work since the purchase from Russia, because professionals had limited access to distant villages (Conn & Hippler 1973a). I consulted with several magistrate advisory committees created by the court system and composed of rural lawyers. Their work, now available for study in the UAA archives, demonstrates that professionals did not perceive Alaska Native magistrates, including Magistrate Sadie Neakok and District Court Judge Nora Guinn, as productive legal-culture brokers, but as embarrassments and threats to due process—even when the formal justice system was far away in towns or cities and would remain there for reasons of cost and caseload (Second Magistrate Advisory Committee 1989). The professionals did not want to travel to appear before nonprofessionals. Neither did the court want to travel or bring potential jurors from villages to town. Jury selection stopped in many villages. Magistrate posts in villages where Native non-lawyers held the posts were reduced. The court system retreated from villages.

Alcohol policy had guided Western law imposed on Alaska Natives from the Russians to statehood (Conn & Moras 1986). Historic and modern legal policy was examined, along with the impact of town-based decisions to go wet or dry on surrounding villages, dividing the villages based on alcohol-related violence reported in hospital records, records far better than crime statistics. The state legal process failed to keep up with changes as problems increased. (Remember, villages had warned the state in the late '60s of their own diminishing power without adequate external support.) Decriminalization of public intoxication drove violent drinking behavior indoors in towns and villages. The state failed to appreciate the impact on what we termed "satellite villages" by denying them any legal say in town decisions to go wet or dry, even when hospital statistics demonstrated exactly which villages were impacted by changes in town policies in Bethel and which were not. Changes in demographics and improvements in transportation and communication all had policy implications that the state failed to translate into needed legal-policy changes and allocation of state resources. The villages knew they were part of a larger region when it came to alcohol-related violence and its consequences—but it did not matter.

In the 1970s, after discussing the ways Alaska Natives handled disputes, we advocated ways to make that happen productively with a modern justice system—paralegals and mediation panels. With Antonia Moras (1986) and Bonnie Boedeker (1983), I studied the ways that alcohol control had influenced Alaska law and the actual legal experiences of Alaska Natives in historical and in modern times (Conn 1977; Conn

& Boedeker; Conn & Moras 1986). In the 1980s I focused on publishing articles on why these experiments had failed (Conn 1988). At least one reason was the failure of the Alaska judiciary to trust that rural Alaskans had answers to their own problems. The state court came to model itself on modern court administration—what I now term the *Snowden effect*, named for the first modern court administrator in Alaska and his influence on the shape of the court system (Conn 1980, 1988). In the 1990s I tried to reform each branch of the justice system, linking studies on corrections, juries, and policing to historical and modern studies to matters being litigated in state court. In each instance I testified as an expert. What I presented to the courts or opposing counsel was the history of corrections or jury selection or policing in the bush. In each instance I was challenged because my research seemed neither legal nor anthropological. What it was, was a retelling of the history of Alaska legal culture in the bush—the way a government had behaved as consumers of justice services in the bush experienced it. In one case against the state I drew attention to the absence of correctional services in the bush to supervise probationers in a case brought by one of several seriously wounded and killed victims of a person who had been placed in a small Native village without state supervision (*Division of Corrections v. Neakok* 1986; Conn 1976b). The state eventually settled when confronted with a likely trial in Kotzebue. Did the then–Department of Corrections remedy the situation with paracorrectional aides it had previously used in the bush? No. Corrections brought probationers into the cities where they could be conveniently supervised even if recidivism was likely for persons plucked out of their rural homes. I was forced to conclude Alaska Native recidivism was better for state policy makers than lawsuits against the Department of Corrections or use of paracorrectional aides in the villages.

In other lawsuits, defendants argued that their cases had not been heard by juries of their peers because potential jurors from many villages were never called. My research (Conn 1995) had shown that 128 villages had been excluded for jury pools. This included exclusion of 3,300 Alaska Native jurors for reasons of cost, 3,704 Natives for reason of distance from the court, according to rules set by presiding judges of superior courts, and 2,648 potential jurors because they were assigned to what I termed "phantom court locations"—places denominated as potential court locations where neither magistrates, nor district or superior courts ever held court. The results? Court findings for the state and against jury participation for as many as 24 percent of Alaska Natives in the Fourth Judicial District— except when called as a victim, defendant, or witness to a trial in regional centers (Conn 1995).

When the Native American Rights Fund tried to use an equal-protection argument against the state to remedy unequal law enforcement in the villages, I showed that the use of non-police—unarmed Village Public Safety Officers— followed a long-standing approach to law enforcement dating from territorial police and copied in recent years from a long-abandoned Canadian program of using Native police to extend the reach of "real police" (Conn 1999, 2000). The court decided against the Association of Village Council Presidents.

Apparently only political clout or the resources to remove oneself from the unorganized borough known as "the bush" can force the state to try other approaches. Eban Hopson possessed sufficient tax revenues and political muscle to allow his Arctic Slope region to break the stranglehold of the trooper monopoly on law enforcement and within the state's system of justice. And foreign models—such as the Canadian model of regular traveling courts (Morrow 1974) or Royal Canadian Mounted Police postings in every northern settlement serve only when they meet the needs of individual justice bureaucracies within the justice system. Reliable service seems secondary to an illusion of a modern state justice system that meets the needs of each centralized justice bureaucracy. Thus, the action plans that evolved into the Strecher plan of decentralized rural justice (Strecher et al. 1974) was a nonstarter for a state criminal justice center, even before the ink dried. See Endnote iii.

Each branch of the justice system focused on its own self-interest and not on construction of a complete and working village justice system. With Chief Justice George Boney's death soon after I arrived in Alaska and the appointment of the court's first modern administrator, the court system looked to professionalize and base itself in cities and towns. Thus, despite many attempts to improve the magistrate system and link it to the process through circuit riding, portable jails, etc., by magistrate supervisor and former bush trooper William Nix, the court ultimately reduced the number of magistrates and, with that, direct Alaska Native participation. To counter an Alaska Judicial Council report (1975) to transform official judicial districts into cultural regions reflective of the regional corporation boundaries, the court created service areas in towns that did draw in residential representational and prosecutorial services but left outlying communities without retention votes when judges outside of their official judicial district were appointed. The court was happy with judicial districts drawn when riverboat traffic, not jets, was the way that legal professionals and citizens moved around the Alaskan landscape and feared new districts drawn around Alaska Native cultures in the bush.

Juvenile services remained inadequate, and attempts to link professional services to parents committee (such as the one we set up in Selawik) failed (Conn 1985). This failure to respond to a major demographic shift when juveniles were allowed to stay in villages to attend high school may have had a dramatic impact on the success of village education. The troopers continued to employ para-police, long used in other colonial domains, to hold down its turf by placing unarmed informants (called "bush trackers" in the Australian outback) to be their resident eyes and ears, displacing village authority and its ability to act— entirely. Regional corporations made these Village Public Safety Officers their employees, wittingly or unwittingly weakening the historical link between village authorities and state police.

AFN's Bush Justice Implementation Committee had advocated municipal courts in the mid-1970s (Case 1977). But as villages began to see their powers as tribal, rather than derived from Alaska, the state, Bart Garber, and I suggested that tribal powers must be used or they would be lost (Conn & Garber 1981). The Indian Child Welfare Act (1978) brought some limited Congressionally mandated approval of Alaska tribal justice to the fore, but the state fought its expansion (Case 1984). The late Senator Ted Stevens seemed committed to killing off official tribal authority at the village level and wanted regional corporations, not villages, to be empowered, perhaps capable of placing restrictions on land use and exploitation of subsurface holdings. He employed a revisionist history to kill off the jurisdictional concept of Indian Country in a successful *amicus* brief before the US Supreme Court, and created a "rural," not a tribal, preference as a Congressional substitute for the extinguishment of aboriginal hunting and fishing rights by ANCSA (Conn & Langdon 1988; Conn & Garber 1990). Still, I have argued that any village could take on federal recognition and even pass the tough historical litmus test that requires evidence of ongoing tribal self-government, no matter what the external opposition is to it, because the historical record of self-governance is thorough in Alaska and very well documented (Conn 1987). Coauthored papers on potential tribal authority in Alaska by Conn and Garber (1990) and Conn and Langdon (1988) deserve attention. Each shows how the history of Alaskan tribal self-governance deserves to be put to use again to solve local problems and to weigh into the subsistence controversy.

Conclusion: The Road Not Taken in Alaska

The Navajo legal system was able to evolve on its own terms in part because the tribe had learned how to manipulate the relationship between sovereigns who competed with it. Arizona, where most of the tribe lives on a reservation, had no abiding desire to take over the job of law and order on the reservation. In that Public Law 280 state, it had no capacity to tax tribal members or property and no desire to spend money if not reimbursed by the federal government. It was happy to cross-deputize Navajo police and let them take cases to Arizona magistrates as well as to tribal courts. When an Arizona creditor contended that he needed to use an Arizona court to collect a debt incurred on the reservation because the Navajo tribe had no civil code and civil court, the tribe and its legislative branch set about inventing a civil code before the case reached the United States Supreme Court (*Williams v. Lee* 1959). When I examined Navajo tribal council transcripts from the period, I found that members modified suggestions made by their tribal attorney (Conn 1978). Tribal judges were to be selected from among those steeped in both traditional and Western legal process, even if the candidates were less trainable than younger men and women with higher education. The same was true of police. Items to be seized to pay debts were not to include sheep, this based on experience with federal sheep seizures in the 1930s to avoid overgrazing. In short, the tribe invented a civil law system it did not need as a kind of movie set to show the skeptical United States Supreme Court that it had a civil code that looked like other civil codes. But it appointed persons to man that system who were prepared to adapt it to the legal pluralism alive and well on the reservation in the late 1950s.

The paralegals we had trained in the late 1960s as investigator-interpreters and as tribal court advocates continued to work in both systems. Years later a Navajo bar was established, and both lawyers and paralegals had to be licensed by it and take a bar exam. As Navajo men and women attended law school, they joined the ranks of this bar. A Navajo law graduate eventually took over the DNA—Dinébe'iiná Náhiiłna be Agha'diit'ahii, or "attorneys who work for the economic revitalization of the People"—the same Navajo legal services for which I worked in the late 1960s and early 1970s. The Navajo approach to dispute resolution at the hogan level—very close to what I had found among the Alaskan Athabascan at the village level in 1972—was institutionalized into a peacemaker component of the tribal court system as that tribal court system became more Westernized to meet the modern legal needs of Navajo and non-Navajo litigants.

Reservation Indians lack jurisdiction over felonies. These cases are sent to the federal courts. The federal government has never shown a great interest in prosecuting felonies on the reservation. So Navajo justice had taken up most crimes as misdemeanors. But the level of punishment for many crimes has been kept very low until the tribe was ready to increase it:

> People who possess liquor on the Navajo Nation, for example, would be fined $500 on the first offense. The current penalty for a first-time offense is a $50 fine. The penalty for shoplifting under the proposal would include jail time and fines, and would depend on the value of the goods taken.
>
> A conviction for receiving stolen property could net a punishment of 180 days and a $500 fine, while contributing to the delinquency of a minor would change from no jail time or fine to a maximum of 180 days in jail and a $1,000 fine . . ..
>
> The list of 30 offenses, once allowed to result in no jail time, because of law of resources, were now made jailable. (Fonseca 2013)

The Alaska penal code is defined and amended far away in Juneau. Village ordinances cannot be pursued because villagers lack the resources to enforce them, resources that must include provision for professional prosecution and defense and detention facilities that meet state standards. The villages are priced out of the legal system. Where Alaska has substituted mandatory sentences for judicial discretion, a rural judge cannot address local concerns when he or she sentences—as in the past. An option for community input that I advocated in the 1970s has been lost (Hippler & Conn 1973b).

Tribal and Alaskan village authority share a common trait. Both must be used to be retained, even if both the state and village want to share in the work. As future advocates for bush justice continue the work I and so many others began, it matters not whether village authority is based on internationally recognized group rights, federal Indian law, or state authority. The historical record demonstrates that a relationship flourished when it was reliable and, perhaps, because an absence of state resources to take on the whole job gave field operatives more latitude. The challenge, then, is for the state to see this same working relationship as worth funding to deal with modern problems brought into the village by modern infrastructures. Alaska must want to serve village Alaska and must end its concern with competing sovereigns.

Attacks on any advocate of hybrid reforms that reject neither state nor tribal responsibility for village justice can be anticipated. Many advocates of tribal rights see attempts to meld both systems into one as simply a return to colonialism. Pragmatism is equated with defeatism. As I drew on the experience of disempowered people to learn tactics of reempowerment and survival, I never intended for citizens to lose their legal rights wherever they chose to live in Alaska. Today, accessible justice is used as an excuse for lack of access to due process. Small and local is not always "beautiful" for all people and the remedies they seek (Conn 1978). The central idea for bush-justice reforms was to give villagers options, including those provided urban Alaskans. But, as I discovered, the overall "look" of Alaska state justice as typical American justice trumps the state's ability to meet the diverse challenges of the bush. Just as the United States Supreme Court wanted to see a Navajo system of civil law that looked like the one it was used to seeing when it heard *Williams v. Lee* (1959), so, also, do Alaskan legal professionals seem to want the image of an American system of law in the bush, whether or not it serves the needs of the people who live there.

Endnotes

i. Interdisciplinary "bush justice" makes difficult a discoverable, full bibliography before Alaska Native Studies became a defined discipline. Many papers were unpublished or were contained in memos directed to international jurists or to justice personnel, including several chief justices of the Alaska State Supreme Court. But this problem is now set to be resolved as work, both published and unpublished, that I did during my tenure will be available online at http://:justice.uaa.alaska.edu/publications/authors/conn/ and stephenconn-ak.com. My plan is to archive and place online unpublished materials in a manner that will allow future students to make use of them. I am including in the collection not only published pieces, but also unpublished letters and memos directed at members of the state justice community, memos and letters to my colleagues, and unpublished interviews with justice personnel, including troopers, correctional officers, defense attorneys, and prosecutors. For example, many reports on alcohol policy and its impact were unpublished. So this article is a "teaser" of sorts. Its editorial message is, "Read the original research, once it is placed online, that led to the conclusions expressed here."

ii. George Boney, the late chief justice, focused on bush justice and was inclined not only to lead the court's administration, but the entire justice system. A political animal, he chaired Governor's Commission on the Administration of Justice meetings that divided federal Law Enforcement Assistance grants (meetings that I attended). Other criminal-justice bureaucracies did not seek that leadership, but the LEAA desk sought a coordinated vision of criminal-justice outcomes. Chief Justice Jay Rabinowitz, Boney's successor, was a dedicated constitutional scholar with no administrative pretentions or interests. Art Snowden, who roomed with Rabinowitz when they visited bush Alaska, was a perfect fit for Rabinowitz and other justice bureaucracies with their own urban and rural agenda, set forth in criminal-justice plans of that era. In a personal discussion with Jay about a recent visit by an Australian aborigine, he told me he viewed their traditional law as "a flaming spear in the leg." In addition, Alaska's early state legal history included a minor scandal involving an Alaskan chief justice who was said to have meddled overly much in management (this is outside the scope of this paper). Separation of administration and judging was the new and desired direction for Alaska's state court system.

iii. Unpublished Final Report of Recommendations: A Criminal Justice Center for Alaska (Strecher, Hoover, George & Fox, 1974, pp. 110-114)

Bush Justice Programs
- Constable Training
- Village Para-Legal Training
  - Magistrate Training
  - Village Advocate Training
- Probation Aide Training

The Bush Justice Program design is a result of Alaska's cultural diversity, population distribution patterns, and specific criminal justice problems at the village level.

1. The categories under the Bush Justice heading are programmatic, rather than discrete assignments for individual personnel. In fact, it is intended that a "Village Criminal Justice Team" concept be established. Within this concept, the native CJ personnel of a given village would proceed through the four phases of training together (at times separated for their special role-concept training). This design feature resulted from Eskimo and Indian comments to the consultants, which revealed the social pressures and isolation accorded village policemen, and other CJ practitioners, because of family and social ties in small communities. It is the judgment of the consultants that team training will establish a climate of professional, mutual support among village team members. The individual role requirements

of independence and advocacy will have to be carefully built into the training programs.

2. The four phases of Village Criminal Justice Team training grew out of the realities of geography and multi-ethnicity of the State's rural areas. While the Assistant Director for Bush Justice Programs should occupy an office on the Anchorage campus, much of the program will be accomplished in distant satellite training centers, or in the rural work settings of the trainees. In Year One, the Assistant Director should use census data to determine the number of village teams to be trained, and prepare a calendar for completion of the four-phased program for all villages in the State, with allowances for turnover.

a. Phase 1. Centralized Core Program

1. Village CJ Teams are brought to a training center (Anchorage, Fairbanks, or Sitka) for about two weeks of intensive basic training. Concentration should be upon subject-matter common to all of the four roles in the village team (substantive and procedural law; elemental records-keeping; ameliorative skills; procedures for serious offenses; role-learning and differentiation).

2. A question to explore is whether more than one ethnic group can be taught in the same course. If not, programming should contemplate a number of village teams from the same Eskimo or Indian group at any given time, with specific months of the year allocated to ethnic groups. Center staffing level will not permit more than one class at a time, but should permit coverage of several villages.

b. Phase 2. Decentralized Core Program

1. After having returned to their villages and performed rudimentary duties as a village CJ team, the team would be transported to a regional training center for an additional two to three weeks of intensive training. The regional centers would preferably be located on the community college campuses nearest the ethnic population centers; however, other governmental facilities might have to be used.

2. If community colleges provide the setting for this training, a faculty member might be designated as part-time coordinator of this phase of the program, and perhaps the Phase 4 work as well.

c. Phase 3. Traveling On-Job-Training Specialists

1. Members of each ethnic group should be identified, invited, and selected to become OJT specialists for each of the CJ team roles. This means that at least one magistrate, constable, village advocate, and probation aide would have to be designated within each ethnic group. This minimal level of operation would eventually become inadequate, because of the wearing nature of the duties, and the difficulties of absence from home.

2. OJT specialists would spend one week at a time with recent graduates of the Phase 2 training. This time would be spent in the trainees' villages, under working conditions. The OJT specialist would have a checklist, prepared by the Bush Justice and Research units of the Center, for a systematic review of procedure. Much of this OJT time, regardless of the trainer's own team role, would involve all four, or three, or two members of the newly graduated CJ team.

3. This activity would have to be supported by well-prepared, translated training materials made available for dissemination by the OJT specialist.

d. Phase 4. Continuing CJ Team Training

1. This training might consist of an occasional visit by the OJT specialist, with programmed training material; or the material might be sent directly to team members for their personal use, without supervision.

2. The ideal packaged training material would address a given subject from the perspective of each village CJ team member. Each package would have to be translated by resources available to the Bush Justice and Research units of the Center. Feedback, in the form of programmed responses, would be an important part of this effort. The regional centers, hopefully on the community college campuses, might develop access to translation and distribution of the English language versions prepared at Anchorage.

3. This phase of training could serve an additional, very desirable purpose: that of "instant consultation" with village CJ teams on difficult cases. This would assume a communication network among the villages, which may not be feasible.

4. A final purpose of Phase 4 might well be on-going monitoring and evaluation of village CJ team operations. It was pointed out to the consultants by the corrections administrator that no adequate and consistent basis for evaluating, rewarding, and motivating village CJ workers (in his case, Probation Aides) now exists. It will be recommended that the Center Research unit examine the feasibility of melding this function into the continuing training program.

References

Conn, Stephen, & Boedeker, B. (1983). An analysis of outpatient accident trends in two dry Eskimo towns as a measure of alternative police responses to drunken behavior. Paper presented at the Academy of Criminal Justice Sciences, San Antonio.

Conn, S., & Garber, B. K. (1981). Moment of truth: The special relationship of the federal government to Alaska Natives and their tribes — Update and issue analysis. Anchorage, AK: Justice Center, University of Alaska Anchorage.

Conn, S., & Garber, B. K. (1990). State enforcement of Alaska Native tribal law: The congressional mandate of the Alaska National Interest Lands Conservation Act *1989 Harvard Indian Law Symposium* (pp. 99–133). Cambridge, MA: Harvard Law School Publications Center.

Conn, S., & Hippler, A. E. (1973a). Paralegals in the bush. *UCLA-Alaska Law Review, 3*(1), 85–102. Retrieved from http://heinonline.org/HOL/Landi ngPage?collection=journals&handle=hein.journals/ uclaak3&div=3&id=&page=

Conn, S., & Hippler, A. E. (1973b). An action plan for village justice. Fairbanks, AK: Institute of Social, Economic and Government Research.

Conn, S., & Hippler, A. E. (1974a). Conciliation and arbitration in the native village and the urban ghetto. *Judicature, 58*(5), 228–235.

Conn, S., & Hippler, A. E. (1974b). Wedding U.S. law to

Eskimo tradition. *Juris Doctor,* 4(4), 40–44.

Conn, S., & Hippler, A. E. (1974c). Final report, Emmonak conciliation board, a model for a new legal process for small villages in Alaska. Unpublished report of National Science Foundation Project prepared for presentation to the Alaska State Supreme Court.

Conn, S., & Langdon, S. J. (1988). Retribalization as a strategy for achievement of group and individual social security in Alaska Native villages — with a special focus on subsistence. In F. von Benda-Beckmann, K. von Benda-Beckmann, E. Casino, F. Hirtz, G. R. Woodman & H. F. Zacher (Eds.), *Between Kinship and the State: Social Security and Law in Developing Countries* (pp. 437–450). Providence, RI: Foris Publications.

Conn, S., & Moras, A. (1986). *No need of gold — Alcohol control laws and the Alaska Native population: From the Russians through the early years of statehood.* Alaska Historical Commission Studies in History #226. Anchorage, AK: School of Justice, University of Alaska, Anchorage. Retrieved from http://justice.uaa.alaska.edu/research/1980/8617.alcohol_control/8617.no_need_of_gold.html

Division of Corrections v. Neakok, 721 P.2d 1121 (Alaska Supreme Court, 1986).

Fonseca, F. (17 May 2013). Navajo Nation considers tougher crime sentences. *Associate Press State Wire,* New Mexico.

Hippler, A. E., & Conn, S. (1972). Traditional Athabascan law ways and their relationship to contemporary problems of "bush justice": Some preliminary observations on structure and function. *ISEGR Occasional Papers.* Fairbanks, AK: Institute of Social, Economic and Government Research.

Hippler, A. E., & Conn, S. (1973a). Northern Eskimo law ways and their relationship to contemporary problems of "bush justice"; some preliminary observations on structure and function. *ISEGR Occasional Papers.* Fairbanks, AK: Institute of Social, Economic and Government Research.

Hippler, A. E., & Conn, S. (1973b). Bush justice: Sentencing reforms, a role for the council. Unpublished research paper prepared for Chief Justice Jay Rabinowitz, Alaska Supreme Court.

Hippler, A. E., & Conn, S. (1975). The village council and its offspring: A reform for bush justice. *UCLA-Alaska Law Review, 5*(1), 22–57. Retrieved from http://heinonline. org/HOL/LandingPage?collection=journals&handle=h ein.journals/uclaak5&div=7&id=&page=

Indian Child Welfare Act, 25 U.S.C. § 1901–1963 (8 Nov 1978).

Marquez, J. E., & Serdahely, D. J. (1977). Alaska Court System village conciliation board project: Evaluation. Anchorage, AK. Unpublished report prepared for the Alaska Court System

McKenzie, E. (1976). The report of the third bush justice conference, Oct. 7–9, 1976. Anchorage, AK: Alaska Federation of Natives.

Morrow, W. G. (1974). Riding circuit in the Arctic. *Judicature, 58*(5), 236–241.

Neakok v. State, 653 P.2d 658 (1982).

Nix, W. (1973). Unpublished transcript of interview by Stephen Conn.

Peratrovich, R. (1973). Unpublished transcript of interview by Stephen Conn.

Public Law 280, Pub. L. No. 83-280. 18 U.S.C. §1162, 28 U.S.C. §1360, and 25 U.S.C. §§1321–1326 (15 Aug 1953).

Second Magistrate Advisory Committee. (1989). Recommendations of the Second Magistrate Advisory Committee. Unpublished report prepared for the Alaska Supreme Court.

Strecher, V. G., Hoover, L. T., George, B. J., & Fox, V. (1974). *Final report of recommendations: A criminal justice center for Alaska.* On file with the Justice Center, University of Alaska Anchorage.

Vicenti, D., Jimson, L. B., Conn, S., & Kellogg, M. J. L. (1972). *The law of the people: Diné bibee haz'áanii — A bicultural approach to legal education for Navajo students* (4 vols.). Ramah, NM: Ramah Navajo High School Press.

Williams, A. W., Jr. (1970). *Navajo political process.* Smithsonian Contributions to Anthropology #9. Washington, DC: Smithsonian Institution Press. Retrieved from http://si-pddr.si.edu/jspui/handle/10088/1325

Williams v. Lee, 358 U.S. 217 (1959).

Appendix A:
About the Contributors

Appendix A: About the Contributors

Ray Barnhardt is a professor of Cross-Cultural Studies at the University of Alaska Fairbanks, where he has been involved in teaching and research related to Native and rural education since 1970. Over the past 40 years, he has served as the director of the Cross-Cultural Education Development (X-CED) Program, the Small High Schools Project, the Center for Cross-Cultural Studies, and the Alaska Native Knowledge Network.

Stephen Conn, lawyer, anthropologist, and legal historian was professor of Justice, first associate professor of Law, the University of Alaska, and first winner of the Chancellor's Award for Excellence in Teaching. His published and unpublished studies on the interplay between local and official laws are available online at justice.uaa.alaska.edu/publications/authors/conn/.

Cathy Coulter is an associate professor of Literacy Education in the College of Education at the University of Alaska Anchorage. Her publications include various book chapters and articles in *Educational Researcher*, *Curriculum Studies*, and the *Bilingual Research Journal*. She has coauthored (with Dr. Christian Faltis) a book titled *Teaching Immigrant Children and English Language Learners in Secondary Schools*. She is dedicated to supporting language- and culture-revitalization efforts in Alaska.

George A. Geistauts is professor of Business and Public Policy at the University of Alaska Anchorage.

Holly Miowak Guise (Iñupiaq) was born and raised in Anchorage, and her family is from Unalakleet. She is a History

PhD student at Yale University studying American Indian history with a focus on 20th-century Alaska Native history.

Alexandra Hill is a senior research associate at the Center for Alaska Education Policy and Research at the University of Alaska Anchorage.

Diane Hirshberg is an associate professor of Education Policy and director of the Center for Alaska Education Policy Research at the University of Alaska Anchorage.

Ute Kaden has more than 20 years of diverse educational experiences in Germany, New Zealand, the United Kingdom, Texas, and Alaska. Her fields of expertise are in science (geoscience/physics) and mathematics education. She actively promotes all fields of STEM education and is involved in teacher education and supervision.

Tony Kaliss holds a PhD in American Studies from the University of Hawai'i and is presently retired in Anchorage, AK, after teaching seven years at Ilisaġvik College in Barrow, AK. He has been involved since 1966 in a wide variety of issues concerning the interactions of Native and European-based communities at both the practical and theoretical levels. This includes work on political, social, economic, legal, health, and education issues.

While he has taught at two tribal colleges, his main work and experience has been with people and issues at the community level. His interest in Alaska dates back to 1982, when he visited the Yukon-Kuskokwim Delta area in connection with an interest by Yup'ik fur trappers in setting up a direct market to the fur clothing industry in New York City.

The realization that the Eskimo/Inuit peoples were interacting with four different European flavors (USSR, USA, Canada, and Denmark) suggested that much could be learned about policies concerning Native peoples.

This led to returning late in life to PhD work at the University of Hawai'i, where it was possible to study international Indigenous issues, including US policy toward Native peoples in the South Pacific and to a doctoral dissertation comparing Soviet and American government policies toward the Native peoples on both sides of the Bering Strait.

As part of dissertation research, he spent a year in far northeastern Russia (Magadan city and the Chukotka region) studying Soviet/Russian government policies and then time in northern and northwestern Alaska. Through all of this he has actively studied and followed Alaska Native issues and in 2002 moved to Barrow and has been an Alaska resident since.

Sharon *Chilux* Lind (Aleut) is assistant professor of Business and Public Policy at the University of Alaska Anchorage. She is developing a new curriculum in Alaska Native business.

Liza Mack (Aleut) was born and raised in King Cove Alaska and is an enrolled member of the Native village of Belkofski. She is enrolled in the Indigenous Studies PhD program at the University of Alaska Fairbanks, and she obtained both her bachelor's and master's degrees in Anthropology at Idaho State University.

Patrick Marlow is associate professor of Linguistics at the Alaska Native Language Center and the School of Education at the University of Alaska Fairbanks. Marlow seeks to understand the language-planning goals of Alaska Native communities in an effort to facilitate those goals and community ownership over language programs.

Phil Patterson's current assignment includes recruiting and preparing special-education preservice teachers. He has over 20 years of experience teaching diverse special- and general-education students in urban and rural settings. He has also served as a special-education program specialist and coordinator of Early Start programs.

Sabine Siekmann is associate professor of Linguistics and Foreign Languages at the University of Alaska Fairbanks. Her research interests include instructed second-language teaching and learning and computer-assisted language learning, particularly as they apply to Indigenous language maintenance and revitalization efforts.

Anna Smith-Chiburis (Tlingit). Anna was born and raised in Anchorage, Alaska and is a Raven of the Deishetaan clan. She received her MA in English and her MFA in Creative Writing from the University of Alaska Anchorage.

Eve Tuck (Aleut) is assistant professor of Educational Foundations and Coordinator of the Native American Studies Program at the State University of New York at New Paltz. She is an enrolled member of the tribal government of St. Paul Island, Alaska.

***X'hunei* Lance A. Twitchell** (Tlingit, Haida, and Yup'ik) is an artist and assistant professor of Alaska Native Languages at the University of Alaska Southeast. He studies and teaches the Tlingit language, Northwest Coast Formline Design, and

Appendix B:

About the Editors

Alaska Native social issues. He lives in Juneau with his wife and three children.

Appendix B: About the Editors

Jeane *T'áaw xíwaa* **Breinig** (Haida) is from Kasaan, Alaska. She is of the Táas Láanas (Sand Beach people), Raven, Brown Bear clan, and an enrolled member of Central Council of the Tlingit and Haida Indians of Alaska. Breinig is Associate Dean for Humanities and professor of English at the University of Alaska Anchorage. She received her PhD from the University of Washington in 1995, and her teaching and research expertise is in American Indian and Alaska Native literatures. S h e is coeditor of *Alaska Native Writers, Storytellers & Orators: The Expanded Edition*, and coproducer and interviewer for the video *Gasdáan Xaadas Gusuu: Kasaan Haida Elders' Speak*. Breinig also has published in *Alaska Native Ways: What the Elders Have Taught Us; Telling the Stories;* and *American Indian Quarterly*. She also writes poetry, and her poems have appeared in *Red Ink, Atlantis: A Women's Studies Journal,* and *Studies in American Indian Literature*.

Beth *Ginondidoy* **Leonard** (Deg Hit'an Athabascan) is an enrolled member of the Shageluk Tribe of Alaska. Leonard earned her PhD from the University of Alaska Fairbanks (UAF) in 2007 in the Interdisciplinary Program with a focus on cross-cultural and Alaska Native studies. Her dissertation was titled "Deg Xinag Oral Traditions: Reconnecting Indigenous Language and Education Through Traditional Narratives." Leonard recently joined the faculty of Cross-Cultural Studies (CCS) at UAF and works closely with graduate students in the CCS master's and Indigenous Studies PhD programs.

Leonard's research interests include Indigenous pedagogies, Indigenous teacher preparation, and Athabascan oral traditions and languages. Her publications include "Reclaiming scholarship: Critical Indigenous research methodologies" (coauthor in *Qualitative Research*), "Deg Xinag Oral Traditions: Reconnecting Indigenous Language and Education Through Traditional Narratives" (in the *Alaska Native Reader*), "Mediating Athabascan Oral Traditions in Post-Secondary Classrooms" (*International Journal of Multicultural Education*), and "Language Revitalization and Identity in Social Context: A Community-Based Athabascan Language Preservation Project in Western Interior Alaska" (*Anthropology & Education Quarterly*).

Thomas Swensen (Alutiiq/Sugpiaq) earned a PhD in Ethnic Studies from University of California, Berkeley, in 2011. He has been the recipient of the Western History Association's Autry Prize in Public History, the Chancellor's Postdoctoral fellowship in American Indian Studies at the University of Illinois at Urbana-Champaign, and the Larry Matfay Cultural Heritage Scholarship. He is enrolled with Koniag, Inc., Leisnoi, Inc. and Tangirnaq Native Village and serves on the board of directors at Koniag Education Foundation. Currently he is the assistant professor of Native Arts and Culture at Arizona State University and writes the *Alaska Native Studies Blog* (alaskanativestudies. blogspot.com).

Ac'aralek **Lolly Sheppard Carpluk** (Yup'ik) was born and raised in Mountain Village, Alaska. Her Yup'ik upbringing and perspective are continually supported and nurtured by a large extended family. Her formal Western education began in an elementary school in Mountain Village. Carpluk went on to attend both Mt. Edgecumbe and St. Mary's Catholic high schools, and received a BA in Sociology, elementary and secondary teaching certification, and a Master's degree in Education, all from the University of Alaska Fairbanks (UAF). The majority of her work experience has been in education. Carpluk also has served and continues to serve on a variety of committees, some of which include: Native Educators' Conference Planning Committee, Native Educators' Advisory Committee to the Commissioner of Education, Honoring Alaska's Indigenous Literature Committee, and the UAF Chancellor's Advisory Committee on Native Education. She currently serves as the Ikautaq Project Coordinator for UAA Center for Human Development.

Gordon *Tan'icak* Pullar (Kodiak Island Sugpiaq) is an associate professor in the Department of Alaska Native Studies and Rural Development at UAF, where he has served since 1992. He was instrumental in the design and implementation of UAF's Rural Development MA program and teaches classes on Indigenous issues such as identity, land claims, leadership, and organization management. A Kodiak Island Sugpiaq, Pullar is a past president and CEO of the Kodiak Area Native Association, past chairman of the Koniag Education Foundation, past president of the Tangirnaq Native Village Tribal Council, and serves on the Alutiiq Museum board. While a board member of the Alaska Federation of Natives, he served on the legislative committee that worked with Congress to secure the important "1991 amendments" to ANCSA. He has lectured worldwide and published extensively on Indigenous issues. He coedited the book *Looking Both Ways: Heritage and Identity of the Alutiiq*

People (UA Press 2001). He holds a PhD in Organizational Anthropology, a Master of Public Administration degree, and a BA in Anthropology. In 2013 he received the Angayuqaq Oscar Kawagley Indigenous Scholar Award at the first Alaska Native Studies Conference.

Alisha Susana *Englartaq* Drabek (Alutiiq, Tsimshian, Scandinavian, and Slavic), was born and raised on Kodiak Island. She currently serves as the project manager for the Alutiiq Studies and Student Support Project at Kodiak College. She graduated from the University of Arizona in Tucson with her BA in English—American Literature in 1994 and her MFA in Creative Writing—Fiction in 1996, and from the University of Alaska Fairbanks with her doctorate in Indigenous Studies—Education/Pedagogy. Drabek completed her doctoral research and dissertation on Alutiiq storytelling and values in December 2012, available on the Alaska Native Knowledge Network website and www.alutiiqeducation.org. She has studied the Alutiiq language with Kodiak Island Elders since 2004 as a language apprentice and has been an active participant and supporter of many Alutiiq cultural programs, which all contribute to her work.

Drabek wrote and designed an Alutiiq picture dictionary titled *Qik'rtarmiut Sugpiat Niugneret cali PatRiitat*, published by the Alutiiq Museum in 2007, and republished it in 2013. She is coauthor of a children's book titled *Red Cedar of Afognak: A Driftwood Journey*, which won the Honoring Alaska's Indigenous Literature (HAIL) Award in 2004 and the American Book Award in 2005, from the Before Columbus Foundation. She served as assistant professor and chair of the

English Department at Kodiak College from 2003–2006, as tribal administrator for the Native Village of Afognak from 1999–2002, and managing editor for the *Sonora Review* literary journal in 1995–1996. She has worked as an independent consultant since 1998 for a number of Alaska Native organizations in public-relations materials production, research, grant writing, and facilitation.

Roy Roehl is Assistant Professor of Secondary Education at UAF.

Miranda Wright (Koyukon Athabascan) is from Nulato, Alaska. She serves as the director and Associate Professor at the UAF Department of Alaska Native Studies and Rural Development. Wright holds an MA in Cultural Anthropology from the University of Alaska Fairbanks, where she is currently pursuing a PhD in Interdisciplinary Studies. She has over 30 years experience as a private business owner. Wright is a member of the board of directors for Doyon, Limited, an ANCSA regional corporation. She also served on the board of her ANCSA village corporation and was instrumental in the merger of four village corporations into Gana-A Yoo' Limited. Ms. Wright has served on numerous boards and committees focused on economic development and native education. Ms. Wright and her husband, Gareth, make their home in Fairbanks, along with a large extended family.

Phyllis Fast (Koyukon Athabascan) is a Professor at the University of Alaska Anchorage in the departments of Anthropology and Liberal Studies. Her research interests are related to Alaska Native peoples, literary, visual and performative arts, as well as areas of transnational political and social economy as it relates to Indigenous peoples, particularly in the area of gender relations. She is the author of *Northern Athabascan Survival: Women, Community and the Future*. In 2009 Fast was part of a research team investigating Native perspectives on Alaska's statehood for Sealaska Heritage Institute. Fast conducted research among Athabascan Elders for the project. She received a BA in English from the University of Alaska Fairbanks, an interdisciplinary MA in Anthropology and English on Alaska Native Literary Forms from the University of Alaska Anchorage, and a PhD in Social Anthropology from Harvard University.

Maria *Shaa Tláa* Williams (Tlingit) is of the Raven Moiety, and of the Deisheetaan clan and enrolled in the Central Council of Tlingit and Haida Indians of Alaska, a federally recognized tribe. Williams's main area of research is on Alaska Native Indigenous cultural practices. Her current research is community-centered and based on an Indigenous model. Williams received her PhD in 1996 from UCLA in Music, specializing in Ethnomusicology.

Williams's publications include "Alaska Native Music and Dance: The Spirit of Tradition" in *Native American Dance: Ceremonies and Social Traditions*, edited by Charlotte Heth (1992); *The Alaska Native Reader: Poetry, Politics and History* (Duke University Press 2009). Currently she is the director of Alaska Native Studies at the University of Alaska Anchorage.

Appendix C:

Original Program for the Alaska Native Studies Conference

Appendix C: Original Program for the Alaska Native Studies Conference

2013 Conference: Transforming the University: Alaska Native Studies in the 21st Century

Dear Conference Attendees and Presenters, Elders and Community members:

It is our pleasure to have you join us for the *first* Alaska Native Studies Conference, April 5–6, 2013, at the University of Alaska Anchorage. The conference is bringing together over 150 Alaska Native scholars, practitioners, teachers, students, and leaders from throughout Alaska and the nation. The conference participants are presenting Alaska Native–related research, science, and educational strategies grounded in Alaska Native experience, culture, insights, and perspectives.

In designing the conference, the Alaska Native Studies Council worked with Alaska Native faculty from across the state. Particular care has been taken to include young Native scholars, including Master's- and PhD-level students, as well as elders. The conference will integrate Indigenous perspectives and research into understanding past, current, and future issues, actions, and paradigms. There are only 54 Alaska Native people who have received PhDs. The Alaska Native Studies Council is committed to growing that number. The conference provides a platform for emerging Indigenous scholars to present their research and creative work. We also support the development and implementation of Native-focused curricula and research and pedagogical strategies. We aspire to create a strategic plan to promote a deeper and more sustained commitment to integrating Indigenous perspectives into a variety of educational settings.

We look forward to the next several days and feel truly blessed that so many individuals have worked very hard to make this happen. We deeply appreciate the support of Provost Baker at UAA, in addition to Chancellor Case, President Gamble, and the UA regents.

Conference Chair and Co-chairs

Sharon *Chilux* Lind, Maria *Shaa Tláa* Williams, Beth *Ginondidoy* Leonard, Jeane *T'áaw xíwaa* Breinig, and Lance *X'hunei* Twitchell

Alaska Native Studies Conference, April 5–6, 2013

Friday April 5th

8–9 a.m. Registration at Wendy Williamson Auditorium lobby
UAA shuttle will start at 7:30 from University Lake hotel to Wendy Williamson Auditorium

9–11 a.m. Opening Session.

Blessing: Marie Meade (Yup'ik)

Introductory remarks and welcomes by President Gamble, Chancellor Case, UAA; Provost Baker, UAA; Maria *Shaa Tláa* Williams, UAA,

Recognition of elders and of the chair and cochairs of the Alaska Native Studies Council—Sharon *Chiluxx* Lind, Beth *Ginondidoy* Leonard, Lance *X'hunei* Twitchell, Jeane *T'áaw xíwaa* Breinig

Keynote Speaker: Graham *Hingangoroa* Smith, distinguished professor of Education and Vice Chancellor *Te Whare wananga o Awanuiarangi*: Indigenous university

11 a.m.–12—Box lunches in Wendy Williamson Auditorium

11a.m–4 p.m *Native Student Services will be open as a place people can get coffee, water, a resting place for visitors, elders, etc.*

Keynote Speaker

Graham *Hingangaroa* Smith

Distinguished Professor of Education Te Whare Wânanga o Awanuiârangi: *Indigenous university*

Dr. Smith is currently one of the foremost influential educators in the world. He is a distinguished professor of Education Te Whare Wânanga o Awanuiârangi: *Indigenous university* in New Zealand, where he also serves as the CEO/ vice chancellor. Professor Smith is internationally renowned and is a prominent Maori educator who has been a leader in the alternative Maori initiatives in the education field. Dr. Smith has dedicated his entire life to Indigenous-based pedagogical approaches in education. His groundbreaking work on *Kaupapa Maori*—which is a Maori-based educational and cultural philosophy—has been universally acknowledged as a powerful and effective approach in Indigenous education that has created systemic change in New Zealand. Dr. Smith served as distinguished chair in Indigenous Education at the University of British Columbia, and most recently as principal international research fellow at the University of Sydney. Dr. Smith was a close colleague and friend of the late Oscar *Angayuqaq* Kawagley and has made numerous visits to Alaska and worked very closely with the University of Alaska Fairbanks on the Indigenous PhD program. Dr. Smith has also been a keynote speaker at the Alaska Federation of Natives and has travelled extensively through the US, Canada, and Hawaii. Many Indigenous scholars worldwide have been influenced by the new models of Indigenous education that Dr. Smith has established.

We are so privileged to have him here at our first Alaska Native Studies Conference.

Panel Schedule
Friday, April 5th
1–3 p.m. Concurrent Sessions
in Rasmuson Hall (RH), Sally Monserud Hall (SMH), and Beatrice McDonald Hall (BMH)

SB 130: Alaska Native Language Preservation and Advisory Council

The Alaska Native Language Council, created under Senate
Bill 130 and signed into law by Governor Parnell, will
host a roundtable presentation/Q&A session to inform
the public about the mission, goals, and activities and
priorities of the council, as well as to receive public
testimony on recommendations and ideas from the
public.

Participants: Walkie Charles, PhD, Chair (Yup'ik); April
Counceller, PhD (Alutiiq); Annette Evans-Smith
(Athabascan, Yup'ik, Alutiiq); Delores Churchill
(Haida); Bernadette Yaayuk Alvanna Stimpfle (Iñupiaq)

1–3 p.m.
RH 101

Decolonization: Global Models Panel

Ray Barnhardt, Professor of Cross-Cultural Studies, UAF and
University of Alaska Fairbanks/World Indigenous
Nations Higher Education Consortium Accreditation
Board **"The Implementation of a World Indigenous
Accreditation Authority in Higher Education"**

Abstract: In August 2002 representatives of Indigenous higher-education institutions from around the world, ranging from Maori Wananga in New Zealand to Tribal Colleges from across the US, assembled in Kananaskis, Alberta, and established the World Indigenous Nations Higher Education Consortium. WINHEC was created to provide an international forum and support for Indigenous peoples to pursue common goals through higher education, including "creating an accreditation body for Indigenous education initiatives and systems that identify common criteria, practices and principles by which Indigenous Peoples live." This presentation will describe the rationale for and implementation of the WINHEC accreditation system and its unfolding contribution to Indigenous self-determination in higher education.

Heather E. McGregor, PhD student, University of British Columbia **"Extending the Circumpolar Dialogue on Indigenous Education: Nunavut and Alaska"**

Abstract: Indigenous education in the Arctic regions of circumpolar nation-states can differ substantially from the context of Indigenous education farther south. Recently enhanced dialogue amongst Alaska, Nunavut, and Greenland is drawing attention to these points of difference and commonality. Using both educational history and examples from Nunavut's new high school social studies curriculum, this presentation features the distinctive perspective offered from the only Canadian jurisdiction where the entire public-education system is intended to be responsive to the Indigenous (Inuit) majority. Areas of common struggle that warrant further dialogue are proposed, with a particular focus on decolonizing history education in the Arctic.

Michael Marker, Associate Professor, Director, Ts"kel First Nations Graduate Studies,
University of British Columbia. "**Indigenous Leadership and the Place-Based Collective Self**"

Abstract: I discussed principles of educational leadership with four Nisga'a elders in the Nass Valley of British Columbia. They emphasized the need for both spiritual foundations and an understanding of the history of the land and the people as the most important qualities for leaders. In many ways these two principles, the spiritual and the historical, are underlying the differences between mainstream approaches to leadership and Indigenous ways of guiding both youth and adults. Based on my work with the Lummi Nation, Northwest Indian College, and as an Indigenous high school teacher for Tlingit-Haida students in Juneau, this paper examines the challenges of designing and directing a teacher-education program at a tribal college.

Moderator: Maria Williams, UAA

RH 211

1–3 p.m.

Cultural Revitalization as a Pathway to Self-determination—
Self-determination issues are pervasive among
Indigenous peoples in Alaska. Alaska Natives are
obliged to address sovereignty concerns and goals within
non-Indigenous political contexts, and in cultural
contexts other than their own. How can leadership
and social organizations stemming from Indigenous
cultural institutions be revitalized to meet non-Native
governmental and political challenges on more equitable
terms? By addressing issues of sovereignty in the context
of rapid culture change, how can this change be guided
in such a way as to foster cultural revitalization and
sovereignty simultaneously? This session's papers will
evaluate culture change through the development and
revitalization of practices and institutions that foster
autonomy.
Participants: Miranda Wright, Director and Associate Professor,
Dept. of Alaska Native Studies and Rural Development,
UAF; Gordon L. Pullar, Associate Professor, UAF;
Michael Koskey, Assistant Professor, UAF
Moderator: Gordon L. Pullar, UAF
RH 110
1–3 p.m.

**Stories of Educational Persistence—Voices from the
Villages—**Alaska Native graduate students in the
Educational Leadership Department (EDL) of the
College of Education who are currently in bush villages
serving as teachers and principals in public K–12 schools

will share stories of their educational experiences and discuss barriers and successes in aspects of educational achievement. The panel represents a respectful form of activism honoring the lived experiences of graduate students. The stories of panelists can lead to new directions in integrating Indigenous perspectives into all aspects of educational programming.

Invited Panelists: Lewis Beaver, Site Administrator, Lower Kuskokwim School District; Vicky Charlie, Principal, Yukon Koyukuk School District, Dana Bartman, Associate Principal and Counselor, Southwest Region School District; and Janet Johnson, Administrative Intern, Lower Yukon School District. Panel convener: Susan Garton, Associate Professor, UAA, Advisor students in the Ed Leadership Program.

Moderator: Caitlin Montague-Winebarger
RH 303
1–3 p.m.

ANCSA I Panel

Sharon Lind and George Geistauts **"The Alaska Native Claims Settlement Act Corporation: A Case Example for Indigenous Peoples' Business Development"**

Abstract: Alaska is home to Indigenous Aleut, Eskimo, and Indian peoples, and neither the Russian presence nor the US purchase negated their legal and moral claims to the land. In 1971 the US Congress passed the Alaska Native Claims Settlement Act (ANCSA). Suddenly Alaska Natives, for whom culture and lifestyles had been tied to subsistence and the land, were thrust into a world of corporate structures and management. Today, some of these corporations do business all over the world and have revenues in the billion-dollar range. This paper looks at the ANCSA experiment's unique aspects and implementation, focusing on the regional corporations, and examines the effectiveness of the ANCSA approach.

George Geistauts and Bob Poe **"Strategic Analysis for Balancing Economic, Cultural, and Social Performance of Larger Indigenous People's Corporations"**

Abstract: We present a model of strategic analysis for larger Indigenous people's corporations operating in a dual-culture world where mainstream business practices must be balanced with traditional Indigenous values and social goals. In effect, many such corporations, in the minds of Indigenous shareholders, are also to some degree socioeconomic-development organizations that must be compatible with their cultural norms. The focus should be on balanced performance where acceptable levels of financial, as well as cultural and social, performance are being pursued. The model is discussed with reference to ANCSA corporations but has broad applicability in the US, Canada, and beyond.

Kristina D. Woolston (Vice President, Government Relations, Chenega Corporation): **"Chenega: A Case Study"**

Abstract: Chenega Corporation is arguably the most successful of the Alaska Native Village Corporations. Its storied history includes two tsunamis that wiped out the original village of Chenega and killed a third of its residents, and the tragic Exxon Valdez oil spill, which Chenega Bay was at ground zero for impact. These significant events make Chenega's business prominence all the more compelling. This paper delves into the background of the historical and cultural tenets of the Chenega people, examines the trajectory of business growth, explains Chenega Corporation's duality of purpose, and posits what the future may hold for Chenega's corporate and community investments.

Moderator: George Geistauts, UAA

RH 111
1–3 p.m

Education and Indigenous Pedagogy and Self-Determination Panel

Diane Hirshberg, PhD, Associate Professor of Education Policy, and Director, UAA Center for Alaska Education Policy Research (CAEPR)

Alexandra Hill, Senior Research Associate, CAEPR.

"Indigenous Self-Determination in Education in Alaska: How Can Communities Get There?"

Abstract: We recently looked at promising models of formal schooling for Indigenous students around the globe and found that self-determination and local control over education appear to be very important in helping improve education outcomes. But in Alaska, Indigenous control over schools is almost nonexistent, and communities generally have not succeeded in creating schools that reflect their aspirations for their children's education. In this presentation we examine the historical, social, legal, and political factors that challenge efforts by Alaska Native communities to control their children's schools.

Holly Guise, Yale University and Khalil Anthony Johnson Jr., Yale University

"Education and Epistemology in Alaska Native Communities"

Abstract: Epistemology—as informed by race, tribe, class, and region—has shaped and informed approaches to educating Alaska Natives. These papers present contrasting pedagogical approaches practiced historically by teachers within the BIA, the impact of these approaches on Native students, and the ways in which an understanding of education in the past can inform decolonizing methodologies in the present. Khalil Anthony Johnson Jr. discusses how, from

1945 to 1975, the BIA employed dozens of African American educators as teachers in Alaskan schools. Holly Guise will present her findings from 29 elder interviews to detail the segregationist regime that Alaska Natives overcame.

Maureen P. Hogan, PhD, Associate Professor, Chair of Graduate Programs, School of Education, UAF

"How and Why I Teach Epistemology in a Graduate Research Methods Class: A Self-Study"

Abstract: In any research-methods course, one must teach the underlying assumptions of various research paradigms, including the interrelated philosophical principles of epistemology, ontology, and axiology. At an Alaskan university, many people do research and work in and with Alaska Native communities, and so a grasp of an Alaskan Native epistemology is crucial. Focusing just on epistemology for this paper, I propose to do an analytical self-study of how I teach epistemology (in general) and Indigenous epistemology (in particular) in my graduate research methods course. I will also explore why I may or may not be successful in this task.

Moderator: Beth Leonard, PhD, UAF

RH 204

1–3 p.m.

Workshops

Sally Monserud Hall

Workshop I: Focus-on-Focus: Rural Alaska Teacher Orientation Through the Lens of Indigenous Educators—Why put so much energy and effort into teaching non-Native teachers about our culture, our lands, and our people? Does this effort have a positive impact on how the non-Native teachers view and work within our remote villages and communities? The presenters will share their experiences and expertise in orienting teachers to teach in remote-village Alaska since 2003. This will be followed with activities where participants will be engaged in a culturally based activity. The participants will then determine how this activity can be integrated into the regular school program. The participants will have time for discussion on *why* the orientation classes need to be regionally based.

Presenters: *Yurrliq* Nita Rearden, Retired Alaska Native Yup'ik Educator and *Arnaq* Esther A. Ilutsik, Director of Yup'ik Studies Southwest Region Schools

SMH 109

1–3 p.m.

Workshop II: Critiquing Indigenous Literature for Alaska's Children—This 30-minute workshop will provide participants with a framework for reviewing literature written about and for Alaska's Indigenous children. The content of the workshop provides a brief look at how children's literature influences the image of the Indigenous children of Alaska. The goals of the workshop are to introduce participants to the genre of Alaska children's literature and the review/critiquing process. The workshop will contain the following topics: Children's literature and cultural identity; Why review Alaska's Children's Literature; Tips on writing a professional Book Review: Guidelines.

Presenter: Vivian Faith Prescott (Saami) (Martindale). PhD Adjunct Professor, University of Alaska Fairbanks

SMH 108

2:30–3 p.m.

Workshop III: Accessing Language and Culture Resources at the Alaska Native Language Archive—The Alaska Native Language Archive (ANLA) is a permanent and enduring repository for Native language and culture materials, including nearly everything written in or about each of Alaska's Native languages. Thanks to recent cataloging and digitization efforts, more than 10,000 items are now available online and can be accessed remotely. This presentation will begin by reviewing the contents of the ANLA and then describe how to access the materials. The presentation will conclude with a workshop format, focused on a dialogue regarding digital repatriation and new ways to utilize archive materials in language-revitalization contexts.

Presenter: Gary Holton, Director, Alaska Native Language Archive, University of Alaska Fairbanks
SMH 108
3–5 p.m.

Workshop IV: Envisioning Indigenous Evaluation in Alaska—Indigenous evaluation is an approach that privileges Indigenous epistemologies and ensures that evaluation processes and methods are tailored to fit projects that serve Indigenous peoples. It involves giving voice and advocating for more meaningful and relevant evaluation assessments, honors Native ways of knowing, and acknowledges Native sovereignty. This interactive presentation will feature developing Alaska Native evaluators who will share their perspectives on the future of Indigenous evaluation in Alaska and lead the audience through hands-on exercises to increase understanding of what Indigenous evaluation is, why we do it, and how we do it.

Presenters: Amelia Ruerup (Tlingit); Charlene Stern (Gwich'in); James Johnson III (Koyukon).
SMH 109
3–5 p.m.

3–5 p.m. Concurrent Sessions
in Rasmuson Hall (RH) and Sally Monserud Hall (SMH)
and Beatrice McDonald Hall (BMH)

Issues of Native Governance—

Abstract—The panel will address issues of Native governance and self-determination through the lens of local, regional, national, and global Indigenous movements. From the abstract discussion of the right of peoples to self-determination as *jus cogens* or a peremptory norm and the impacts of discrimination perpetrated against Indigenous peoples. Tribal courts and tribal justice practitioners, the work of the Yukon River Inter-Tribal watershed Council, to governance in the corporate boardrooms will be discussed.

Moderator: Dalee Sambo Dorough, Assistant Professor, UAA Department of Political Science
Edgar Blatchford, UAA, Journalism and Public Communication
Kevin Illingworth, UAF Tribal Management Program
Mara Kimmel, Senior Fellow, Institute of the North
Kimberly Martus, BBNA, Tribal Court Enhancement Program

RH 111
3–5 p.m.

Speaking Truth to Each Other: Making Higher Education Accountable to Indigenous Communities in Thought, Word, and Deed

Abstract: We will discuss how Native American Studies programs can influence responsible connections with Indigenous communities and how Native American Studies programs can influence institutional change. We will discuss our program's efforts to grow and maintain the teaching of tribal languages (Ojibway and Dakota) and how teaching Indigenous methodologies and traditional knowledge promotes Native students returning to serve their communities. Finally, we will discuss how Native American faculty and administrators can build institutional infrastructure to support Native American students and communities.

Presenters: Kathryn W. Shanley (Nakoda) –organizer and chair, Professor of Native American Studies and Special Asst. to the Provost for Native American & Indigenous Education, University of Montana; Gyda Swaney (Salish), Director of Indians Into Psychology Program, University of Montana.

Moderator: Jeane Breinig, PhD, Professor of English, Associate Dean, UAA

3–5 p.m.

RH 110

Community Arts Action: Developing a Localized Art Agenda for Alaska

Abstract: Current movers and shakers in the Anchorage arts will discuss the projects they have recently completed. Anna Hoover, independent contractor/filmmaker will discuss First Light-Artists, a Dillingham-based community project that involves workshops taught by internationally acclaimed artists. The other presenters will address their recent art-related programs.

Presenters: Anna Hoover; Dawn Biddison; Sonya Kelliher-Combs; Nadia Jackinsky-Sethi; Jonella Larson-White; Julie Decker.

Moderator: Dr. Emily Moore, UAA

BMH 104
3–5 p.m.

Arts and Indigenous Alaska Native Cultures Panel

Jennifer *Aposuk* McCarty

"Iñupiat Iliquisiat: Those Things That make Us Who We Are"

Abstract: For thousands of years before contact with non-Native explorers, traders, missionaries, and others, essential bodies of knowledge found within Inupiaq stories that were passed orally from generation to generation both provided instructions on how to exist in partnership with the land and the animals of the Arctic world, and relayed over time lessons of survival—triumph, failure, and humorous details of everyday living. In this lecture, I will explore how these stories and their inherent values, both of which were passed down through the generations, can help contemporary Inupiaq people navigate today's world, and, by applying the knowledge contained within to their everyday lives, how they can exemplify a good Inupiat—a good human being.

Heidi *Aklaseaq* Senungetuk, PhD candidate, Wesleyan University

"Qanukiaq Ililuta: How Shall We Proceed?"

Abstract: This paper explores the revitalization of traditional Alaska Native music and dance as a form of cultural sovereignty. In the 1990s a group of young urban Iñupiat living in Anchorage, Alaska, with ancestral ties to their village of Kingigin, or Wales, started a dance group to reclaim Kingikmiut music and dance with the help of elders and video recordings. I present an Indigenous research perspective to traditional performance as an innovative art form. I focus on issues of cultural sovereignty through the lens of an Iñupiaq song, "*Qanukiaq Ililuta*," whose title translates into a question: "How shall we proceed?"

Moderator: Maria Williams, UAA
RH 204
3–4 p.m.

Poetry and Creative Writing

Reading from new creative fiction (30 minutes)
Anna Smith Chiburis (Tlingit)

An Offering of Words (30 minutes)
Alice Rose Crow—Maar'aq (Yup'ik)

RH 204
4–5 p.m.

The Future of Alaska Native Languages

X'unei Lance A. Twitchell, Assistant Professor of Alaska
Native Languages, UAS **"Alaska Native Language
Revitalization: Changing the Fabric of Our People"**

Abstract: Alaska Native languages will go through a massive
shift in the next decade. Some of those languages will
continue to endure, or they will die, unless our people,
organizations, and governments initiate radical change
to preserve them. It could be argued the death of those
languages is a form of institutional murder—and even
suicide—as our people lose their connection to those
languages. But that can change by understanding and
revitalizing those languages. That is, it is important to
understand the complexities of changing our individual
and collective lives to allow our heritage identities
to not only exist, but to thrive. This presentation
examines the social and individual realities of language
revitalization in Alaska.

Lawrence D. Kaplan, PhD, Director, Alaska Native Language

Center, UAF **"Revitalizing Native Languages:
Comparisons between Alaska and Other Situations"**

Abstract: As awareness grows of the decline in numbers of
Alaska Native language speakers, Alaskans are becoming increasingly concerned with finding approaches
that are likely to strengthen Native language use.
There is academic literature on the subject of language revitalization that focuses on what is possible
and what is being tried elsewhere. In addition to reading, a number of Alaskans have visited language programs in other states and countries to see what they
can learn. With the caution that every language situation is different, I will look at some of the efforts being conducted elsewhere, in particular the Hawaiian
programs, which are widely known and with which I
have firsthand experience.

April G.L. Counceller, PhD, Assistant Professor of Alutiiq
Language and Culture, Kodiak College, UA **"Alutiiq
Studies: Creation of a Program"**

Abstract: Alutiiq language and culture classes are now regular
offerings in Kodiak, due to a five-year Department of
Education Title III project at Kodiak College. Initiated
in the fall of 2011, the Alutiiq Studies & Student
Support Project is creating an associate's degree in
Alaska Native Studies, certificates and endorsements
in Alutiiq language and cultural revitalization, and a
Native student mentorship program modeled after
successful programs on other campuses. It also includes

physical changes to campus, such as meeting areas, a language recording studio, and multilingual signage.

Moderator: Thomas Swensen, PhD Assistant Professor, Arizona State University

RH 101

3–5 p.m

The Strength of our Grandmothers and Grandfathers: Culturally Competent care for Alaskan Native and American Indian Elders—Western medicine defines health as the absence of disease and focuses on the eradication of physical ailments. In contrast, traditional Indigenous teachings define health as a balance between mental, physical, emotional, and spiritual components not only within the individual but also within the community. Two such diametrically opposed ideals collide when it comes to the care and wellness of Alaskan Native elders. In a two-part panel, learn how the leadership of the Chickaloon Village Traditional Council (CVTC) changed the focus of elder wellness through the mobilization of the community to educate, feed, and enhance health of the community elders.

Participants: Benjamin Olmedo, PA-C, Chickaloon Village; Lisa Wade, Director Health and Social Services, Chickaloon Village; Albert Harrison, Chickaloon Elder and Council Member; Patricia Wade, Chickaloon Elder and Traditional Storyteller

Moderator: Theodore W. Sery, UAA
BMH 101
3–5 p.m.

Traditional Knowledge Panel

Benjamin Schleifman **"Internships in Indigenous Art"**
Abstract: Apprenticing with the Uncles: A brief discussion
    about the differences in teaching styles and artistry of
    Jim Schoppert and Kenny Jackson.

Judith Ramos, Indigenous studies PhD Student, UAF
    **"Documenting Indigenous Knowledge of the
    Yakutat Tlingit on Historical and Contemporary
    Seal Hunting"**
Abstract: Indigenous knowledge about the environment and
    the changing climate is encoded in oral traditions and
    toponyms. This information can be chronologically
    correlated with archaeological and geological data. As
    the Hubbard Glacier was retreating from its maximum
    extension during the little ice age, it opened up
    and attracted major concentrations of harbor seals.
    This gave the opportunity for local and migrating
    Tlingit, Athabascan, Eyak, and Sugpiag peoples the
    opportunity for seasonal hunting this area. Over time,
    this resource became more and more intensively used
    as other villages became attracted to this area. A clan-
    based and traditional values–based management system
    was used to manage these resources.

Christine Stewart, Assistant Professor, University of Alberta
and Jason Moccasin, Graduate Student, English and
Film Studies, University of Alberta. **"Transforming
Scholarly Practice: Autobiography as Indigenous
Intellectual Tradition"**

Abstract: In "Writing Autobiographically," Cree Métis scholar
Deanna Reder argues that autobiography is an
Indigenous intellectual tradition based in a collective
and complex sense of self. In this paper, graduate
student Jason Moccasin (Saulteaux/Cree) and assistant
professor Christine Stewart (Irish Canadian) analyze
the use of autobiography within the Indigenous
intellectual tradition in a special class that consists of
Indigenous and non-Indigenous adult learners from
the inner city of Edmonton and Indigenous and non-
Indigenous students from the University of Alberta.
Moderator: Diane Benson

RH 303
3–5 p.m.

New Models in Indigenous Education

Presenter: Cand. Pæd. Karl Kristian Olsen (Government of
Greenland) & MSc. Social Anthropology Aviâja E.
Lynge, Greenland (Institute of Learning Processes)
"Reforming Education as a Decolonialization Process"
Abstract: This presentation on Greenland's effort to implement
a new school reform will focus on the dialogues Inuit
in Greenland were creating to formulate policies on

education in all levels based on values, language, and culture in Greenland. The major goal in the educational reforms was to change the colonial educational system based on Danish legislation and to create and implement a reformed education system based on research on education and the Greenlandic values and culture. What succeeded in the ambitious reform works in Greenland and what was not succeeding?

Larry Steeves, PhD, Associate Professor, University of Regina, Canada. **"The Kokum Connection: A Consideration of Western and Indigenous Pedagogy within Chief Kahkewistahaw Community School"**

Abstract: Chief Kahkewistahaw Community School was established in 2005 to fulfill a vision that saw their children experiencing academic success while retaining their traditional culture and beliefs. The Kokum (Grandmother in Cree) Connection, with its emphasis on family and community involvement, as well as its focus on culturally appropriate teaching and learning methods, provides a means of meeting these goals. Recent research conducted in New Zealand, Hawaii, Alaska, and Arizona supports these aspirations. This presentation will report on this research and consider its implications for programming, both within Chief Kahkewistahaw School and the Faculty of Education, University of Regina, which is currently reviewing its programming with a view to better preparing future teachers to work with Saskatchewan Indigenous students.

Moderator: Diane Hirshberg, UAA

RH 211

3–5 p.m

UAA shuttle back to hotel is available from 5–6 p.m.

**5:30–7 p.m. Graduate student mixer and social
(live jazz and food)
RH Lobby**

Evening Performance: *The Defenders of Alaska Native
Country*
RH 101

7–8:15 p.m. Ishmael Hope Reading

The Defenders of Alaska Native Country tells the story
of the Alaska Native Brotherhood and Sisterhood
through William and Louis Paul, Roy and Elizabeth
Peratrovich, Andrew Hope, and Frank Johnson, and
their struggle for civil rights and aboriginal title. The
ANB and ANS, now over 100 years old, achieved
landmark legislation and lawsuits that helped to ensure
the survival, safety, and a measure of dignity for the
Native people of Alaska. The leaders were heroic, feisty,
brilliant, and often all too human. The play seeks to
tell a Native story from a Native perspective, to honor

the elders, and to shed light on the history and legacy of the Alaska Native Brotherhood and Sisterhood.

Written by Ishmael *Angaluuk* Hope
Directed by Flordelino Laugndino
Developed at Perseverance Theatre
Actors: Ishmael *Angaluuk* Hope, Anna Smith-Chiburis, Jack Dalton, *Xh'unei* Lance Twitchell, Mike *Aak'wtaatseen* Hoyt and Ryan Romer, and Jeff Allman.

With the support of the Alaska Humanities Forum, Sealaska Heritage Institute, and 62 Kickstarter Donors, and the Alaska Native Oratory Society

++
8:15–8:30 p.m.
Hotel shuttle will provide transpo back to Springhill Suites Marriott
++

Saturday April 6ᵗʰ
UAA shuttles to the Social Sciences building 7:30–8:30 a.m.

8–10 a.m. Concurrent Sessions in the Social Sciences Building

Justice Education Online to Rural Communities—Roundtable—The Justice Department, University of Alaska Fairbanks, is working toward delivering the Justice Degree completely online. Within a year's time it will be possible for a student to obtain a BA in Justice from even the smallest and most remote village setting, provided that Internet service is available. Faculty experience suggests that selected high school students can benefit by taking three Justice courses— Introduction to Justice, Rural Justice, and Introduction to Addictive Processes. This roundtable will further develop the possibilities of a coordinated and dedicated effort to expand this type of delivery to more rural communities.

Presenters: Jeffrey May, Assistant Professor, University of Alaska Fairbanks Justice Department

Michael Daku, Professor and Program Director, UAF Justice Department

Gary Copus, Emeritus Professor, University of Alaska Fairbanks Justice Department

9 a.m.–10 a.m.
SSB 250

Teacher Education and Preparation—This panel will highlight the partnership efforts of Ilisaġvik College and Avant-Garde Learning Alliance as they work toward their shared goal of increasing the number of local teachers in our rural communities. Speakers will focus on current and future efforts and initiatives. Programs like Ugauchim Uglua (Language Nest) at Ilisaġvik College will be featured, the Alaska Native Teacher Initiative by Avant-Garde Learning Alliance

and some of the findings of the IlisaġvikAvant-Garde
Feasibility Study. Entire study will not be made public
until June.

Presenters: Devin Bates, Uqauchim Uglua Director, Ilisaġvik
College; Mary Sage, Uqauchim Uglua Language Nest
Coordinator, Ilisaġvik College; Kameron Perez-Verdia,
President/CEO, Avant-Garde Learning Alliance

Moderator: Ray Barnhardt, UAF

SSB 253

8–10 a.m.

Growing Our Own Educators—University of Alaska
Statewide is responsible for many Alaska K–12
outreach efforts, including Alaska Native goals and
objectives. At K–12, our goal is to "Grow Our Own
Educators." There are four components of our K–12
outreach efforts designed to support Alaska Native
students from the K–12 public schools, through UA
Schools and Colleges of Education, and into their
teaching careers. Our K–12 outreach's current goals
include embedding the AK Cultural Standards for
Educators throughout all four strands. We would
like to share with interested attendees how these four
components interconnect and work, their differing
objectives, together with their common connections.

Participants: Nita Rearden; Dr. Barbara Adams; Janice Littlebear, Nancy Douglas (members of Advisory Board of
Cultural Knowledge Providers)

Moderator: Sean Asiqtuq Topkok, UAF

SSB 224

8–10 a.m.

ANCSA II Panel

Edgar Blatchford **"The Future of Alaska Native Corporations: Who Will Share the Wealth of the Subsurface Estate?"**

Abstract: The unresolved issues of the settlement act are complex and interwoven with public policies and the politics of special interests. The most complex issues are 7(i), corporate democracy, and how the "new" Natives (those born after 1971) are to be treated. Some of the regional corporations have attempted to resolve the issue of new-Native status by creating life-estate stock. The regional corporations and village corporations are independent but are irrevocably connected. What should be considered in resolving the inequities should not be approached independently but with all Native interests seated at the table. Facts that should be considered are the growing population of new Natives and the migration of original shares to the Lower 48.

Zach Hozid **"Cultural Relationship and Impact on the Environment: A Look at How ANCSA and Capitalism Has Impacted the Relationship to the Environment"**

Abstract: This paper assesses how the current neoliberal capitalist practices are being played out in the Alaska

Native–owned corporations, mostly focusing on Sealaska. This paper is concerned with how and why the corporate model was chosen for the governing bodies for Alaska Native land, cultural changes that occurred due to the neoliberal capitalist model and ideology. We must realize that this economic system has been altering the planet in ways that may not be able to sustain our existence much longer. The ANCSA corporations provide a unique opportunity to bridge these two often contrasting systems into one that is applicable to the global economy and healthy for the environment and social organization.

Eve Tuck **"Claiming an Alaska Native Futurity: Settler Colonialism and the Alaska Native Claims Settlement Act"**

Abstract: This paper will analyze settler colonialism in the context of Alaska and the Alaska Native Claims Settlement Act (ANCSA), the largest land-claim settlement in United States history. Contrasting understandings of land and place in the settlement act and by Alaska Native intellectuals, the paper will present a critical overview of the ANCSA and theorize what is meant by surface and subsurface rights to land. The paper will argue that an underexamined strategy of settler colonialism is the entrusting of land to Alaska Native corporations instead of tribal governments, and the recasting of Alaska Native peoples into shareholders.

Finally, the paper will describe Alaska Native futurity as a framework for understanding the contradictions built into the settlement act.

Victoria Hykes-Steere **"Refusing to be Defeated by Lies, Statutes, and False Doctrine"**

Abstract: In 1955 Tee-Hit-Ton, one of the most racist Supreme Court cases not overturned, illegally used the Doctrine of Discovery to determine Tlingits were not entitled to any compensation when their lands were taken. However, in 1946 the United States voluntarily listed Alaska in the United Nations Charter as a territory with the right of nationhood. By listing Alaska as a territory under the charter, the Doctrine of Discovery no longer applied to our peoples, as the charter was ratified by Congress, thus having the force of the constitution. To this day the obligations the United States put upon itself under the charter and under the decolonization mechanism of the UN have never been fulfilled as they were by Denmark with Greenland.

Moderator: Dalee Sambo-Dorough, UAA

SSB 118
8–10 a.m.

RUSSIAN ENCOUNTERS (60-minute panel)
Leighton Suen, Vassar College
"Alternative First Contact: The Role of Tlingit Oral

**Narratives in Reaffirming Claims of Tribal
Sovereignty in the Pacific Northwest"**

Abstract: The Tlingit oral narratives collected by Richard and
Nora Dauenhauer reaffirm claims of tribal sovereignty
in the Pacific Northwest by proclaiming the existence
of an alternate first contact to what has been taught in
most American schools. Through their very existence,
these narratives disrupt the concept of manifest destiny.
By adapting a method that was used to marginalize
accounts of history that did not agree with Western
discourse, the Dauenhauers demonstrate the resilience
of Native peoples against the effects of colonization
throughout history and ensure that the Tlingit
perspective will be preserved for generations to come.

Cheryl Jerabek Indigenous Studies PhD Student, UAF
**"Russian Impact on Alaska Native Identity and Heritage
in the Middle Kuskokwim Region of Alaska: A
Historical Perspective"**

Abstract: The Russian colonization of Alaska, although brief,
greatly impacted the local population of the middle
Kuskokwim River region in ways much different from
other parts of the state. The blending of Russian and
Native cultures resulted in a group of people known as
Creoles who were for the most part actively involved
in the society and economy of the region and served
as cultural brokers and intermediaries between the two
divergent cultures. The paper will focus on the early
Russian history and impact to the region and some of

the changes that occurred after the "sale" of Alaska.

Moderator: Thomas Swensen, PhD, Assistant Professor
Arizona State University

SSB 119
9–10 a.m.

Indigenous Justice

Polly Hyslop, Graduate Student in UAF Justice Department
"Restorative Justice in Rural Alaska"

Abstract: A new wave of justice is finding its way to the
interior region of rural Alaska, creating a climate of
cooperation between state court magistrates and tribal
people of rural Alaska. This community form of justice
allows for more local participation using restorative
justice principles and models that include input from
victims, offenders, and members of the community.
Each model will show a working relationship between
the Western justice system of magistrates (local judges)
and the communities. In addition, this paper will
introduce a model used in Yukon, Canada, called
the Family Conference model of restorative justice.
Restorative justice can be seen as a healing process.

Stephen Conn, Retired Professor of Justice, UAA **"Bush
Justice in Alaska—A Proven Takeoff Point for
Alaska Native Studies"**

Abstract: Bush justice, the historical interplay between state
and village law, both critical to defining behavior and

resolving problems in rural Alaskan villages, focused
my teaching and research. For Alaska Native Studies,
it is an interdisciplinary lodestone, drawing upon
law, history, and anthropology. I studied historical
village experiences with law, especially with alcohol,
and conducted field experiments with bicultural
legal education, village problem boards, and native
paralegals. None induced state change nor did
studies in Canada, Greenland, Australia, and Brazil.
Interdisciplinary "bush justice" makes difficult a
discoverable, full bibliography. Sadly, Alaska justice
agencies resisted power sharing with villages, however
useful.

Presenter: Liza M. Mack M.S. Anthropology, MESAS Fellow
**"Native by Policy: How Legislation Contributes to
Indigenous Identity"**

Abstract: Precedent-setting legislations in the United
States and around the world have effectively changed
the way that we as Native people define ourselves.
Using my own history as a case study, this paper
will take an in-depth look at the ways in which
these biological, cultural, and personal definitions of
"Native" have changed over time and how they play
into our everyday lives.
Moderator: Emily Moore, UAA
SSB 211
8–10 a.m.

Research and Indigenous Learning

Michael Covone, Chantel Justice, Mariana Ivanovic, Samantha
 Bacon PhD students, UAA-UAF in Clincial-
 Community Psychology. **"Project Puqigtut: Alaska
 Native Student Success in a Culturally Responsive
 Academic Program"**

Abstract: Project Puqigtut is an educational project
 implemented by Anchorage School District's (ASD)
 Department of Indian Education to increase Alaska
 Native students' academic achievement and reduce
 dropout rates through online learning. The current
 research project is based on the involvement of
 UAA doctoral students and in a program evaluation
 led by an independent evaluator, Patricia Partnow,
 Ph.D, contracted by Anchorage School District. A
 unique aspect of this research will be analyzing the
 relationship, if any, between students' success in the
 program and their self-reported cultural identity.

Douglas Cost, NSF IGERT Fellow, UAF, Resilience and
 Adaptation Program **"Feasibility Study of Alternative
 School Programming for Village Schools"**

Abstract: The scope of this study was to explore how alternative
 school programming might be applied in a village
 school setting. Peggy Cowan, the superintendent of
 North Slope Borough School District, asked me to
 explore the feasibility of such programs in the villages
 of Pt. Hope and Pt. Lay. Specifically, I conducted field-
 study research at Kali School in Pt. Lay and Tikigaq

School in Pt. Hope. The purpose of the research was to evaluate the feasibility of employing an alternative school or alternative-type programming for village schools.

Moderator: Caitlin Montague-Winebarger

SSB 223

8–10 a.m.

10:30 a.m.–12 noon BRUNCH in Library 307

10:30 a.m.–4 p.m. **Poster Sessions** outside of Library 307

Poster Sessions

Alaska Native Heritage Center—Updates on the survey recently completed by the Alaska Native Heritage Center on Alaska Native languages. There will also be a roundtable during the conference as well.
Participants: Ember Thomas, Rochelle Adams, Marcella McIntyre.

Festival of Native Arts, Unity through Cultures: Celebrating 40 Years—A reflection of how students working together for over 40 years has provided cultural education and sharing through Native dance, music, and the arts.
Participants: Cathy Brooks, Faculty Advisor for Festival of Native Arts/Assistant Professor, UAF; Sarah

Walker, Student Coordinator for Festival of Native Arts, UAF; Carol Murphrey, Advisor, Rural Student Services, UAF.

Growing Our Own Educators—University of Alaska Statewide is responsible for many Alaska K–12 outreach efforts, including Alaska Native goals and objectives. At K–12, our goal is to "Grow Our Own Educators." There are four components of our K–12 outreach efforts designed to support Alaska Native students from the K–12 public schools, through UA Schools and Colleges of Education, and into their teaching careers. Our K–12 outreach's current goals include embedding the AK Cultural Standards for Educators throughout all four strands. We would like to share with interested attendees how these four components interconnect and work, their differing objectives, together with their common connections.

Participants: Janice Littlebear, Lead Mentor—Curriculum Developer, University of Alaska Statewide

---

1–3 p.m. Concurrent Sessions in SSB

Alaska Native Heritage Center—60-minute roundtable.
Updates on Alaska Native languages and the recent survey

results. The Alaska Native Heritage Center developed a major survey instrument, and over 700 individuals responded. The results of the survey and other updates will be discussed, along with a Q&A.

1–2 p.m

SSB 211

The Craft Shop: The Big Impact of a Little Shop at the Alaska Native Medical Center—The Craft Shop—officially known as Tausigniaviat, "The People's Shopping Place"—is a small shop that has sold Alaska Native art in the Alaska Native Medical Center since 1975. Well known among artists and collectors for its quality collection and its mission to provide a trustworthy sales outlet for Alaska Native artists, the nonprofit, volunteer-run Craft Shop has made a bigger impact on Alaska Native art than is commonly known. This panel will explore the history of this unique shop, including its origins in a telephone operator's phone booth, its early work to combat racism against Alaska Native artists, its development of an award-winning Heritage Collection now on display throughout the ANMC hospital, and its funding of a scholarship program that aided several Alaska Native artists who went on to have successful careers.

Panelists: Agnes Coyle, Jeanne Dougherty, Audrey Armstrong, Sean Topkok, Da-ka-xeen Mehner

Moderator: Emily Moore, UAA

SSB 251
1–3 p.m.

Bringing Culture Into the 21ˢᵗ Century Roundtable—
Currently, online, virtual curriculum is dominated
by mainstream culture, and very slowly Indigenous
populations are beginning to become producers
rather than consumers regarding technology. As we
continue to incorporate technology as a tool in the
classroom, Ilisaġvik College is taking advantage of
the opportunities that technology can provide to
our students. On-campus faculty and staff are using
the Rosetta Stone Iñupiaq Language Program. These
types of programs will be discussed, along with a
conversation around bringing together generations, our
elders and our youth, who collectively have the cultural
knowledge and the technological knowledge to make
these connections for the support of our students and
the perpetuation of our culture.
Participants: Birgit Meany, Dean of Instruction, Ilisaġvik
College; Anna Edwardson, Iñupiaq Studies
Coordinator, Ilisaġvik College; Dr. Edna MacLean,
Adjunct Iñupiaq Studies Instructor, Ilisaġvik College
Moderator: Liza Mack, PhD candidate, UAF

SSB 118
1–3 p.m.

Growing the Road Home: Alaska Native Education Foundations Linking Higher Education to Workforce Development—Panelists will discuss the Alaska Native Education Foundations' scholarship initiatives that provide shareholders and shareholder descendants with support. These initiatives encourage shareholders and their descendants to return to Alaska after leaving the state for higher education and/or to consider pursuing employment in an Alaska Native organization. This work raises questions about the role of foundations in higher education and workforce development, draws attention to the need to network Alaska Natives pursuing higher education away from home, and highlights some efforts to create pathways home for those affected by diaspora.

Presenters: Tyan Hayes, Koniag Education Foundation; Alisha Drabek, PhD, University of Alaska Fairbanks; Malia Villegas, National Congress of American Indians Policy Research Center;

Invited: Fred Brooks, Old Harbor Tribal Council; Rosita Worl, Sealaska Heritage Institute; Sarah Obed, Government Relations Director, Doyon Limited, Inc.; Carol Wren, Senior Director of Programs, Cook Inlet Tribal Council; Shauna Hegna, Vice President of Shareholder Services, Afognak.

Moderator: Thomas Swensen, PhD, University of Arizona

SSB 250
1–3 p.m.

Who We Are and What We've Become: A Discussion from SLATE PhD and Master's Graduates—The Second Language Acquisition Teacher Education (SLATE) project focused on second-language teaching and learning that involved four (4) PhD students and 18 master's students. This roundtable discussion will present three threads. First, master's and PhD graduates will share their challenges and successes as Alaska Native graduate students in this challenging program. Second, they will highlight their language advocacy and leadership activities since graduation. Finally, they will invite audience members interested in pursuing graduate work in Alaska Native language teaching to share their own experiences and discuss ways the group could network together to develop and further common goals for Alaska Native language survival.

Presenters: Walkie Charles, PhD, chair; Theresa John, PhD; April Laktonen-Counceller, PhD; Hishinlai' Kathy Sikorski; Patrick Marlow, PhD; Sabine Siekmann, PhD

Moderator: Dalee Sambo-Dorough, UAA

SSB 119
1–3 p.m.

Preparing our Youth for the Future Workforce, Summer Camp Programing at Ilisaġvik **College**—In order to expose middle and high school students to career options and higher education, Ilisaġvik College hosts a series of summer camps as part of the institution's mission of assisting to bridge the gap between secondary and tertiary education. Students from across the state are recruited to take part in these educational opportunities to explore educational and career paths in topic areas such as Allied Health, Construction Trades, STEM, Climate Change, Digital Media, and Iñupiaq Land Use Values and Resources.

Presenters: Amanda Sialofi, Allied Health Coordinator, Ilisaġvik College; Gloria Burnett, Dean of Students, Ilisaġvik College; Linda Nicolas-Figeroa, Science Instructor, Ilisaġvik College

Moderator: Ray Barnhardt, UAF

SSB 223

1–3 p.m.

Indigenizing Health Practices Panel

Brittany N. Freitas-Murrell, M.S., Doctoral Student, Joint PhD Clinical-Community Psychology Program Rural Indigenous Emphasis **"Predicting Attitudes and Intentions: Seeking Professional Psychological Help in Alaska Natives"**

Abstract: Previous research has yet to examine attitudes toward mental-health treatment options in Alaska Natives. This study furthers our understanding of the attitudes that Alaska Natives hold toward seeking professional psychological help. Specifically, in this study variables previously found to predict attitudes and intentions in other ethnic groups (locus of control, social support, public and self-stigma, psychological distress, and acculturation) were tested as potential predictors of attitudes and intentions in a sample of Alaska Native university students ($n = 30$). This study contributes to the literature in the hope of providing services and interventions that suit the values, beliefs, and preferences of Alaska Native people.

Presenter: Benjamin Olmedo, PA-C

Traditional Health/Healing vs. Western Teachings on Health—

Abstract: Western teachings on health focus on "fighting disease" instead of supporting wellness through harmony and balance. Traditional Indigenous teachings focus on the belief that mind, body, and spirit can never be truly separated and unbalance can bring about a state of disease. There is no better example than the dichotomy in the care for our elders. Western medicine underestimates the role of culture in health, overmedicates elders, and isolates them in the fight against disease. Where are the alternatives? Learn how to integrate community engagement, state-of-the-art geriatric assessments, and holistic views of health to improve elder health care.

Meda DeWitt Schleifman, TH

"Women's Rites of Passage Pilot Project in Southeast Alaska by ANTHC"

Abstract: Late last summer "out the road" in Juneau a group of women gathered for the purpose of revitalizing culture. Bringing light to a part of women's lives that has been treated as unclean and kept in the shadows of modern life. These milestones in women's lives once were celebrated and treated as sacred and necessary for the continued health and strength of the family, clan, community, and nation. There are many rites of passage in a person's life, but for this project we focused on puberty and the transmission of knowledge from elder women to the young lady transitioning into her womanhood. Please join us to discuss the purpose and outcomes of this intense topic and gathering.
Moderator: Sheila Selkregg, UAA

SSB 224
1–3 p.m.

3–5 p.m Concurrent Sessions in SSB

Cup'ik Dreams: Chevak Teacher Education Initiative—A partnership between the College of Education (COE) and the Kashunamiut School District and Chevak community supports 12 paraprofessionals who are working toward their bachelor's degrees in elementary education. This partnership, known as the Chevak Teacher Education Initiative, embraces the concepts of inclusivity and culturally relevant teaching. Course work reflects both Western and Cup'ik cultures and philosophies. This initiative is providing important insights about the power of collaboration as an Indigenous community, school, and university come together to create a space that supports cultural and language revitalization. We will hear perspectives from both students and faculty.

Presenter Nancy Boxler, UAA College of Education and members of the Chevak Cohort:Laura Atcharian, Elsie Ayuluk, Cora Charles, Twila Chayalkun, Susie Friday-Tall, Catherine Joe, Jacquelyn Kashatok, Priscilla Matchian, Mary Matchian, Neva Mathias, Pauline Miles, Liana Pingayak, Darlene Ulroan and Lisa Unin. Chairman of Kashunamuit School District and John Atchak, Superintendent Larry Parker. University Faculty and Staff: Dr. Claudia Dybdahl, Dr. Irasema Ortega, Dr. Cathy Coulter and Ms. Nancy Boxler Travel is sponsored by the Kashunamuit School District and the College of Education at the University of Alaska.

Moderator: Pat Chesbro, Alaskan Educator

SSB 223
3–5 p.m.

Factors Related to Teacher Retention in Arctic Alaska— Preparing and retaining teachers for teaching in rural-Indigenous communities throughout Alaska is a complex and challenging task. Panelists will

418

share and discuss preliminary research results from
an NSF-funded study on teacher retention in rural
Alaska with the objective to inform participants about
challenges in teacher preparation and retention in
rural Alaska and discuss possible effective strategies
for teacher preparation, induction, and retention. It
is the intent of this presentation to share and discuss
factors related to teacher retention in rural-Indigenous
schools, including teacher preparation and community
integration, and to identify best practices.

Participants: Lenora "Lolly" Carpluk, M.Ed.; Ute Kaden
Ed.D. (UAF); Beth Leonard PhD (UAF); Phil
Patterson PhD (UAF); Barbara Adams PhD (UA)

Moderator: Beth Leonard, UAF

SSB 253
3–5 p.m.

Spirituality, Land, and Ethics Panel

Chad Cook

Abstract: The major theme of my paper highlights
conservation ethics and notions of environmental
stewardship amongst rural Yup'ik hunters of the Yukon
River delta. My research findings are based on ethnographic research documenting beluga whale hunting,
seal hunting, commercial and subsistence fishing,
moose hunting, and the gathering of wild berries. The
importance of maintaining direct relationships with

the natural world, eating Native foods, and passing on hunting and gathering skills to future generations helps develop the narrative of my analysis. I explore how the cultural heritage of the Yup'ik people is embodied in such practices, providing a direct link between culture and nature.

Michael Kirby "The Ecuadorian Indigenous Movement: Its Origins and Coincidence with Liberation Theology for Social Transformation"

Abstract: To establish a correlation between Ecuadorian Indigenous spiritual traditions and that of Jesuit Liberation Theology is an informed methodology for change within the Indigenous peoples of the Arctic. To disarm the adversarial relationship that exists between Arctic Indigenous spiritual traditions and Christianity, by informing Christianity of the historical validity of those traditions in order to develop a mutually complimentary spiritual composition of progress and sustainability as joint stewards of the land for future generations. To reframe the dialogue in the Arctic over resource development through a comprehensive reassessment of values and needs based on the fundamental consistencies found within both Native and Christian spiritual traditions.

Tony Kaliss "From the Spiritual to the Practical and Back: The Interaction of European and Native Societies"

Abstract: This paper develops a model of the interactions of European and Native societies. Central is an exploration of how practical and spiritual issues are deeply interrelated in these interactions. The goal is to go beyond what happened or how it happened to the roots of a dynamic ongoing complex process. Deeper understandings of these interactions are necessary to develop strategies to strengthen Native societies and to show Native societies and Indigenous worldviews as essential active contributors dealing with basic issues affecting all peoples in the modern world. Specific examples are drawn from Alaska and the Russian Far East (Chukotka).
Moderator: Edgar Blatchford, UAA

SSB 119
3–5 p.m.

Education and Indigenous Peoples

Pearl Brower, President, Ilisaġvik College. **"The Longest War: Overcoming the Era of Assimilation through Education"**

Abstract: This paper examines various Indigenous nations and reviews the diverse forms of assimilation through education they have faced through history. Assessments on Indigenous nations around the world, including Mozambique, Canada, Hawaii, continental United States, and Alaska are included. As these nations work to reverse the detrimental effects this has had on their communities, specific methods of revitalization are discussed. Various models that are discussed include community-based education, language-immersion programs, culturally relevant curriculum, and the creation of tribal colleges. In addition, included in this document is a survey from one tribal college regarding how it incorporates the Indigenous value system of its region into each of its departments at the institution.

Caitlin Montague-Winebargar **"Average People Don't Think About Those Types of Things." Examining Notions of Culture and Cultural Difference Among Pre-Service Teachers in an Alaskan University**

Abstract: This presentation will center on research conducted within the University of Alaska system that examines the ability of undergraduate students within a specific education program to articulate a working definition of culture and cross-culture within an Alaskan context. Through the use of semistructured interviewing and participatory/observational autoethnographic fieldwork, the presenter will provide several viewpoints from which to look at this complex issue.

Gail Weinstein, Cook Inlet Tribal Council, Anchorage, Alaska **"Alaska Native Youth Transforming Public Education— Effecting Change from Within; More Than a Decade of Indigenous Self-Determination in Public School"**

Abstract: The dynamics used to implement and grow the

ability to significantly improve the well-being and graduation outcomes of Alaska Native youth in urban public schools is presented. Cook Inlet Tribal Council's strength-based, culturally responsive, and academically rigorous program demonstrates students' self-determination in urban American public education. The daily presence of the CITC team, with its unshakeable advocacy on behalf of the Alaska Native community, provides a best-practice program, pulling together ASD/school and community resources, modeling and reinforcing mainstream educators/administrators to implement systemic and behavioral change from within. Recognizing the need for continued tribal vigilance within schools, educational achievement with prideful and empowered futures among Native youth is the reality discussed.

Moderator: Phyllis Fast, PhD, Professor, UAA

SSB 224
3–5 p.m.

Identity and Language Documentation Panel

Alice Taff, PhD, Research Assistant Professor, Alaska Native
    Languages, UAS

"Collaborative Language Documentation; Alaska and Around the World"

Abstract: Alaska has a long history of invaluable language documentation. Have the activities of researchers changed over this period? This paper will showcase successful collaborative Indigenous language-documentation activities around the world. Collaborators include members of the Indigenous communities, along with academics, videographers, funders, and others. In balanced collaboration, who decides what to document? Who holds the microphone and camera, designs and manages the budget, authors the results? Who gets funded for documentation projects? We will discuss the benefits of such collaboration in language documentation. What are others doing that we might learn from? What might they learn from Alaskans?

Jessica Lewis-Nicori

"Qaneryaram Tamangellra-Yuum Kituucia-llu Tamangellra: Cimiingelria Yupiit Qaneryarait, Qitevvnermek Ilallranek, Qaillun-llu Yuum Kituucia Cimingellra: Language Loss-Identity Loss: The Evolution of the Yup'ik and English Languages and the Effect on Individual Identity."

Abstract: The paper is about Westernization and the effect that losing language has on today's youth. I will also touch on issues of language loss, i.e. boarding schools, introduction of religion and its effect on language. I will briefly discuss the Sapir-Whorf theory, the Whorfian hypothesis, and Chomsky's independent theory and what I think of them. This paper is my exploration of language loss and identity loss. In the process of writing it, I thought of what my grandparents would tell me and remembered their personalities and wisdom.

Frederick White, PhD, associate Professor, English Department, Slippery Rock University, PA

"Haida Discourse Patterns: Identity, Sovereignty, and Perpetuity"

Abstract: Haida discourse patterns found in Swanton's recorded narratives at the end of the 19th century as well as contemporary stories reveal a continuity of themes regarding identity, sovereignty, and perpetuity. With traditional tales of Raven or historical accounts, these three themes suggest an awareness of what it means to be Haida and how that identity is bonded to the land and sea, and stewardship to both. That stewardship has been bestowed in perpetuity, and these narratives affirm Haida identity, their sovereignty, as well as their survival and thrival from generation to generation.

Moderator: Jeane Breinig, PhD, Professor of English and Associate Dean, UAA

SSB 211
3–5 p.m.

Decolonizing History Panel

Thomas Michael Swensen, Assistant Professor of Native Arts and Culture, Arizona State University

"Indigenous Subject/Citizens in Alaska"

Abstract: Alaska Natives have long considered their colonial subjectivity within a nation granting them citizenship. For example during the 1970s, Fred Bigjim exclaimed, "This is exactly where the danger is for Native people," as he struggled to consider "the relationship between Native rights and Citizen rights" in Alaska. This essay explores the history of political mutuality of the subject/citizen in Alaska.

Jordan Craddick, Research Assistant, UAF **"The Reluctant Assimilationist: Sheldon Jackson's Motives for entering Alaska"**

Abstract: Presbyterian missionary Sheldon Jackson became Alaska's federally appointed general agent of education in 1885. He infamously implemented schools throughout Alaska with the intention of stamping out Indigenous culture in favor of an Americanized Christian archetype. To explain his actions, historians have woven Jackson's Alaska policies into a narrative that correlates with the late-19th-century assimilation zeitgeist. Regrettably, this reform-minded thesis is based on backward induction. Primary sources indicate that Jackson's attraction to Alaska was born of rivalries in an elaborate scheme to coax financial support from Protestant women.

Dr. Janis Judson, Director of Law Program and Associate Professor of Political Science, Hood College, MD

"Justice for Native Americans and Alaskan Natives: What the US Could Learn from the Canadian TRC"

Abstract: This paper is an exploration of the US's failure of restorative justice with respect to Native Americans and Alaska Natives, using the Canadian Truth and Reconciliation model as a normative lens for comparison. In 2012 the TRC of Canada held one of its inaugural commissions bearing witness to the legacy of human-rights violations by the residential school system. The Canadian TRC is an important nexus in understanding why the US has no comparable truth commission for harms done to our own Indigenous populations. And with no formal mechanism for truth we can never understand these wrongs. A geographical proximity of Alaskan Natives with Canadian First Nations also makes the Canadian research even more relevant for this discussion of truth and reconciliation.

Moderator: Maria Williams, UAA

SSB 118
3–5 p.m.

++

UAA shuttle to Alaska Native Heritage Center starting at 3:30

4–5 p.m. Tour of the Alaska Native Heritage Center

5:30–6 p.m. Light refreshments available at Alaska Native Heritage Center

6:00 Banquet starts—MC, Jack Dalton. Program will feature the Oscar Kawagley Award

7:30–8:00 Inupiaq dance group will perform

UAA shuttles back to Hotel starting at 8:15 p.m.

Sunday April 7th: Business meetings—

10 a.m.–12 Social Sciences Building room 223 for graduate students to organize

10 a..m.–12 Social Sciences Building room 119 for the decompress for Alaska Native Studies Council (elect officers, plan for future conferences, etc.)

9–10 a.m. and 12–5 p.m. Social Sciences building room 223, debrief for Indigenous Studies PhD students, UAF. Ray Barnhardt, coordinator

Alaska Native Studies Conference Closing Banquet

Saturday, April 6, 2013
Alaska Native Heritage Center
Emcee: Jack Dalton

4–4:45	Tour of Alaska Native Heritage Center
5:30	Light refreshments
6:00	Buffet-style dinner

6:00   Opening blessing (Marie Meade)
Welcoming: Provost Baker, Chancellor Case
Acknowledgement of sponsors - Sharon Lind
Recognition of Elders
Recognition of Distinguished Professor
Graham *Hingangaroa* Smith

6:45–7   Presentation of the 2012–2013 *Angayuqaq*
Oscar Kawagley Award

In recognition of *Angayuqaq* Oscar Kawagley's role in articulating the significance of Indigenous knowledge systems, ways of knowing, and worldviews in the contemporary world, the Alaska Native Knowledge Network has established the AOK Indigenous Scholar Award in his honor.

7:30–8   King Island Dance Group performances

8:15   Buses depart to Hotel

Pre-Conference Symposium

The Things We Make:
Alaska Native Art in the 21st Century
April 4, 2013
Anchorage Museum
625 C Street
Anchorage, Alaska

9:30–10am	**Registration and coffee**
10–10:20am	**Welcome/Opening remarks: Dena'ina welcome and blessing by Aaron Leggett, welcome by James Pepper Henry, comments by UAA Chancellor Tom Case**
10:30–12pm	Artist Roundtable: Forty Years of Reflection Moderator: Perry Eaton Panelists: Alvin Amason, Larry Ahvakana, Ron Senungetuk, Nathan Jackson, Glen Simpson, Delores Churchill
12–1pm	Lunch break
1–1:50pm	Diverse Dialogue: Perspectives of Contemporary Alaska Native Artists Moderator: Da-ka-xeen Mehner Panelists: Nicholas Galanin, Sonya Kelliher-Combs, Drew Michael, Joel Isaak, Benjamin Schleifman
1:50–2pm	**Artist Performance: Ishmael Hope**
2–2:50pm	Oral History and Modern Media: Filmmaking and Community in Alaska Moderator: Anna Hoover

Panelists: Deborah Schildt, Sonya Senkowsky, Julien Jacobs

2:50–3pm   **Artist Performance: Allison Warden**

3–3:50pm   Native Curators Interpreting Native Collections for a Public Audience
Moderator: James Pepper Henry
Panelists: Darian LaTocha, Eleanor Hadden, Aaron Leggett

3:50–4:20pm **Artist Performance: Heidi Senungetuk**

4:30–5:30pm Birthright: Artists & Activism
Moderator: Jack Dalton
Panelists: Allison Warden, Ishmael Hope, Ethan Petticrew, Susie Bevins-Ericsen

Thank-You

*chin'an quyana qaĝaasakung doykshn way dankoo quyanaq
háw'aa dogIdinh tsin'aen mahsi' igamsiqanaghhalek tsin'ee
'awa'ahdah maasee' gunalshéesh*

Special people: Jennifer Wisel, CBPP, UAA; Marilynn Woods,
AKNS, UAA; Jeanne Taylor, CAS, UAA; Provost Elisha "Bear"
Baker, UAA

Sponsors:

Office of the Provost, UAA; Office of the Provost, UAS; Office
of the Dean, College of Arts and Sciences, UAA;

NANA

Arctic Slope Regional Corporation

Aleut Corporation

Alaska Dispatch

Cosponsors:

Perseverance Theatre, Alaska Native Oratory Society for
staged reading of The Defenders of Native Country;
Kashunamiut School District and Barney Gottstein
for the travel for the Chevak teachers initiative
presentation.

Volunteers: Jennifer McCarty; Tony Kaliss; Hillary Presecan;
Tricia Gillam; Molly Sparhawk; Sandra Ehrlich; Theo
Sery; Anna Smith-Chiburis

UAA Native Student Council Volunteers: Janelle
Huntington; Gordon Iya; Audrey Leary; Olivia Shields; Kyle
Worl

Special Note: With compliments from *Alaska Quarterly Review*, we are providing Alaska Native writers, storytellers, and orators the expanded edition. A special edition of *Alaska Quarterly Review* was made possible by a Heritage and Preservation Grant from the National Endowment for the Arts.

Alaska Native Studies Conference Organizing Committee:
Jeane Breinig, UAA; Beth Leonard, UAF; Sharon Lind,
UAA; Maria Williams, UAA; Lance Twitchell, UAS; Gordon
Pullar, UAF; Sean Topkok, UAF; Alvin Amason, UAA; Da-
ka-xeen Mehner, UAF; Dalee Sambo-Dorough, UAA; Ray
Barnhardt, UAF; April Counceller, UAK; Phyllis Fast, UAA;
Emily Moore, UAA; Lenore "Lolly" Carpluk, Educator; Marie
Meade, UAA; Liza Mack, UAF; Trisha Gillam, UAF.

Pre-Conference Symposia Organizing Committee:
Emily Moore, UAA; Da-ka-xeen Mehner, UAF; Alvin
Amason, UAA; Perry Eaton, Artist; Julie Decker, Anchorage
Museum; Maria Williams, UAA; Anchorage Museum staff.